Routledge Revivals

Oman

Oman was, until the coup which brought Sultan Qaboos (1940–2020) to power in July 1970, one of the most remote and least known countries in the world. This book, originally published in 1977 and written by someone who worked in Oman for a period spanning the old and new regimes, discusses the legacy inherited by the late Sultan from his father. The government which was formed in 1970 was made up of a ruler and ministers who had little confidence in themselves, little training and no experience of government. Yet despite this over the next 50 years, Oman saw massive progress in the construction of essential economic and social infrastructure as well as the fight against an extremist guerilla uprising in Dhofar. The book analyses how challenges were tackled and considers Oman's relations with its immediate oil producing neighbours, Iran, Saudi Arabia and the United Arab Emirates.

Oman

The Making of a Modern State

John Townsend

Routledge
Taylor & Francis Group

First published in 1977 by Croom Helm Ltd

This edition first published in 2026 by Routledge
4 Park Square, Milton Park, Abingdon, Oxon, OX14 4RN

and by Routledge
605 Third Avenue, New York, NY 10158

Routledge is an imprint of the Taylor & Francis Group, an informa business

ISBN: 978-1-041-33149-0 (hbk)
ISBN: 978-1-003-78638-2 (ebk)
ISBN: 978-1-041-33161-2 (pbk)

Book DOI 10.4324/9781003786382

OMAN
The Making of the Modern State

JOHN TOWNSEND

CROOM HELM LONDON

Croom Helm Ltd.
2-10 St John's Road, London SW11

ISBN 0-85664-446-3

Reprinted 1977

Printed in Great Britain by Biddles Ltd, Guildford, Surrey

CONTENTS

For Barbara

Who knew, and shared, and cared.

AUTHOR'S NOTE

The quotations from Machiavelli which appear at the beginning of this book and at the heads of chapters are taken from the Folio Society edition of *The Prince,* published in London in 1970. Some parts of Chapter 3 have already appeared in the book *Oman,* written by the author of this book, and first published by the then Omani Department of Information in November 1972.

The author's archives, to which reference is made at the end of certain chapters, have been lodged with the Centre for Islamic Studies at Durham University.

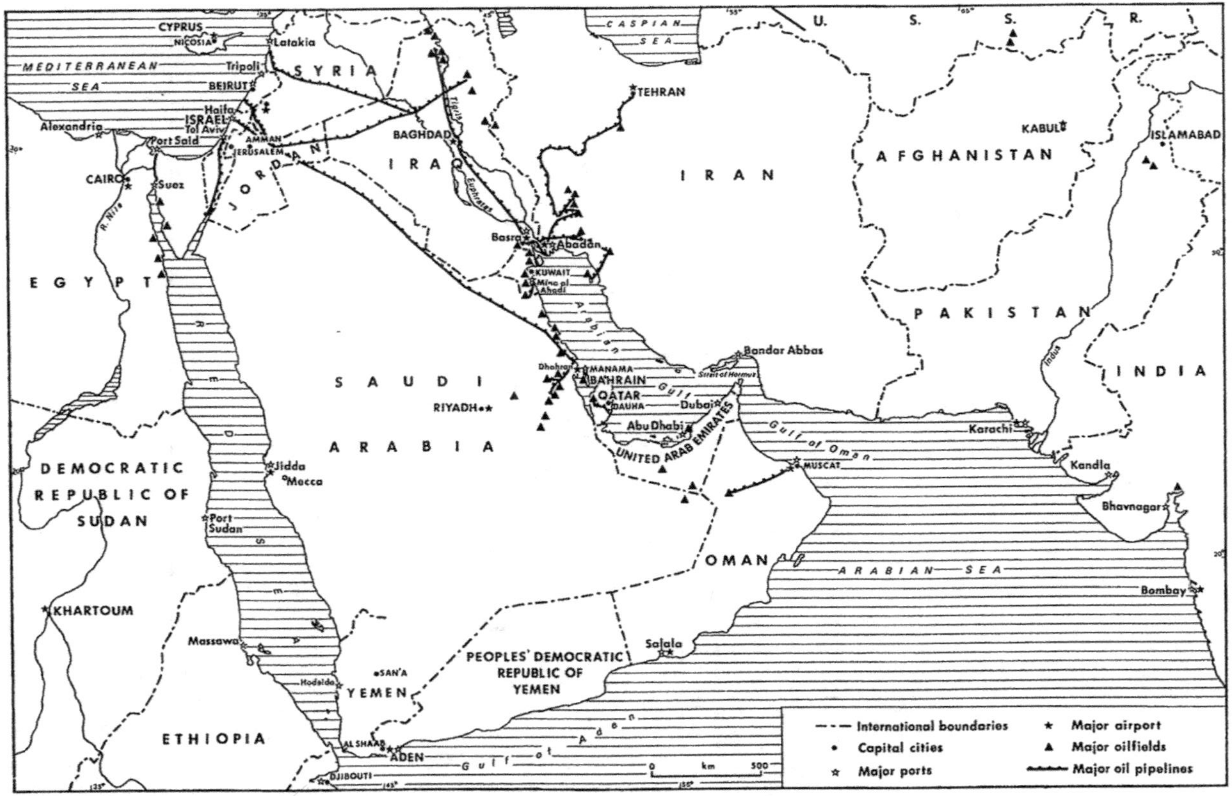

Oman and its Neighbours

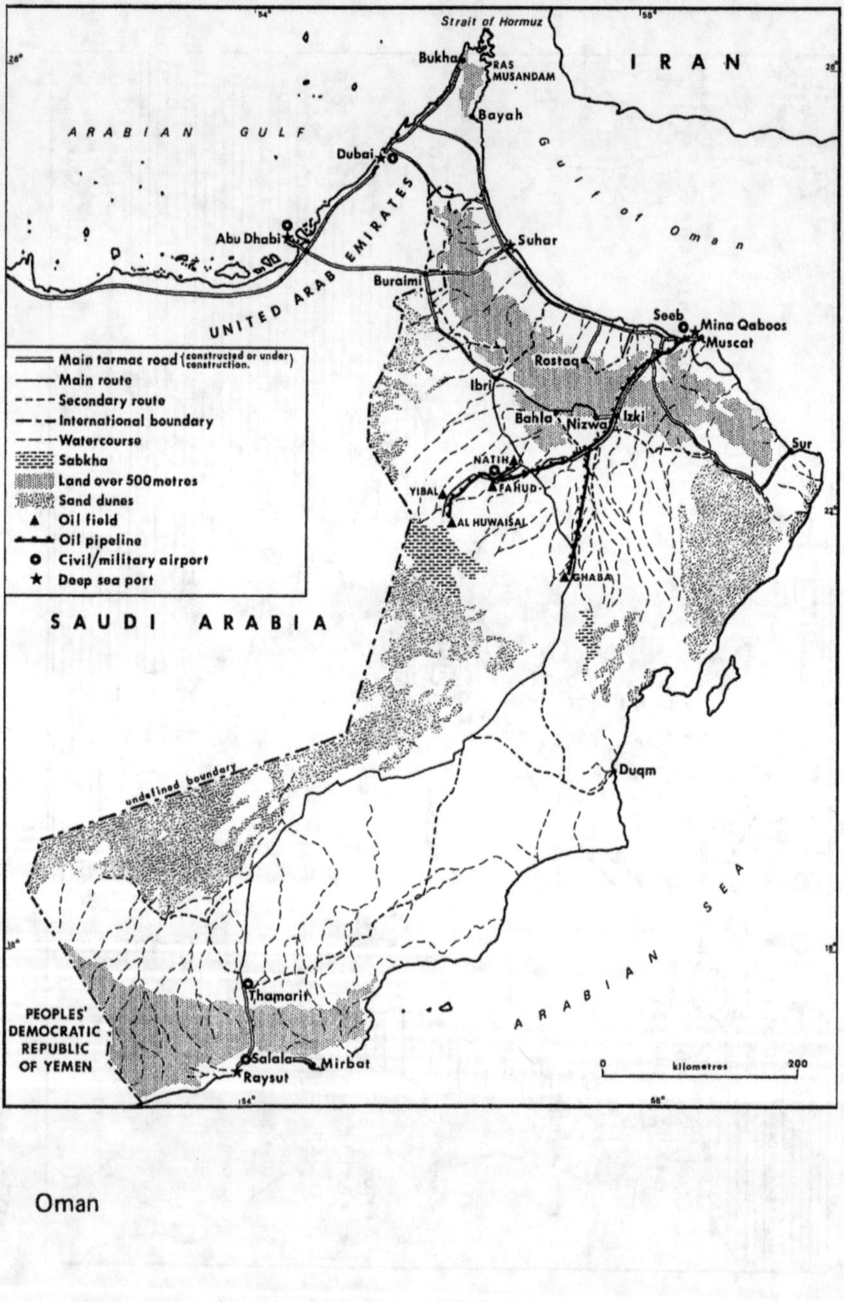
Strait of Hormuz
IRAN
Bukha
RAS MUSANDAM
Bayah
ARABIAN GULF
Gulf of Oman
Dubai
Abu Dhabi
UNITED ARAB EMIRATES
Suhar
Buraimi
Seeb
Mina Qaboos
Muscat
Rostaq
Ibri
Bahla
Nizwa
Izki
Sur
NATIH
FAHUD
YIBAL
AL HUWAISAL
GHABA
Main tarmac road (constructed or under construction.)
Main route
Secondary route
International boundary
Watercourse
Sabkha
Land over 500 metres
Sand dunes
Oil field
Oil pipeline
Civil/military airport
Deep sea port
SAUDI ARABIA
undefined boundary
Duqm
ARABIAN SEA
Thamarit
PEOPLES' DEMOCRATIC REPUBLIC OF YEMEN
Salala
Mirbat
Raysut
0 kilometres 200

Oman

The Musandam Peninsula

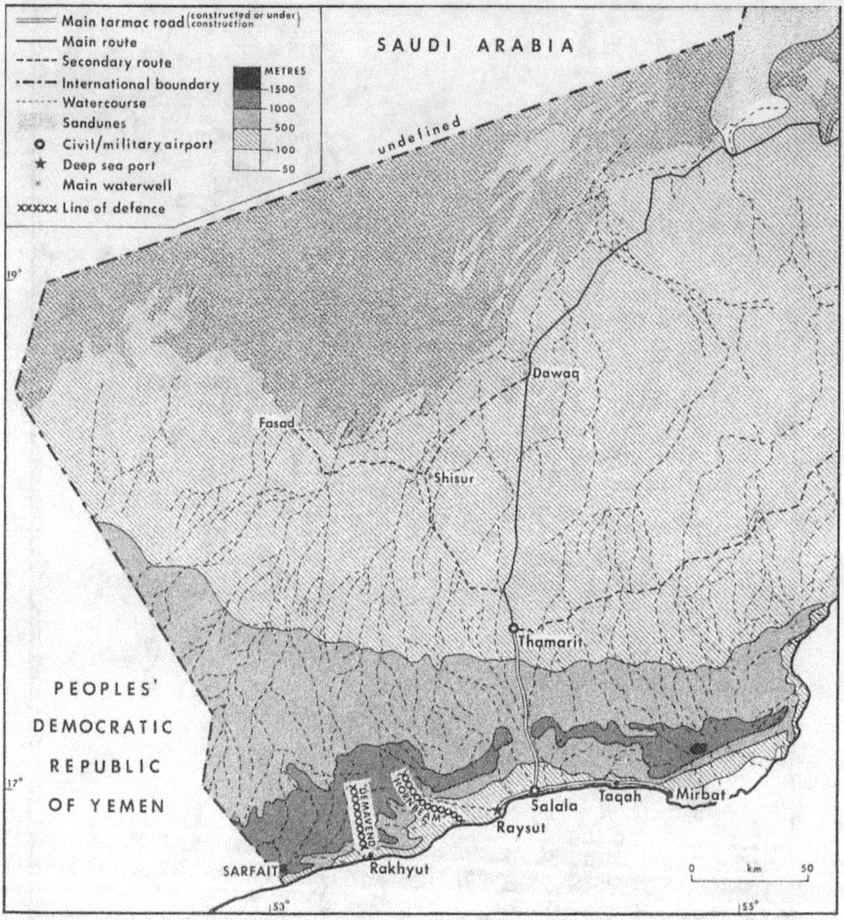

The War in Dhofar

PREFACE

It was at the end of April 1969 that I first went to Oman. I had been invited to lead a small team of consultants whose task was to advise Sultan Sa'id bin Taimur on the establishment of various elementary organisations to begin a cautious move forward into the modern world. Oman was at that time one of the least known countries of the world. Few people had been given permission by the Sultan to visit this torrid and barren corner of the Arabian peninsula, and fewer still had made the journey to Salalah to meet the Sultan in his palace on a beach bordering the Indian Ocean. My first visit to Salalah and first meeting with the Sultan had a dreamlike unreality: I met a strange, small old man with a splendid set of Father Christmas whiskers, tended and guarded by burly young men of undoubted African origin who were known as 'slaves'. He gave me, in excellent English, careful instructions as to whom I should meet and what I might say. All the people with whom I was to work were expatriate, I was not to meet any Omanis. 'Our people are not ready for development,' was the explanation.

I worked in Oman until May 1970, sending regular reports to the Sultan proposing simple organisations to staff nascent development programmes, an agricultural department, a small unit to run the Muscat water supply, a roads planning and maintenance organisation, a strengthened municipality for Muscat, a very small development secretariat. I made the journey to Salalah a few more times to present proposals to the Sultan. Progress was distressingly slow. I had been given permission to travel through northern Oman, and had had my eyes opened to conditions throughout the Sultan's realm. The visitor to Muscat who was not allowed to travel could never begin to appreciate the condition of the people of Oman at that time. I had no personal experience of political tyranny; Sultan Sa'id's tyranny was not that of the history books, a harsh rule imposed by naked force, but a tyranny of indifference to want and suffering backed up by a very genuine threat of punishment if his people complained. There was no obvious demonstration of the Sultan's power. A discreet presence in a few key towns of his Armed Forces, led by British officers, was enough to let his people know that they were under observation, and that they had better behave. Everywhere there was great poverty and disease. Equally, it was possible to see that much could be done to alleviate the poverty by creating income-generating investment in agriculture (most food was at that time imported) and eradicate much of the disease, which was mostly due to a vitamin-deficient diet and ignorance of basic hygiene. Yet nothing was done, because the Sultan would not permit it. No man could leave his village and seek work without the permission of the Sultan. No man could repair his house without the permission of the Sultan. This remote old man, who never left his palace in Salalah, and ruled by radio-telephone through expatriates, had instilled such a fear in his people that very few of them dared defy him and undertake any initiative to improve their lot.

After over twelve months of effort, with limited success, amounting to little more than the recruitment of a few expatriate experts in specific fields, I realised that there was no more to be achieved in Oman. Equally, it was becoming apparent that those forces which had hitherto acted to protect the Sultan and keep him on his throne were preparing to desert him and encourage a change of government. I left Oman with a heavy heart, realising that the little I had achieved was nothing compared to the needs of the Omani people. The next twelve months were spent mostly in Iraq and in Abu Dhabi. I kept a close interest in Oman, and was not surprised to learn of the *coup* of 23 July 1970, which ousted the Sultan and which placed power in the hands of his son Qaboos. I visited Oman again in November 1970, and yet again in February 1971, keeping contacts alive and observing with the keenest interest all that was happening.

In July 1971, I was invited by the government of Oman to carry out two studies, one on structure of government, commissioned by the then Prime Minister, the Sultan's uncle, Sayyid Tarik bin Taimur, and the second an economic survey, commissioned by the then Minister of the Economy, a distant cousin of the Sultan, Sayyid Faisal bin 'Ali. As team leader on two simultaneous projects, I spent the next few months travelling throughout Oman, and meeting many Omanis, from the Sultan and his ministers, down to simple and unsophisticated tribesmen. As a result of this work, and the reports and recommendations which were made, I was invited to join the government of Oman by the Sultan in July 1972. I served the Sultan and his people for over three years, until July 1975.

A great deal of what follows in this book is therefore a first-hand account. My objective has been to present an analysis of the evolution of the government of Oman from a structure almost feudal in its simplicity and implied relationships into what it is today, a government trying very hard to put a modern image before its own people and the world. A process which took Western societies several hundred years, which has taken other developing societies at least two or three generations, has been forced in Oman to occupy the space of some five years. Institutions of government, evolved over many years in other societies, with consequent axiomatic understanding on the part of the people, have been created overnight in Oman, often to the bewilderment of the Omani people. Inevitably in this process problems have arisen and problems have been created. If my Omani friends consider that I am at times too critical, they should recall that I have great sympathy for their situation and its enormous difficulties, and that I have striven in this book to be as fair and objective as I can. There is nothing in the pages that follow which a responsible political analyst would not write about the government of any country he had the good fortune to be associated with, and which would be published in any country without political censorship.

Many friends, Omanis and expatriates, have helped with the writing of this book. They will all understand why I do not acknowledge them publicly. I owe a great debt to them for their interest, stimulation and comment. For errors and omissions, I am alone responsible.

'A prince who is not wise himself cannot be well advised.'

PART 1: THE ENVIRONMENT

1 THE ECONOMIC GEOGRAPHY OF OMAN

'. . .whether a prince's power is such that, in case of necessity, he can stand alone, or whether he must always have recourse to the protection of others.'

Oman occupies most of the south-eastern part of the Arabian peninsula between latitudes 16°40' and 26° 20' N and longitudes 51° 50' and 59°40' E. It has a coastline of some 1,800 km facing the Gulf of Oman and the Arabian Sea. Many of its land frontiers have not been precisely defined or agreed by international treaty; its neighbours are the United Arab Emirates to the north-west, Saudi Arabia to the west, and the Peoples' Democratic Republic of Yemen to the south-west. The northernmost part of Oman, the Musandam peninsula, is isolated from the main part of the country by a strip of land some 80 km wide forming part of the United Arab Emirates. The Musandam peninsula commands the strategically important Strait of Hormuz through which oil tankers carrying most of the oil exported from the Gulf and Iran pass. The large island of Masirah lies off the south-east coast and is the site of a British Royal Air Force base. The Kuria Muria islands are a small group off the coast of Oman's southern province, Dhofar.

Most of the territory of Oman is either desert or bare and infertile mountains. In the northern part of the country, the Hajar mountains, sometimes known as the Oman mountains, run from the Musandam peninsula south, south-east and east almost to Ras al-Hadd, the extreme south-eastern tip of Arabia. The highest point in this range, in the Jabal Akhdar massif, is just over 3,000 metres high. In the south the Qara mountains form an escarpment cutting off the narrow plain flanking the town of Salalah from the gravel deserts to the north; parts of this escarpment reach 1,200 metres in altitude. In the north of Oman, the Batina coastal plain, some 250 km long and varying in width from 2 to 30 km, contains much arable land. The Salalah plain in Dhofar is almost 70 km in length and from 1 to 10 km in width; it also contains a certain amount of arable land. There are pockets of arable land in the valleys and foothills of the Oman mountains. Of a total land area of about 275,000 sq km, at least 80 per cent is made up of sand and gravel desert and at least another 15 per cent of bare and rugged mountains.

The country has had historically many of the characteristics of an island, there having been until 1970 only three difficult land routes leading to Oman from the outside world. One, in the south, was a prolongation of the ancient frankincense route from Dhofar and the Hadramaut through Yemen to the Mediterranean. Of the two northern access routes, one came through a pass in the Oman mountains from Dubai, and followed the coast to Muscat. The second entered Oman at the Buraimi oasis and connected the village settlements on the inland side of the mountains. Access from the coast to the interior of the country was via four passes through the Oman mountains. The *wadi* al-Jizzi led from Sohar to Buraimi, a short but difficult route. From al-Khaburah on the coast a long and little-used track les to 'Ibri. The main pass followed the *wadi* Sumail from Muscat to Izki and Nizwa; this route was the most used and the most important of the four. Finally, the *wadi* al-Fulayj carried a track from Sur to the eastern regions of the Oman mountains. Muscat, Matrah and Sur were each small all-weather ports with a certain amount of fresh water. Sohar has a maritime history, but its small port has been silted up for centuries. The coast of Dhofar has the silted remnants of two or three small ports; the heavy seas which pound this coast from May to October restrict access to it.

The area under cultivation in Oman has been estimated to be some 36,000 hectares, less than 0.15 per cent of the total land area of the country. Oman can be thought of as having islands of settlement surrounded by desert and inhospitable mountains. Some 40 per cent of this land under cultivation is situated on the Batina coastal plain, about 4 per cent is in Dhofar, around Salalah, and 1.7 per cent in the Musandam peninsula. The balance is found in pockets in the mountain valleys and in the foothills of the Oman mountains.[1] There is rough grazing supporting a marginal pastoral activity in the mountains of Dhofar. Table 1.1 shows the estimated area under various crops in 1971.

There are no forests or wooded areas in Oman. On the Batina coastal plain, in some mountain valleys, and on the Qara escarpment in Dhofar, there is a certain amount of stunted and scrub vegetation which supplies firewood. The seas around Oman provide fish for human consumption and for use as fertiliser and as an animal foodstuff.

The climate of Oman is hot and dry. Summer temperatures reach 50°C with averages over 40°C. Winter temperatures seldom go below 15°C. Humidity on the coast is particularly high, but inland the climate is dry. Rainfall is scarce and unpredictable, save on the Salalah plain and the seaward face of the escarpment, where the monsoon brings

Table 1.1: Crop Areas in Oman, 1971 (estimate)

	ha.	%
Dates	13,350	37.1
Lucerne (alfalfa)	5,550	15.4
Limes	3,550	9.9
Onions	3,700	10.2
Wheat	1,200	3.3
Tobacco	1,000	2.8
Bananas	850	2.4
Coconuts	200	0.6
Other crops	1,450	4.2
Uncultivated in settled areas	5,150	14.1
Total	36,000	100.0

Source: Harold Whitehead & Partners Ltd., London, Economic Survey of Oman, 1972.

assured precipitation from mid-June to mid-September each year. Attempts at systematic recording of rainfall have generally not been successful, but such records which have been kept suggest that annual rainfall over the country varies from about 40 mm in the drier regions to about 120mm in Salalah.[2] Both in the mountains of Dhofar, and in the Hajar mountains of northern Oman (where rainfall is more common in the winter months), soil erosion and limited vegetation ensures a relatively high run-off and regular recharging of natural ground-water reservoirs. In Dhofar there are a number of perennial springs discharging on to the Salalah plain.

The major mineral resource of Oman is oil, and this will be discussed separately. In recent years, surveys have been carried out for other minerals, and copper, chrome, nickel, iron ore and coal have been detected. Of these, only copper seems to be in quantities which might justify commercial exploitation.[3] Very much more work needs to be carried out before sufficient is known about Oman's mineral resources.

There has been no comprehensive population census of Oman. The government of Oman quotes a figure of 1,500,000 people. A number of independent surveys, using modern maps produced from aerial surveys, specially flown aerial surveys, and a considerable amount of field work to check results, have all suggested a population of between four hundred and five hundred thousand. The first economic survey of Oman carried out in 1971 estimated a figure of 450,000. At that time, the Sultan suggested a figure of 750,000 people. The first World Bank team in Oman in 1972 took a figure midway between these two figures, 600,000 people, and this figure has been much quoted in documents and year books published by international agencies. Table 1.2 amalgamates the various surveys undertaken by consultants which included attempts to measure population.

Table 1.2: Population of Oman (estimate)*

Batina coastal plain	102,500
Seaward foothills	28,000
Mountains and mountain valleys	27,600
Inland foothills	120,400
Desert	20,000
Sur region	11,500
Dhofar	50,000
Musandam	15,000
Capital area, Muscat and Matrah	50,000
Total	425,000

Sources: Harold Whithead & Partners Ltd., London, *Economic Survey of Oman, 1972;* Gibb, Petermueller & Partners, Athens, *Regional Road Studies, 1973/4;* Sir Alexander Gibb & Partners, London/ILACO, Arnhem, *Water Resource Surveys, 1974/75;* Sir William Halcrow & Partners, London, *Dhofar Surveys, 1973/4;* ITALCONSULT, Rome, *Transportation Survey, 1974;* Professional Group Australia, Sydney, *Musandam Survey,* 1975.

*These population estimates include about 10,000 fishermen.

The economy of Oman is almost exclusively dependent on oil. The petroleum sector provides well over 90 per cent of government revenues and almost 100 per cent of Oman's foreign exchange earnings. Yet Oman is not in the position of its neighbours and near neighbours in terms either of volume of production or of proven reserves, or of production costs. Saudi Arabia and the United Arab Emirates have higher production and higher reserves of crude oil, as well as production costs which are less than one-quarter of Oman's production costs. Table 1.3 gives crude oil production for Oman, for Oman's immediate neighbours Saudi Arabia and Abu Dhabi (part of the United Arab Emirates), and for near neighbours Kuwait, Qatar, Iraq and Iran for the ten-year period 1966 to 1975 inclusive.

Table 1.3: Crude Oil Production (millions of barrels), 1966-75

	Oman	Saudi Arabia	Abu Dhabi	Kuwait	Qatar	Iraq	Iran
1966	–	949.7	132.9	906.8	105.9	507.4	771.2
1967	20.9	1,023.8	139.1	912.4	118.3	447.9	947.7
1968	87.9	1,113.7	182.6	956.6	124.4	551.2	1,042.2
1969	119.7	1,173.9	219.0	1,011.8	129.9	557.4	1,231.7
1970	121.3	1,386.7	253.3	1,090.6	131.4	571.6	1,403.6
1971	104.7	1,740.6	340.9	1,166.4	157.0	624.5	1,666.5
1972	103.1	2,202.0	384.3	1,201.6	176.8	523.4	1,849.3
1973	106.9	2,772.6	477.1	1,102.5	208.1	705.2	2,152.2
1974	106.0	3,095.1	518.1	929.4	190.3	675.0	2,210.6
1975	124.6	2,583.2	512.0	749.6	160.3	820.6	1,965.4

Source: Petroleum Economist, London, June 1976.

These crude oil production figures tell their own story. Oman is by far the smallest of the major Middle East oil producers. Proven reserves of crude oil in Abu Dhabi, Saudi Arabia and Iraq are sufficient to sustain significant production increases, given a corresponding increase in demand. Oman, the smallest producer of the seven mentioned, has modest reserves and is currently (1976) at peak production. Reliable unofficial estimates suggest that production will be half its present rate in five years from now, that is, unless significant new discoveries are made and brought into production by 1980, in 1981 Oman's crude oil production will be little more than 60 million barrels. By the end of the century, production will have ceased, for all practical purposes. Further exploration is continuing, in Dhofar, offshore near Masirah, and in the Strait of Hormuz. Although some oil has been found both in Dhofar and in the Strait of Hormuz, production costs in both areas are likely to be particularly high, and there is as yet no guarantee that either field will ever be brought into production.

The story of oil exploration in Oman is an interesting one, and is worth telling. The difficulties encountered by exploration companies due to difficult terrain and poor communications, and the consequent concentration of effort to solve the problems created, provided many lessons for individuals and agencies concerned with the economic development of Oman.

The first oil concession in Oman was granted in 1924 to the D'Arcy interests by Sultan Taimur bin Faisal, but no serious exploration took place until one of the D'Arcy Exploration Company successors, the Iraq Petroleum Company subsidiary, Petroleum Development (Oman and Dhofar) Limited started work in 1956. Between this date and 1960, the IPC group spent £12 million on exploration and drilled four wells in central and southern Oman. Results were disappointing; there was nothing, it seemed, which would justify the expenditure of further sums of money on exploration, particularly taking the extremely difficult nature of the country into account. Enough was known to appreciate that any oilfields discovered would lie beyond the Oman mountains, in the desert regions of Oman, and that export would involve constructing a pipeline either northwards through the mountains, or eastwards to the coastline of the Arabian sea. The first route promised no small degree of engineering problems, and the second led to an exposed coastline with heavy seas for almost six months of the year. Given the alternative oilfields in Abu Dhabi then being explored by IPC, and world prices and demand for crude oil at that time, the IPC shareholders, British Petroleum, Standard Oil of New Jersey, Mobil, Compagnie Française de Pétroles, Royal Dutch Shell, and Partex (the Gulbenkian interests), were not unanimously enthusiastic about prospects in Oman. Most of these shareholders wished to give up exploration in Oman.

In April 1960, a majority of the shareholders withdrew from Oman, leaving Shell with 85 per cent of the concession and Partex with 15 per cent. In June 1967, Compagnie Française de Pétroles bought two-thirds of the Gulbenkian share and thus returned to the Oman operation with 10 per cent of the concession. The group was renamed Petroleum Development (Oman) Limited (PDO) at the time of the shareholders' withdrawal in 1960, and was from that point onwards managed by Shell.

Shell continued to explore, and eventually found oil in commercial quantities at Fahud in a well drilled only some 400 metres from one bored by the IPC group. A faulted geological structure and a large measure of bad luck had been responsible for this near miss by the earlier drillers. Subsequent discoveries at Natih and Yibal assured profitable exploitation of the field and a decision to commence commercial production was taken in 1964.

Before production and the export of oil could commence, an underground pipeline had to be constructed from Fahud through the Sumail gap in the Oman mountains to a new oil terminal built near Muscat, 276 km from the oilfields. This pipeline, the collecting system required to bring the crude oil from Yibal and Natih, and from a further small field at Al Huwaisah, and the terminal facilities on the coast at Mina al Fahal, were collectively designed to be as highly automated as possible. The cost was considerable; over £25 million was spent on export facilities in the two years prior to the first exports of oil from Oman in August 1967.

Oil from these fields in Oman has a low sulphur content, compared with oil found in fields within the Gulf, and has thus earned a 'sulphur premium'. On the other hand it has a comparatively high salt content, which has caused production difficulties and added to production costs.

PDO has continued exploration and in 1975 a new field at Ghaba was brought into production, after a spur pipeline had been constructed northwards for about 110 km to join the main pipeline to the coast from Fahud. Further small finds have been made; the best that can be hoped for is that the small fields may stop production failing at such a steep rate.

PDO is also active in Dhofar. A concession in Dhofar had been given by Sultan Sa'id bin Taimur to Wendell Phillips, an independent American oil man. This concession was relinquished in 1951 and subsequently twenty wells in the area were drilled by two American oil companies, City Services and Continental Oil. Some very heavy oil was discovered at Ma'mul, but it was considered at the time that this was not of sufficient quality and in sufficient quantity to justify commercial exploitation. PDO is looking again at this field, and others like it, as well as conducting new exploration. Although a potential resource, this field would require much capital to develop and production costs would, on an unofficial but informed estimate, be at least ten times those in northern Oman, which are themselves high compared to other fields in the Gulf area.

An offshore concession outside the territorial waters of the Gulf of Oman is held by international consortium and managed by the German company, Wintershall AG. Two wells have been drilled, one in 1968 and the second in 1971, without success. Attempts continue to interest other groups in concessionary areas relinquished by PDO.

Following developments in other oil-producing countries, the government of Oman acquired first a 25 per cent share in Petroleum Development (Oman) Limited early in 1974, and subsequently in the same year a further 35 per cent, bringing the total government share to 60 per cent. Oman was not, as of mid-1976, a member of the Organisation of Petroleum Exporting Countries (OPEC), but had been.

treated by the shareholders of PDO as though it were, thus benefiting from the oil price increases of October 1973 and January 1974, which had the effect of multiplying Oman's oil revenues by a factor of almost five.

The constraints to economic development in Oman after oil exports began were serious. The most significant was the ultra-conservative rule of the then Sultan of Muscat and Oman, Sa'id bin Taimur. This is discussed in detail in Chapter 3. Other constraints were poor or non-existent communications, both within Oman itself and between Oman and the outside world, and the poverty and low standard of education of the vast majority of the people of Oman. These bars to economic development had kept the economy of Oman at a subsistence level for over a century and, of course, precluded any saving by the society for ultimate investment in projects to lift the standard of living.

The fact of a static subsistence economy masked perhaps the most fundamental constraint to further economic development, the absolute shortage of water. The natural ground-water reservoirs of Oman were recharged by the meagre annual rainfall generally at a rate more or less equal to the consumption rate of a stagnant society. A high general and infant mortality rate, and also a high rate of emigration, kept the population static. Traditional irrigation methods, although wasteful of water, were not so inefficient as to cause a noticeable decline in the ground-water reservoirs. This problem, often not recognised by Omanis themselves, risks becoming extremely serious as development places hitherto unprecedented demands on Oman's natural water resources.

Efficient management of the water resources, through the twin vehicles of a strong national water conservation policy and modern irrigation systems, could double the area of land under cultivation and increase agricultural production in Oman by a very much larger factor. Failure to implement propositions for the professional management and conservation of the water supply could mean that this most precious and most scarce natural resource could be destroyed, and with it any hope of agricultural production on an economically viable basis in Oman.

The possibility of the destruction or impoverishment of Oman's natural water resources, coupled with the probable early exhaustion of the country's crude oil reserves, means that there are very severe constraints both to economic development and to political independence. Machiavelli's question about the ability of a prince to stand alone or have recourse to the protection of others may become most relevant in the next seven years in Oman.

Notes

1. Harold Whitehead & Partners Limited, London, *Economic Survey of Oman*, 1972.
2. Renardet Sauti ICE, Paris, *Water Resources Survey, 1975.*
3. *Middle East Economic Digest,* London, Vol.20, No.26, 1976.

2 THE HISTORICAL BACKGROUND

'. . .the prince should read history. . .'

Oman was, until the changes brought about following the forced deposition of Sultan Sa'id bin Taimur in July 1970, one of the least-known and most isolated countries in the world. The *coup* which overthrew the Sultan ended not only his 38-year reign but also a social structure which had not changed very much in over a thousand years. In a space of some five years, Oman shook off most of its medieval remnants and began to develop some of the institutions of government demanded by a modern state. There can be no understanding of what these changes meant to the Omani people without a knowledge of their history and traditions, their social organisation, and the influences which shaped their society and gave it its character.

It seems unlikely that the way of life of Sultan Sa'id's subjects had changed significantly since the first Arabs came to this corner of the Arabian peninsula, and certainly not since the Omani people embraced Islam in the eighth century AD. The greatest single constraint inhibiting the development of social structures in Oman is a shortage of water. The characteristic Omani settlement is a semi-fortified village around a water source. Jealousy of this scarce resource, as well as difficult communications caused by the rugged nature of the landscape, has made each village a self-contained entity. The pattern of settlement was thus a number of small communities, almost islands in a desert of rugged mountains and gravel plains. In a land not blessed by natural resources, people have had to fight to hold on to what they had, even amongst themselves. Invasions from outside and raids from neighbours have been common occurrences. The people of Oman have always known strife, either strife produced by external forces or induced by internal squabbling.

The early history of Oman is shrouded in mystery. Archaeological work carried out since 1970 has begun to lift the veil from the past, but many years of patient and painstaking work will be required before much more is known about pre-Arab Oman.

The first waves of Arab settlers, coming from what is now the Yemen Arab Republic, reached Oman about 2,000 years ago. Legend suggests that one such wave was led by Nasr, the son of al-Azd, and another by the sons of Malik bin Fahm, another descendant of al-Azd. These names live on in current everyday tradition in Oman. The early wanderers were followed by increasing numbers through the centuries. They came, as did the first nomads, from an area around the Marib dam in Yemen, about 150 km east of the city of Sana'a, capital of the modern Yemen Arab republic. The ruins of the Marib dam are still visible, and, as far as is known, the dam must have been a formidable engineering feat in its day, providing the means of life for a considerable population. Successive breaches, caused probably by inadequate maintenance, reduced the dam's capacity to support this population. It seems that there was a catastrophic breach sometime during the last decades of the sixth century AD. The Koran (Chapter 38, verses 15 and 16) says:

> Certainly there was a sign for Saba in their abode: two gardens in the right and the left; eat of the sustenance of your Lord and give thanks to Him; a good land and a forgiving Lord.
>
> But they turned aside, so we sent upon them a torrent of which the rush could not be withstood, and in place of their two gardens we gave to them two gardens yielding bitter fruit and growing tamarisk and a few thorn trees.

It is possible that these verses refer to this final breach of the Marib dam which caused so many people to leave their homes and wander in search of new lands in which to settle. They are also of interest in that they sum up in a few words the attitude of the traditional Arab society to authority, be it spiritual or temporal, an attitude relevant to an understanding of the development of government in Oman even down to the present day. In western political experience, the sanctity of private property as a realm over which public authority exercises minimal jurisdiction is a fundamental tenet of freedom; the dichotomy between authority as sovereignty and authority as ownership is unrecognised outside the stream of Western political thought. In the traditional Arab society, people can be dispossessed of their property by the whim of a ruler, whose power is absolute. This is a factor of considerable importance in understanding government in Oman or, indeed, in any developing country.

The migration of the Arab tribes from Yemen to Oman would not have been a sudden departure from an old home followed by an immediate settlement in a new abode. Rather, generation would follow generation as a tribe moved reluctantly from the destroyed world of its old home out across the desert pasture of 'tamarisk and a few thorn trees', finding little to sustain it, pausing a season or two in a favoured area where propitious rainstorms had brought the harsh lands to life, pausing until their flocks had destroyed the grazing and then moving on. There would have been constant fights with the people living in the path of their migration, until at last they came to 'a goodly land, a land abounding in fields and groves with pastures and unfailing springs'.[1]

This end of the odyssey brought no sudden peace or rest, for Oman was already peopled. The society the Arabs found in Oman was probably a series of relatively prosperous small rural communities with a type of feudal aristocracy having a well-ordered agricultural economy based on a Persian irrigation system. This system, known as *qanat* to the Persians and *falaj* to the Arabs, is expensive to build and to maintain, and the agriculture it sustained would also require much hand-labour. There is no reason to think that this ancient pattern of settlement in Oman was radically different from that of other ancient organised agricultural communities. The fact of the irrigation system, and the careful management it required, suggests an ordered society, a series of villages, each village the seat of some petty lord. The house of the lord, probably fortified, would dominate the cluster of houses and shelters of his serfs and servants. Gardens and irrigated fields would spread out from this centre. The constraint to growth would always be the limited water supply.

Dim and far off though it may be, an understanding of the picture that the Arabs found when they arrived first in Oman is important, because, as the wandering tribes settled, they had to accept much of the social organisation of the people they conquered. For the pre-Arab people of Oman, the wandering Arabs would have come like a plague of locusts out of the desert. Hungry and determined, they would take what they needed, fighting to do so when necessary. Just as the Bedu (nomadic) tribes of today live alongside the settled tribes of the towns and villages, sometimes trading, sometimes squabbling, sometimes acquiring wives, and gradually themselves becoming owners of property and thus losing much of their mobility, so it is likely that the first Arabs would have established themselves in Oman. In some cases there would have been conquest and immediate subjugation of the conquered peoples, in other cases a gradual assimilation over some generations. This went on until the Arabs, reinforced by fresh migrating waves behind them, became the dominant force in the community, jealously keeping their new possessions from others.

It is probable that later migrating tribes would care little whether they found Arabs or non-Arabs inhabiting a desired village. If they wanted it, and were strong enough, they would take it.

One important lesson that the early invaders had to learn was not to destroy that which sustained life, the elaborate irrigation system. The building and repair of this system was a skilled and costly business, demanding both skills and capital that the wandering tribes did not possess. The Arabic word *falaj*, loosely used to describe an irrigation system, or even the open channel ditches leading water from its outflow through the fields, is better thought of as a system for distributing water amongst those who have established rights to a source of supply.[2] The Arabs of Oman talk of the *falaj* system as 'coming from God', that is to say, it is something which they did not create themselves. The root of the word *falaj* has nothing to do with water or water supply, as such, but with division and distribution. The need for a disciplined management of a water supply does not come easily to nomads whose normal habit is to foul a well when they have finished using it at the end of a day's march. The evidence of ruined *falaj* systems in Oman suggests that not all tribes learned to adapt their tribal structure to this co-operative discipline. Western people, with generations of industrialised society behind them, tend to forget that in traditional societies, there can be no concept of independence from the harsh laws of nature. The early Arab settlers in Oman had no choice but to adapt themselves to the conditions of their new home. Those who did not do so did not survive; those who did had to make a concession to a way of life and accept a social discipline which was not natural for them. The result was that a naturally gregarious people settled down and developed a decentralised society, a comparatively large number of small units, each unit largely self-supporting and tied to the rhythm of the management of its water supply system.

The Arabs settled mostly in the heartland of Oman, that is to say in the foothills and valleys of the Jabal al-Akhdar massif and its extensions. The height of the mountains was sufficient to cause a modest precipitation, which in turn filled and replenished the ground-water reservoirs, the source of the *falaj* irrigation system. Arab influence on the coast was less. When the Portuguese arrived off the shores of Oman in the early sixteenth century, they found that the people of the coast still owed allegiance to a Persian-orientated monarch, the King of Hormuz, and that the peoples of the mountainous interior of Oman were fiercely independent. A recognition of this difference between the people of the mountains and the inland areas of Oman, who are inward-looking, mistrustful of strangers, slow to mix, with the more outward-looking people of the coast, who have had to live through a contact with the wider world, is yet another factor essential to an understanding of the history and government of Oman.

Omani legends speak of two different migrations of Arab peoples to Oman. The first, as described above, came from Yemen. The people of this migration were of southern Arab, or Qahtani stock, and still today the tribes who claim Yemeni origin are known as 'Yemani'. The second major migration, again according to legend, was of northern Arab or Adnani stock and entered Oman from the north. Tribes claiming this descent are today known as 'Nizari'. This may seem a relatively unimportant point, but, as will be seen, the history of Oman is so often a story of internecine tribal fighting and feuding, leading at times to civil wars. Mostly the fighting was between Yamani and Nizari tribes. Even today in the small town of Izki, little more than an hour from Muscat on a new modern highway, the traveller finds the town divided into two distinct sections, one called Yaman and one called Nizar. The tribesmen who live in each section claim respectively Yamani and Nizari origins and each group lives in perpetual mistrust of the other. Throughout Oman, tribal rivalry is still a significant factor. Every child in every tribe knows his tribal traditions, knows whether he is of Yamani or Nizari descent, and knows those tribes with which his tribe historically has been at fued. It is not uncommon for a tribesman to refuse the arbitration of a representative of the central government in the settlement of a dispute because that representative has a tribal background at odds with his own.

Contrasting to the fragmentary and nuclear nature of the Omani society imposed by the facts of physical geography, the greatest unifying force has been Islam. Oman was one of the first countries to embrace Islam during the lifetime of the Prophet Muhammad. There is no greater unifying force in the Arab world than Islam, and for those who believe, the Koran is at once the source of all wisdom, all laws, all customs. Just as traditional societies such as Oman have no concept of the difference between the sovereignty of the state and the authoritity of an individual over property, as mentioned above, so does Islam have no concept of the difference between spiritual and temporal power. It is as much a political and a legislative system as it is a religion. All religions are, in one way or another, codes of social behaviour, and Islam dictates to the True Believer almost every detail of his daily life, his ablutions, the manner of eating, what he should or should not eat, how he should dress, how his women should dress, how he should make love. It has become a religion of habit, though its faithful would deny this vehemently. Because it holds that all knowledge comes from God, because of its essential fatalism ('That which God gives, He also takes away'), because above all of its conservatism and refusal to accept that it can be other than perfection, Islam has acted as a great barrier to change. It suited societies in isolation, such as Oman, where any change could upset a delicate economic balance and thus cause disaster.

The innate conservatism of Islam was reinforced in Oman by a sectarian variant, Ibadhism. This sect grew from the Khawarij, or seceders, which in turn was born in the succession struggles which followed the death of the Prophet in 632 AD. The Khawarij denied the claimed hereditary right of the Quraish, the tribe of Muhammad, to the leadership of Islam (the Khalifate) and instead fought for what they asserted was the original democratic system for the election of a leader. This leader, or 'Imam', could be elected by the whole community from candidates who possessed the appropriate spiritual and personal qualities.

Oman in the eighth century AD was a loosely knit tribal society on the edge of the world of Islam. Such societies did not accept easily the yoke of Khalifate domination, and with it the obligation to pay taxes. Because of its remoteness from the centre of the Khalifate government, and because of the difficulties of communication both to and from Oman and within the country itself, any secessionist movement would have stood a reasonable chance of avoiding the domination of a distant government. A movement which had at its heart the principle of a spiritual leader elected democratically from its own numbers would be in an even stronger position to reject the demands of a despotic central power.

The Omanis, as Ibadhis, do not regard themselves as a breakaway sect, but as true Muslims. Others are the deviationists. Their leader was styled 'Imam of the Muslims', the word 'Imam' meaning 'One who sets an example.' His people gave him their allegiance on the understanding that he would guide and defend them, protect them from their enemies, and comply with the rules of the Koran and the customs of Islam. These rules and customs say, in effect, that all law is divine law, is hence immutable and may not be challenged, because by its very nature it is perfect.

The Imam was elected by a small council of tribal elders, the 'Ulama', and then had to submit himself to the people for the approval of his candidature by the acclamation of the crowd. This last was no hollow gesture; there are recorded instances of the general concourse of the people refusing to accept a nomination put to them by the Ulama. In this public gathering, the people vowed allegiance to the Imam and he vowed in turn to uphold and defend the integrity of the community. The people's allegiance could be withdrawn if the Imam did not measure up to the standards of his office. The first Imam of Oman elected in this way was Julanda bin Mas'ud who took office in *c.*750 AD as 'the first of the rightful Imams of Oman'.

An account has come down of the election of an Imam, Rashid bin al-Walid, in the late tenth century AD:

> Wherefore, when they had resolved to elect Rashid bin al-Walid Imam, they deemed it expedient to summon a general council, to come to an agreement as to the course to be adopted in the matter. Accordingly, a great number of the elect of the true faith assembled in the house of Nizwa in which Rashid. . .used to reside. . . They thereupon proceeded to swear allegiance to the Imam Rashid bin al-Walid, binding him to administer the duties of his office in obedience to God and his Apostles; to govern uprightly and to repress crime; to prosecute wars in defence of the faith as a Dafi'i Imam; and further to tread in the footsteps of the just Imams, his predecessors, in imitation of their virtue and uprightness. On such condition did [the sheikhs] swear fealty in the house at Nizwa. . . The Imam having accepted their vows, they went forth to the open plain at Nizwa, where the vast concourse of the people of Oman had collected. They had come not only from Nizwa, but from the various towns of the east and the west of Oman, and the assemblage was composed of persons of unimpeachable integrity, holding positions of rank and authority. They all assented to and obeyed the decision of the Council without the slightest sign of repugnance or disapproval. Then [one of the Council] arose. . .and approaching Rashid hailed him as Imam, and announced to the people that the Council had elected him, commanding them to vow their allegiance. This they did openly and willingly without a dissentient voice. . .For some time people kept arriving for the purpose of making the compact, until the whole realm had declared for the new Imam.[3]

Apart from his spiritual obligations, which in addition to those mentioned in this account, would include leading the prayers in the principle mosque in Nizwa each Friday, the main responsibilities of the Iman to his people were to lead them in battle against their enemies and to punish criminals. In such a loosely knit polity, all other matters would be in the hands of the local village sheikhs. Oman at that time, and indeed for many centuries afterwards, had no need for a more formal government structure. Each small village was economically more or less self-sufficient, and provided that the country was at peace, and the water supply did not fail, life could continue peacefully. The natural proclivities of mankind for power, wealth and position, and for wishing to take possessions of others were the enemies of this precarious political balance. Later rulers, abandoning the elective principle, needed soldiers, taxes and regional governors, thus changing fundamentally the original structure of the Omani state.

Before this happened, however, the Ibadhi creed became a rallying point around which Omanis fought for their independence. From the time of the first Iman, Oman suffered no fewer than ten successive waves of invasion over a period of little more than two hundred years. Each onslaught had as its stated purpose the destruction of this community of religious independents who would not acknowledge the Khalifate, and who would not pay their taxes. Each invasion was ultimately defeated, as much by the fierce resistance of Omanis in defence of their lands and their faith and way of life as by difficult terrain, distance and poor communications.

Fundamental weaknesses in the structure of the Omani polity were revealed once an invader had been defeated and the external threat thus removed. The forces of tribal mistrust and rivalry, fanned doubtless by the great scarcity of resources, and careless of what had been gained in unity and the crystallisation of common objectives during the period of invasion, gave birth to internal strife and civil war. The results were disastrous. As an Omani historian put it:

> They fought among themselves for power and supremacy, each one aiming at having the authority in his own hands or in the hands of those he favoured, so God delivered them into the power of one more unjust than themselves, and since they had become corrupt in their religion, therefore God deprived them of the realm and set an enemy over them to rule them.[4]

This conflict between the democratic concepts of the Ibadhi creed and the nature of medieval man in all countries to group himself with his fellows around a strong leader has been, and indeed remains, at the heart of political development in Oman for some 1,200 years. Traditional societies have no concept of a state in the sense understood in Western Europe or North America. The difference mentioned earlier in this chapter between the sovereignty of a state and the authority of a private property-owner cannot be translated into terms that have any significant meaning that relate to the experience of people and their rulers in traditional societies. An individual, by the strength of his will and his arm, could dominate a region for a time, and the people living in that region would support him because he was the strongest and could thus protect them. All property was thus his, the strong man's, by right of conquest, actual or implicit; those who accepted his authority were given a right to property on condition that they provided armed support to their lord when he needed it. The right to property could be withdrawn at the whim of the lord. This brief generalisation describes the situation in any society which has not developed a fundamental and unchallenged respect for the rule of law and the concept of the state being greater than the individual, but with the individual having clearly defined and unalienable rights within the fabric of the state.

On the other hand, the Ibadhi political concepts recognised the rights of groups of individuals (i.e. tribes) to their own tribal lands, those lands within working distance of their water supply, and saw the need for a supra-communal authority only for setting an example in spiritual matters. As there was no difference between religious law and civil law, the spiritual leader, whose task it was to set the example, would thus logically be the supreme judge on earth for crimes of any nature, and the supreme arbitor in the settlement of disputes. This system could work in times of peace, and it could work also in times of war if the Imam happened to combine his spiritual qualities with martial vigour and effectiveness. His authority depended wholly on the will of a majority of the people to support him. If he could gain military victories, this support was assured. A judicious sharing of the spoils of such a victory would ensure that support continued. A defeat naturally would mean a great drop in support, and eventual challenging by a rival who could offer some chance of victory. The age-old right of victors to help themselves to the chattels and women of the vanquished proved a stronger motivator than religious faith, and the successful Imams were those who were able to go on adding to the material wealth of their people.

Thus the history of Oman has always been one of conflict. The fragmented nature of the pattern of settlement, the poor internal communications, the resultant self-sufficiency of village communities sharpened already deeply felt tribal rivalries. The Ibadhi creed itself, well rooted in the habits of the people though it was, was not the element to forge a natural national cohesion. There was, and there still is, in the Omani character, an innate propensity to quarrel with one's neighbour. The centuries-long history of internal strife has at once encouraged despotic rulers, opened the door to foreign interference in the affairs of Oman, and, perhaps most serious of all, slowly destroyed the most priceless and irreplaceable heritage of the Omani people, their water supply and distribution system. Around Nizwa, around 'Ibri, from Bahla down the *wadi* Bahla to Bisya and beyond, in the Sharqiya, are vestiges of a much greater water-supply system, and a more extensive area under cultivation, than exist today.

A continuing brief examination of Oman's history emphasises these points. The country is covered in a veil from about the end of the tenth century AD until the early seventeenth century. This seems to have been a 'dark age' of tyranny, despotism and internal strife. The veil began to lift when the Portuguese, followed by English, Dutch and French traders and adventurers arrived off the coasts of Oman. Following the fall of Constantinople to the Ottoman Turks in AD 1453, and the consequent great expansion of the Turkish Empire, the trade routes of the European nations to the Indian subcontinent and the islands of the East Indies were either destroyed or seriously impeded. Alternative routes were sought and found around the coast of Africa. This brought the Portuguese to the Gulf of Oman as forerunners of the European influences which have had such an effect on recent developments in Oman.

A Portuguese fleet commanded by Alfonso de Alboquerque anchored off Ras al-Hadd towards the end of August, 1507.

> And they found there. . .thirty or forty fishing ships, which come thither from the city of Ormuz, Calyate, and all that coast to fish for bonitos and albeciras; for there is a great traffic in these fish to many parts. . .and they burned all these ships, and on the following morning set sail with a fair wind, and took the ships' boats with mast and sails.[5]

Later the Portuguese fleet arrived off Muscat.

> Mascate is a large and very populous city, surrounded on the inner side with very large mountains, and on the seaboard it is close to

> the water's edge. . . The harbour is small, shaped like a horseshoe, and sheltered from every wind; it is the principal entrepot of the Kingdom of Hormuz, into which all the ships which navigate these parts must of necessity enter, to avoid the opposite coast, which contains many shallows. It is of old a market for carriage of horses and dates; it is a very elegant town, with very fine houses, and supplied from the interior with much wheat, maize, barley and dates, for lading as many vessels as come for them. This city of Mascate is part of the Kingdom of Ormuz, and the interior belongs to a king called the Benjabar. . .[6]

From the little that is known of Oman during the period from the tenth century to the arrival of the Portuguese, it can be gleaned that for part of this period the interior of the country was tyrannically ruled by a family which styled its members 'king' and which came from the al-Nabhani tribe. An Omani historian summed up the general feeling towards these despots:

> Of the rulers of the Benu-Nebhan there was not one Imam or Malik [king] whom the God of grace and benevolence could approve of. On the contrary, most of them were tyrants and oppressors, and that led to their downfall – 'Do not imagine that God overlooks the actions of the evil-doers.' When, therefore, He decreed that the evils which had so long afflicted the people of Oman should come to an end and their wounds be bound up by justice. He caused the sun of salvation to shine upon them, and by its pure beams to scatter the mists of injustice. . .[7]

By this time, in addition to the anarchy of the interior of the country, the Portuguese had occupied Muscat and the coastal towns for well over a century. The 'sun of salvation' which scattered the enemies of Oman and replaced chaos with order was Nasr bin Murshid bin Sultan al-Ya'arubi, who was elected Imam at Rostaq in 1624. His tribe, the Ya'arubah, were perhaps the oldest representatives of the southern Arab migration of perhaps 1,200 to 1,500 years previously, and his proud genealogy ended '. . .al Ya'arubi, al-Arabi, al-Himyari, al-Azdi, al-Yamani, the upright Ibadhi'. Nasr was a remarkable man and an outstanding military and political leader. His election in Rostaq was engineered by a much respected figure, the 'learned and pious Sheikh'[8] Khamis bin Sa'id al-Shaqsi, who led the deliberations of the people when they:

> were greatly divided, and much contention and strife existed among them on many matters. . . The learned and devout Mussulmans then consulted together about setting up an Imam who should be invested with full powers to decree what was lawful and prohibit what was unlawful. . .[9]

At the time of Nasr's election, there were at least five petty rulers who styled themselves 'king' in Oman, based at Rostaq, Nakhl, Sumail, Samad and Ibra, with other forts and towns in the hands of other tribal leaders and the whole country beset by internal strife. The Portuguese occupied the coastal towns, including Muscat. Nasr had the foresight to realise that the problems which beset Oman could only be resolved by unity, and that this unity in turn could only be engendered by a common cause: the driving out of the foreigners. A man who was as able a soldier as he was a politician, with all the personal courage and cunning at his command, he set about giving the country a unity it had not enjoyed for some seven hundred years.

The task took him the remainder of his life. On 22 April 1649, whilst his armies were besieging the last of the Portuguese in Muscat, and at a time when his authority was unchallenged throughout Oman, Nasr died and was buried at Nizwa. He was succeeded by his cousin Sultan bin Saif al-Ya'arubi, a redoubtable leader of men and a warrior, who had no difficulty in winning the acclaim of the people at a time when the national fortunes flourished. Imam Sultan completed the capture of Muscat and the complete expulsion of the Portuguese in January 1650. The expulsion of the Christians was not enough for the Imam; doubtless with the intention of maintaining the hard-won prize of national unity, and also with the idea of being able to reward those who had served him well in battle with further spoils of war, he ordered a *Jihad* (Holy War) against the Portuguese. His ships pursued and harried them in India and down the east coast of Africa, and he was able to build up a considerable navy from captured ships as a result. So successful was he that Oman soon had the most powerful fleet in the northern Indian Ocean and Omani trade flourished as never before. At this time too was laid the foundation of the Omani colonial empire down the east coast of Africa, and Omani large-scale involvement in the trade in slaves, events which were to have consequences of great significance two centuries later.

The hitherto undreamed-of wealth which flowed into the country during the reign of the Imam Sultan permitted the building of the great fort at Nizwa, which took some twelve years to complete, as well as many other substantial houses and forts. The previous decentralised nature of the government was replaced by a strong and dominant central power, who appointed *walis* and *qadhis* (governors and judges) to rule and a minister justice in his name in all major towns. Equally significant, the community's wealth now permitted, for the first time in the history of the Arab occupation of Oman, large sums of money to be spent on renovation and repair of the *falaj* system, with consequent encouragement to agriculture and a resultant movement away from a subsistence economy. The Omani historian comments:

> . . . Oman revived during his government and prospered; the people rested from their troubles, prices were low, and roads were safe, the merchants made large profits, and the crops were abundant. The Imam himself was humble. . . He used to traverse the streets without an escort, would sit and talk familiarly with the people. . . Thus he persevered in ordaining what was lawful and forbidding what was unlawful. . .[10]

The Imam Sultan died in 1679. Nothing revealed the changed and centralised nature of the government more than his succession, which was not by an Imam elected democratically and acclaimed by the people *en masse,* but by his son Bil'arab. The hereditary principle thus established persists to this day, and with it a denial of a nine-hundred-year-old principle of the right of the Omani people to choose their own leader. It can be argued that they forfeited this right by being unable to elect a leader who could undertake the most fundamental of all tasks of government, the defence of the integrity of the state. In fact, this right had not so much been denied as sold: Imam Sultan realised, as did the more effective of his successors, that filling the pockets of a few key tribal leaders made both their religious fervour and their democratic principles seem less important. It was only when pockets became empty that the cry for an elected Imam and a return to the true religion became heard.

The reign of the Imam Bil'arab was an unhappy one. His one notable achievement was the building of the beautiful fortified house at Jabrin, which was completed about 1688. For much of the period of his Imamate, he was fighting with his brother Saif for control of Oman. He died, some have said by his own hand, at Jabrin in 1692.

His brother Saif assumed the title of Imam, and continued with his father's policy of making money for himself through trade and hence making money for many of his subjects through his active encouragement of their business endeavours. The country's prosperity continued, and the Imam Saif continued also the work of water-supply and *falaj* renovation and repair and the consequent encouragement of agriculture. Agriculture became more than a mere subsistence activity; the emergence of a merchant class with large houses and households provided a market for surplus agricultural production. Thousands of young date palms were planted along the flat plain of the Batina coast, where they could be irrigated from shallow wells rather than from the *falaj* system. Production costs were lowered as the frequent shallow wells required less labour than the intricate *falaj* system with its long supply channels. People were encouraged to move from the interior villages to settle in the new lands of the coastal plain. The Omani historian comments: 'Oman was strong under his administration and became the best of countries.' Imam Saif died at Rostaq in October 1711.

The hereditary principle was now established, and Saif was succeeded as Imam by his son Sultan. This Imam's claim to fame is modest: he spent all the money he inherited from his father and borrowed much as well. He used part of this to build the fine fort at Hazm. His navy, always aggressive, became feared throughout the Gulf of Oman and the northern Indian Ocean. Some of his less well-disciplined captains earned themselves a reputation as fierce and ruthless pirates. These captains, often out of control, underemployed, and probably underpaid, attacked whatever ships they could find, and thus brought their master and his country into increasing contact and conflict with the London-based Honourable East India Company and the power of England behind it, an occurrence which was to have fundamental and far-reaching effects on the history of Oman.

Before this effect made itself felt, however, Oman suffered a long period of civil war. The Imam Sultan bin Saif died in 1718, and was succeeded by his twelve-year-old son, Saif bin Sultan II. No boy of twelve could hope to have the necessary statecraft to maintain stability, particularly when his easy-going father had tended to let matters slip. The absence of the strong central control encouraged rivals, king-makers and adventurers. The battles and alliances which occurred during the ensuing long period of bloody internal strife are too numerous and too complex to be followed here. It is sufficient to say that the rival sides in this civil war were divided broadly on Yamani-Nizari lines. The Yamani tribes were led initially by Khalf bin Mubarak, of the Bani Hina tribe, and thus became known as 'Hinawi'. The Nizari tribes were led by Muhammad bin Nasr of the Bani Ghafir, or Miyayihah, and were henceforth known as 'Ghafiri'. Although both leaders were killed in a battle in Sohar in 1724, the names of the factions continued. The bitterness and suspicion engendered during this costly and cruel civil war has its echoes even today in tribal rivalries and mistrust.[11]

Although the original division of tribes in the civil war was broadly on Yamani-Nizari lines, there was, during the conflict, and has been ever since, much switching of loyalties, the most notable being the example of the Bani Ghafir themselves. Although they gave their name to the Ghafiri faction, they are now counted among the Hinawi tribes. An important tribe in the Ghafiri faction is the Bani Riyam, who claim Yamani origin. Similarly, an influential and powerful tribe in the Hinawi faction, a tribe whose leaders have played no inconsiderable role in the recent history of Oman, is the al-Hirth, who claim Nizari descent.

As has happened subsequently on occasions when Omanis were divided among themselves, one faction appealed to outsiders, in this case the Persians. Again, as has happened elsewhere on other occasions, the erstwhile helpers showed signs of wishing to stay in the country to which they had been invited. A Persian invasion in 1737 marked the beginning of the end of the destructive fratricidal struggle. An effective military leader, Ahmad bin Sa'id bin Muhammad Al Bu Sa'id, heartened the remnants of the Hinawi faction, and defeated the Persians in a battle fought at Sohar. The Persians left Oman and Ahmad was elected Imam shortly afterwards in about 1744.

A great deal of the achievements of the Ya'arubi dynasty was destroyed during this disastrous civil war. Irrigation systems, water sources, gardens, fields and buildings were indiscriminately destroyed by both factions. Yet the lessons of how Oman could be best governed were not lost on the Imam Ahmad. On the political plane, it has been demonstrated that the spiritual ideals of the Ibadhi Imamate had to be backed with statecraft and with considerable temporal power and authority for the polity to have stability. The elective democratic principle, the very heart of Ibadhism, came up against the sharp rocks of human frailty and encouraged intrigue. The Ya'arubi experience showed that the dynastic principle with hereditary succession had its inherent weakness also, but on balance was more suited to the needs of the Omani people at the time.

Economically, the fundamental weakness of the inward-looking subsistence way of life based on an inherited irrigation system which could not generate a sufficient capital surplus to maintain that irrigation system on a long-term basis had been demonstrated, but few were perceptive enough to see the implications for the future of Oman. Agriculture could only be sustained on capital earned from other activities, plunder or trade; with its pattern of fragmented holdings and little specialisation, with poor communications and lack of markets, Oman could never survive on agriculture alone.

The Imam Ahmad recognised this, and recognised also that Oman's geographical position would give it a considerable advantage in intra-regional trade. A considerable merchant in his own right, he encouraged his subjects to trade in a far more peaceful way than had the Ya'arubi before him. Muscat flourished as a commercial centre, and the whole country prospered. In his capital at Rostaq, the Imam Ahmad preserved a balance between the traders of the coast and the cultivators of the interior. He maintained a not inconsiderable court and organised a regular army and navy, innovations wholly contrary to the spirit of Ibadhism, but practical and necessary at the time. The defeated Ghafiri faction and the remnants of the Ya'arubi still smarted under their losses, and the innate Omani propensity to intrigue revealed itself again. There were several uprisings during the Imam Ahmad's 39-year-long reign, and in the last years of his reign he was challenged by a revolt led by two of his sons, Saif and Sultan.

Upon his death in 1783, the Imam Ahmad's second son, Sa'id, was elected Imam. Hilal, Ahmad's elder son, was disqualified by blindness, and the vigorous sons, Saif and Sultan, by their revolt against their father. The Imam Sa'id was weak and ineffectual, and commanded no respect. His son Hamad usurped political control from his father and moved the capital to Muscat, where he ruled, using the title 'Sayyid' (Lord). He made no attempt to assume the role of Imam, which his father retained, quite ineffectually, in Rostaq, until he died sometime between 1811 and 1821. No attempt was made to elect or appoint another Imam upon his death, nor did his successors ruling as temporal lords in Muscat attempt to use the title of Imam.

Sayyid Hamad bin Sa'id ruled in Muscat from 1784 to 1792. He appears to have been a shrewd politician and an effective ruler, for the trade of Oman continued to flourish and there is no record of any challenge from the tribes of the interior, suggesting that all benefited in one way or another from the general wealth, either directly or through a generous subvention payment from the ruler. Yet in his rule were sown the seeds of yet another future division of the country. The erstwhile 'Oman' came to be known as 'Muscat and Oman', the people of Muscat and the coastal towns being traders and Oman being the home of the tribal traditionalists; the latter became more and more isolated from the world, as they spurned the profits of trade and their agriculture sank lower and lower to a subsistence level. This split caused much discord in the latter part of the nineteenth century and was not finally healed until Sultan Qaboos renamed the country 'Oman' in 1970.

Sayyid Hamad died of smallpox in Muscat in 1792 and his place as ruler was taken by his uncle, Sayyid Sultan bin Ahmad, one of the Imam Ahmad's rebellious sons. There was no question of an election, and in any case there was still an Imam in Rostaq. Sultan was the strongest man and no one was prepared to challenge his assumption of the role of ruler. To strengthen his position against any flickering ambition on the part of his brothers Sa'id (the Imam) and Qais (the third son of the Imam Ahmad), Sultan concluded a family agreement with them at Barka in 1793. This agreement involved a virtual dismemberment of Oman: Sa'id was to continue in Rostaq as Imam, Qais was to have Sohar, and Sultan to have Muscat. A modern historian has commented:

> The compact of Barka was a tangible manifestation of the changes effected by two generations of Al Bu Sa'id rule. Sovereign power was now divided, the Imamate was falling into desuetude, and the most vigorous member of the ruling family, Sultan, was concerned almost wholly with maritime and commercial enterprises. Not unnaturally, a growing estrangement between the Al Bu Sa'id and the inland tribes developed, becoming more marked in succeeding generations. Oman's great need in the nineteenth century was for strong leadership and military strength.[12]

The lack of leadership and military strength was heavily underlined over a period of some three years from 1800 to 1803 when Oman was invaded by Wahhabi tribes burning with a new-found religious fanaticism from what is now Saudi Arabia. It is possible that Oman might have come under Wahhabite domination had not a fortuitous assassination (at least from an Omani point of view) of a Wahhabite leader caused the enemy to withdraw.

No matter what the leadership of the Omani nation might have wished in the nineteenth century, their weakness was assured by an event of great long-term significance for Oman. This was the conclusion of a treaty with the British Honourable East India Company in 1798 and the confirmation of this treaty in 1800. The British aim at that time was to contain French ambition and above all to keep French ships and soldiers away from India. The victories of Napoleon in Egypt and his diplomatic advances throughout the area prompted the first treaty. Sayyid Sultan was probably not given much choice in the matter of this first treaty. As a merchant prince in his own right, he would have been knowledgeable enough and realist enough to see the power of the British presence in India. Certainly he would have been in no position to resist British demands. This first treaty was innocuous enough; unlike some of those which followed, it did not affect the trade of Muscat or the ruler's personal wealth, and there was no challenge to his rule from within Oman up to his death in 1804.

Immediately following his death, however, the characteristic Omani pattern of intrigue was again revealed. The cousin of Sayyid Sultan, Badr bin Saif bin Ahmad Al Bu Sa'id, claimed the right to rule, but this was not generally accepted and there was much internal squabbling and killing until Badr was assassinated by the son of Sayyid Sultan, Sayyid Sa'id, in 1807, at a time when the obvious weakness of Oman had tempted a second successful Wahhabite invasion. At the time of the murder by which he obtained power, Sayyid Sa'id was aware that the invaders controlled most of the interior of Oman.

No more than seventeen when he came to power (Omanis are seldom sure of their age), Sayyid Sa'id proved to be a remarkable young man. Murdering a rival to secure the rule for himself proved the least of his attributes. He immediately had to fight for his realm against the Wahhabite invaders, and it was not until 1820, with some help from the British East India Company and the Persians, that he was finally able to secure his position. At some time during this period of strife the Imam Sa'id died in Rostaq. He was of so little account that even the date of his death is uncertain. Whether it was because there was sufficient confidence in Sayyid Sa'id among the tribes of Oman, or whether the religious fervour of the Wahhabis had tempered the enthusiasm of Omanis for an Imam, or whether the disgraceful intrigues of the civil war had robbed the office of much of its traditional respect is not clear. The fact is that, for whatever reason, there was no move to elect another Imam or to acclaim Sayyid Sa'id as Imam.

Sa'id continued his family's mercantile tradition with great success, and sought vigorously to expand Oman's trade and influence, not hesitating to use force against Bahrain and the Persian coast when he thought that this would strengthen his argument. In 1829 he secured a foothold in Dhofar, a miserable, poverty-stricken and trouble-ridden region to the far south of Oman, and in 1832 he began seriously to cultivate his East African colonies. Most of the rest of his life was spent on the greener coast of Zanzibar and many of his Omani subjects migrated to join him and to find an easier life in those rich lands. Sa'id was responsible, as no other Omani ruler, for the spread of Arab influence along the East African littoral. Funds remitted to Oman by the settlers assured wealth at home, but wealth which in general was used for consumption and display, rather than investment in assuring the water supply and improving agriculture. Sayyid Sa'id was almost permanently absent from Muscat from 1832, his Oman dominion tended to become a poor relation, a tendency enhanced by Sa'id's closer association with the power of the British exercised through the officials of the Honourable East India Company.

Sa'id knew, as did Sayyid Sultan before him, that he could not challenge the British position with any hope of success. There were certain obvious advantages in this association for the Omani side, in the short term at least. The British naval and military prowess was formidable, compared to anything that the Omanis could muster, and such allies could assure Omani success against enemies, provided they did not ask too much. The price asked by the British officials seemed extraordinary to the Omani government, but they were not in any position to negotiate, it seems. The price was simply that they should give up the extremely profitable trade in slaves from Sa'id's African colonies to the rest of the Arabian Peninsula. This request, laudable though it doubtless was in British eyes, struck at the whole basis of the economy of Oman and the organisation of its society. Slavery in the Arabian context does not have the same basic infringement of human rights, the same sordidness and cruelty as it does in the European or North American tradition. Slaves were family retainers and servants, clerks and administrators, and often held important positions of trust, as well as performing menial tasks; they were an essential element in the society.

In addition to this, of course, the trade in slaves was a highly profitable undertaking, and Sayyid Sa'id both employed a large number of slaves and was a principal in the slave trade. The first anti-slavery treaty with the British government, acting through the East India Company, was in 1822. It sought to restrict the trade in slaves and was followed by further treaties in 1839 and 1845. These treaties may have caused a glow of righteousness in British hearts but for Oman they were little short of disastrous. It is not clear what concession, if any, Sayyid Sa'id was able to extract from the British in the negotiation of these treaties. A large personal payment might have been offered and accepted; this would be in keeping with a way of life in Oman, but there is no historical evidence of such a *quid pro quo.*

Coupled with the loss to the Omani economy caused by the suppression of the trade in slaves, there were further losses due to the ever-increasing commercial presence in the seas and countries around Oman of European ships and traders whose business methods and efficiency made Arab competition lose its edge. Too much should not be made of this point, however, as even today most of the coastal trade of the whole Persian Gulf region is carried in the traditional craft by Arab and Iranian seamen.

In any event, Omani trade, and with it Omani prosperity, declined sharply during the last years of the reign of Sayyid Sa'id. The fact of the ruler's almost constant presence in Zanzibar did not help Oman at all. There was a great migration of Omani families to Zanzibar. On the death of Sayyid Sa'id in 1856 his small empire was divided between his two sons, Thuwaini and Majid, the former to have Oman and the latter Zanzibar. Sayyid Thuwaini attempted to regain Zanzibar by force of arms and the government of British India, concerned with stability in the area, acted as arbitrator in the dispute. Recognising the economic loss caused to Oman by the severance of the Zanzibar connection, the Governor-General of British India, Lord Canning, ruled in his arbitration that the government of Zanzibar should make an annual payment to the government of Oman of 40,000 Maria Theresa dollars, a not insignificant sum in those days.

Payment of the Canning Award by the Zanzibaris fell almost immediately into arrears; it is likely that lack of the will to do so was as much a factor in this default as actual shortage of funds would have been. The government of British India, having stopped the Omani side taking Zanzibar back by force, had a moral responsibility in the matter, as well as a desire to maintain peace and stability in an area lying astride the sea route to India. Thus it happened that the British came to make the payment themselves from 1871; it was paid from Bombay until 1947, when it became the responsibility of the Foreign Office in London. It was discontinued in 1956. Although Oman was never a British colony or protectorate, the British government provided the one stable and sure part of the national revenue for 85 years, a fact of the greatest importance in understanding political developments in Oman during this period and the evolution of government.

Before this happened, however, there was one flare-up of Omani national feeling, one attempt by the people of the interior to arrest the seemingly inevitable slide into the sterility of dependence on foreigners of their country. This was the brief reign of the Iman 'Azzan bin Qais, a cousin of the direct succession, from 1868 to January 1871. Following a period of disorder and fratricide quite exceptional even by Omani standards, 'Azzan took over the rulership of Oman and was accepted as Imam by a significant number of tribes. He was not elected, and did not have the honour of public acclamation; he had many enemies and had to fight for his position. Yet, seemingly alone among his peers, he realised that Oman could never be strong and independent until the authority of the central government was re-established and the tribes of interior Oman accepted the obligations due to this central government, and were prepared to pay taxes for its sustenance. Imam 'Azzan failed, and his failure must be seen in part due to a complete misunderstanding of his motives by the government of British India, advised by the then political resident in the Persian Gulf, Colonel Lewis Pelly. A report from Pelly to the Political Secretary in Bombay states:

> I asked the Agent [of 'Azzan bin Qais] how it happened that while the Sultans of the old dynasty permitted the tribes on the frontier to remain in quasi-independence and refrained from intruding on them with force, the present government pursued an opposite policy. He explained that under the old dynasty the Sultans were not in sufficient strength to subjugate the border tribes. But that the policy of Syud Azan's Government had from the first been to subjugate all the tribes of Oman to the central authority, and that the Government were determined to adhere to this line of action, as they considered that the Oman territories could never be at peace or possess a strong Government so long as the Tribal Chiefs considered themselves independent.[13]

Pelly had no sympathy with the motives of 'Azzan: his attempt to unify the country was seen as a move against the established order, the thought of a strong and coherent state on the flank of the sea route to India was an anathema, his government was not recognised by the government of British India, and the payment of the Canning Award was stopped. Further, the British gave encouragement and financial support to the leader of the opposition against 'Azzan bin Qais, his rival Sayyid Turki bin Sa'id, a younger son of that Sayyid Sa'id, whose death in 1856 caused the dismemberment of the Zanzibar limb and the consequent economic and political problems. Sayyid Turki was weak and ineffectual, a sycophant, but he could claim legitimacy in the succession. In any event, his opposition with the support of the British succeeded in defeating the forces of 'Azzan bin Qais, and the latter was killed in a battle outside Matrah in January 1871.

Sayyid Turki was immediately installed as 'Sultan' (a term which British officials came to use to describe the ruler of Oman during the early part of the nineteenth century), his government was recognised by the government of British India, and payments of the Canning Award were resumed. In spite of this, Oman sank into an ever-deepening economic and political torpor. Lack of purpose and direction in the government, no effective means of maintaining any semblance of authority, an inability to control the tribal leaders of the interior, either by example, or force of arms, or by material inducements, the almost complete stifling of Omani trade by yet another treaty signed in 1873 aimed at 'the effective suppression of the slave trade' – all these influences contributed to a general debility. Tribal leaders in the interior of Oman, unable themselves to maintain authority in a period of such distress, saw more and more of their people making the one-way migratory trip to Zanzibar. Whole villages became depopulated.

It was not long before the increasing desperation of the people produced an uprising. The *tamimah* (paramount sheikh) of the al-Hirth, a powerful Hinawi tribe of the Sharqiyah, Sheikh Salih bin 'Ali al-Harthi, led attacks on the capital in January 1874 and again in June 1877. In each case the rebels captured Matrah and threatened Muscat, and in each case they were bought off by the Sultan with a cash payment, coupled, in the second case, with a certain amount of moral persuasion caused by the presence of a British warship, HMS *Teazer*. In October 1883, a third attack was made on Muscat by Sheikh Salih bin 'Ali. The pattern was repeated: a cash payment and a few rounds from a British warship, HMS *Philomel*, caused the rebels to disperse and kept Sayyid Turki in power. At this time, the term 'Muscat and Oman' described the country very well. The Sultan, Sayyid Turki, lived in Muscat, his palace on the water-front being adjacent to the residence of the British Political Agent. His authority, in so far as he had any at all, extended along the Batina coast to Sohar. The rest of the country went its own way, under its many different tribal leaders. The subsistence agricultural economy sustained a barely adequate life; surplus population emigrated to Zanzibar. To relieve the dullness and pressures, the Sheikhs of Oman would combine to attack the Sultan in Muscat.

Sultan Turki died in 1883, and was succeeded by his second son, Sayyid Faisal. The elder son was disqualified by idiocy, caused probably by congenital disease. Poverty and unrest continued, but a fortuitous squabble between the Hinawi and Ghafiri factions prevented them from combining to attack the new ruler. It was just as well, for Sultan Faisal's government was in no shape to meet any challenge. However, by 1894, the tribes of the interior had found sufficient common cause to forget their differences and to combine for yet another attack on Muscat, led, as previously, by Sheikh Salih bin 'Ali al-Harthi. Sheikh Salih was now an old man and the fighting was under the command of his son Abdullah. A surprise attack on Muscat on 13 February 1895 carried all before it. This time, the government of British India did not intervene, in spite of frantic requests from Sultan Faisal. The Sultan had recourse to the age-old Omani method of overcoming enemies; he borrowed money from merchants and bought off the rebels. His forces reoccupied Muscat on 10 March in the same year. In spite of this success in maintaining his position, the authority of the government in Muscat was at a nadir. Nowhere was the Sultan respected, and his authority, where accepted, was only on a *faute de mieux* basis. He was heavily in debt, and his only income, the Canning Award and a customs revenue rendered minute by the dearth of trade, was inadequate to meet his commitments. Government structure was non-existent.

The failure of the British to come to his assistance in 1895 so alienated the Sultan that he was prepared to listen to the French overtures which a wily French political agent made to him at this time. The French authorities were prepared to be very much more relaxed about the slave issue than were the British. The British also frowned heavily upon a lucrative arms trade, which the French were prepared to countenance and sustain. The British position over arms was understandable, because Muscat became something of an entrepôt for arms on their way from Europe to the tribesmen of the North-West Frontier of British India. The French attitude is also understandable; at a period of intense colonial rivalry between the two European nations, any move to embarrass the other side was fair.

The Sultan's extremely grave financial position softened British hearts to a certain extent and he was granted two loans by the government of British India, one of 60,000 Maria Theresa dollars in 1895 and a second loan of 60,000 rupees in 1897. Repayment of each loan was to be made in monthly instalments deducted from the Canning Award payments. As is often the way with those who lend money, the sum lent in each case was inadequate to pay off the Sultan's debts, and served only to put the government of Oman deeper in the control of the British. It is probable, too, that the Sultan diverted at least part of the money he received into his own pocket rather than that of the government. At that time, it was not always possible to define clearly the boundaries of the privy purse and the exchequer. In any event, the Sultan became more and more disenchanted with the British, and his attitude was not helped by the hectoring and patronising manner of the current British Political Agent in Muscat. His flirtation with the French increased its intensity, and he granted them coaling facilities for their fleet in Bandar Jissah, a small but excellent natural harbour some 8 km from Muscat. This was too much for British imperial pride, and the Sultan was publicly humiliated and forced to adjure his French connections on the deck of a British warship in Muscat harbour. Eighty years later, this action of the British seems incredible, but at the time it was regarded as an essential part of the statecraft necessary to ensure the security of the empire.

Relations with the government of British India improved after this diplomatic defeat for the Sultan, simply because he ceased to fight and accepted that he had to accept British interference because he had no way of throwing it off. This he did with an inevitable good grace, and the arrival of a new British Political Agent, Captain (later Sir) Percy Cox, did much to make relations easier. In the best traditions of colonial patronising diplomacy, Cox took Faisal's elder son Taimur, the future Sultan, to India to attend the Coronation Durbar of King Edward VII in Delhi in January 1903, and later the same year, Lord Curzon, the Viceroy of British India, visited Muscat. Although still legally independent, Oman was seen to be very much a far-flung outpost of the British Indian Empire. The Sultan's debts to the British were written off and the way seemed clear for the building of a classic dependent relationship.

Had Sultan Faisal been the ruler of a city state, as were the Emirs of the mini-states of the Persian Gulf at that time, the relationship might well have succeeded. But the British officials knew little of, cared less for, and totally ignored the tribes of Oman. The people of Oman had little love for Sultan Faisal, and his dealings with the British meant little to them. His public humiliation and loss of face made them even more contemptuous of him and all that he stood for. They knew great poverty and he was unable to help them. He could not defend the integrity of the state, because his own integrity had been seen to be prostituted to the agents of a foreign power. He was a far cry from the classic figure of an Imam who would lead the people in prayer on Fridays, he had no authority to decree what was lawful and prohibit what was unlawful.

The flickering discontent of the tribes of Oman went on. Sheikh Salih bin 'Ali al-Harthi had been killed in a tribal fracas in 1896 and had been succeeded as *tamimah* of the al-Hirth tribe by another of his sons, Sheikh Isa. Then Sultan Faisal, under British pressure, created a *casus belli* by a decree establishing a controlled arms warehouse in Muscat, aimed at stopping a trade which was profitable to some tribes. At the same time a ban was placed on the export of arms. This was, in the eyes of the tribesmen, a major betrayal of their interests. Doubtless some saw it stand more specifically at them, and at the inalienable right (in that society) of a man to carry arms.

A respected tribal leader, the *tamimah* of the Bani Riyam tribe, Himyar bin Nasr al-Nabhani, a man with a proud genealogy and the leader of the Ghafiri faction, recognised the national *malaise* and called a meeting of tribal sheikhs and elders. As the Sultan in Muscat could no longer command any respect or allegiance, it was felt that the office of Imam should be revived, and that Oman should be free of the foreign lackey in Muscat. Salim bin Rashid al-Kharusi was elected Imam at Tanuf in May 1913, and the white flag of the Imam raised in revolt against the Sultan. Isa bin Salih al-Harthi at first did not join the revolt, but as it gathered momentum, he threw in his hand with the rebels, thus ensuring a joint Hinawi-Ghafiri challenge to the Sultan.

Sultan Faisal died in October 1913 and was succeeded by his son Taimur, of whom the British officials in Bombay and Muscat hoped much. After all, he had been taken to see the Coronation Durbar in Delhi. Taimur inherited the indebtedness that his father had let accrue, the legacy of an open rebellion of the tribes of Oman, and a fair share of his father's weak and irresolute character. The new Sultan attempted to negotiate with the tribes, but matters had gone too far. Isa bin Salih al-Harthi had taken over the military command of the rebel tribes, and in 1915 he organised a full-scale attack on Muscat. Left alone, there would have been no way for the Sultan to defeat this attack. However, the government of British India interfered in defence of the *status quo* and sent a battalion of Beluch infantry with British officers to the Sultan's aid. When the tribesmen launched their attack at Bait al Falaj in 1915, they came up against this disciplined, well-armed and well-led force, carefully dug-in in a pre-prepared defensive position. The result was a foregone conclusion; a ragged, ill-equipped host was no match for an organised and professional military force and the tribesmen were flung back. From an Omani point of view, and with the virtue of hindsight, it would almost certainly have been better if the tribesmen had been allowed to throw out Sultan Taimur, and end the Al Bu Sa'id dynasty. Materially they probably would not have been much better off, but at least they could have lived in their own way, as did other peoples in the Arabian Peninsula, rather than have this quasi-foreign domination of a ruler whose instincts caused him to look more to British India than to the world of his people.

The 'ifs' of history may be fascinating, but we are concerned with reality. The reality in Oman was that the Sultan's victory was tactical only; the tribes had not lost their antagonism to him. As long as he had outside military support, they could not defeat him. Equally, the Sultan's British advisers would not let him use British-officered troops for offensive operations against the rebel tribesmen. An uneasy situation of 'no peace – no war' followed for five years, with the Sultan ruling Muscat and the coastal towns, and the Imam ruling 'Oman', that is, the country of the mountain valleys and plains of the interior of the country. After the conclusion of the war in Europe in 1918, the British officials in India turned their attention to these isolated trouble spots again. Wingate, the Political Agent in Muscat, was instructed to arrange a peace, which he did, and the Treaty of Seeb, which brought peace to Oman, was concluded in 1920. Sheikh Isa bin Salih al-Harthi represented the tribes, not the Imam. Isa was now the strong man of Oman, and when the Imam Salim bin Rashid al-Kharusi was assassinated later in 1920, a nominee of Isa's, Muhammad bin Abdullah al-Khalili of the Bani Ruwahah tribe was elected Imam in his stead.

The Treaty of Seeb opened the door to a form of government in Oman which endured for fifty years. This was simply a situation of a ruler without respect or support in his own land maintaining his authority through foreign officers and governing his country through foreign officials.

The Treaty of Seeb itself is worth looking at briefly. Its preamble states:

> In the name of God, the Compassionate, the Merciful.
> This is the peace agreed upon between the Government of the Sultan, Taimur bin Faisal, and Sheikh Isa bin Salih bin 'Ali on

> behalf of the people of Oman whose names are signed hereto, through the mediation of Mr Wingate, I.C.S., political agent and consul for Great Britain in Muscat, who is empowered by his Government in this respect and to be an intermediary between them. Of the conditions set forth below, four pertain to the Government of the Sultan and four pertain to the people of Oman.[14]

It is interesting to note that nowhere is the Iman mentioned. Further, half a century later, it reads a little strangely to think of this sort of an agreement between a ruler and his people. It must be remembered that this was 'Muscat and Oman', with its deeply felt division between the people of the coast and the people of the interior. In the Treaty, four articles concerned 'the people of Oman': they shall be at peace with the Sultan, they shall not attack the coastal towns, they shall have full right of movement and security in the coastal towns, and claims against them by merchants and others were to be settled according to the law of Islam. For his part, the Sultan agreed not to interfere in tribal matters and the treaty permitted people from the coastal towns to enter Oman on lawful business or for commercial purposes.

The British government helped the Sultan swallow the bitter blow to his pride which the Treaty of Seeb must have been with a loan from the government of British India, to be repayed over ten years. The amount of this loan was sufficient to permit the Sultan to pay off all his debts to merchants. To help the Sultan keep track of his finances, a British adviser, D.V. McCullum, was engaged to attempt to set up a simple accounting system, but he stayed only six months, probably because of the climate and because the Sultan would not want to have any system which required financial (or any other) discipline. It would be in character for him to prevaricate, to agree one day to a course of action, only himself to be the first to break the rules the following day. By 1924, the Sultan was in default on his loan payments, and his administration in a bigger mess than ever. In 1925, Bertram Thomas was engaged on a five-year contract to try to bring some order and sanity into the financial and administrative chaos of the Sultan's affairs. It seems that he was no more successful than his predecessor in steeling the Sultan's will to the realities of financial control. In any case, it seems that Thomas cared more about travelling around the country and reading papers to the Royal Geographical Society than he did about helping the Sultan to govern. Financial stability was only achieved in the 1930s by Taimur's son, Sa'id, when be became Sultan.

Before leaving this account of the legacy of history to the development of modern government in Oman, it is necessary to clarify a little the expressions 'tribe' and 'tribesman'. An immediate question is: 'what is a tribe?' Mention was made earlier of an Omani tribe, the Bani Hina. The prefix 'Bani' (sometimes Beni in English – precise transliterations from Arabic are never easy) means 'the sons of', but more in the sense of a clan, i.e. having a common ancestor, like a Scots clan, than in the sense of the sons of one father, where the word *owlad* is used. A tribe becomes then either a large clan, or a number of such clans, with a strong family association. Although their paramount sheikh *(tamimah)* lives in the village of al-Ghaffat, the Bani Hina regard Nizwa as their chief town, but share the town with members of several other tribes. They have wandered far afield, and members of the tribe are found in sub-clans in the villages of the *wadi* Sumail as well as on the Batina coast. They have a strong martial tradition and are great warriors by Omani standards. They are also farmers, and grow much wheat in the *wadi* Bahla. Variations of Arabic names are often confusing; individual members of the tribe are called al-Hinai, and a group of the tribe together would be referred to as 'Hinawi'.

The *tamimah* of a tribe is likely to be a senior member of a sheikhly family, mature but vigorous, who by force of his personality commands the respect of the members of the tribe. He will be a man to whom the confederation of families which make up the clan or tribe look to for the settlement of all disputes between them. Following Omani custom, such a dispute will be settled after a tribal discussion and the *tamimah* will rarely try to impose a solution but endorse a solution which represents a consensus of the views of a majority of the tribe. He will be expected to represent the tribe in any dispute with the government or with another tribe, to argue their case and to ensure that they receive what they regard as their right. The *tamimah* has no formal authority other than that which comes from respect for his personality, his years, and above all his achievement in defending and safeguarding the interests of the tribe. He is allowed to enrich himself through his office; this is no moral or criminal offence, providing he ensures that the riches are shared and that the whole tribe benefits.

A tribesman, an adult male member of the tribe, has considerable pride, and there are a number of tasks which he will not perform, or the performance of which in front of his fellows will lead to shaming loss of face. As a tribesman, a free man, he is above all a warrior, and will always go armed. A man who is not armed is not a man, in the eyes of the traditional society. A free man may herd camels, he may buy and sell (no traditional Arab will send his wife to shop, even for foodstuffs), and in a village community in Oman, he will oversee the irrigation of his crops and gardens. But he will not tend the sheep and goats, he will not cut alfalfa, he will not harvest. In the modern idiom, he may be a driver, driving any sort of vehicle from air-conditioned limousine to tractor to Land Rover, but he is extremely reluctant to engage in manual work, especially in front of his peers. Herding sheep and goats, harvesting and general gardening is work for women and children, or for servants, or hired labour.

Most of the tribes of Oman are settled, that is, they have permanent homes and seldom leave them. Of tribes of this nature, there are at least over two hundred in Oman, some sub-tribes of larger groups, but each jealous of its tribal identity. Some are very small, having not more than one hundred members, others, like the Bani Hina or the al-Hirth, may number ten to fifteen thousand people. Settled tribes and tribesmen make up an estimated 80 per cent of the population of Oman.

There are also a small number of nomadic, or Bedu, tribes, whose total would not amount to 5 per cent of the population, but whose tribal area covers at least 80 per cent of the land area, the poorest, most arid regions of desert or near desert.

All the tribes, settled or Bedu, are scattered and fragmented, so much so that it is not possible to compile a realistic tribal map showing tribal boundaries. It is said that the tribal loyalties become less as the benefits of education and development spread, and as members of tribes leave their traditional homes and settle in towns. To a certain extent this is so, but the force of tribal society remains strong in Oman, and it is not possible to understand the evolution of government structures without an awareness of the fragmented structure of the society.

This fragmentation is not confined to tribes. Oman has many other communities, embracing Islam, often speaking Arabic, but not Arab. Perhaps the largest of these is the Beluch community, very strong in Muscat and along the Batina coast, and well represented in the army. The Makran coast of Beluchistan and the port of Gwadur, which was counted under the control of the Sultans of Oman until 1959, has long supplied mercenary soldiers and emigrants to Oman. There is also a tribe, the Bani Beluch, descendants of a force of soldiers recruited in Makran in 1736 and now settled in the interior of Oman, living as an Arab tribe.

In Muscat and Matrah and also in Salalah there are many people of African origin whose ancestors were brought to Oman as slaves. Many of these people have worked as servants for various Sultans and members of the Sultans' families.

Muscat's historic role as a trading centre is shown by its strong Indian community, some of these being third- and fourth-generation Oman-born. They retain their distinctive dress and make no attempt at assimilation. In Matrah is found a prosperous Khoja community, of Pakistani origin, whose mother tongue is Sindhi. Although they dress as Omanis and speak Arabic, this group also does not readily assimilate into the wider Omani society. Because its members are successful merchants, it is perhaps the richest private grouping in the country, and among its members are some of the best-educated and most able people in Oman.

Also well-educated and able are the Zanzibari Omanis, Omanis generally of mixed blood whose mother tongue tends to be Swahili rather than Arabic, who have returned to Oman from Zanzibar following successive revolutions there and the setting up of the state of Tanzania. Educated in British schools and encouraged to go to university when Zanzibar was a British colony, the Zanzibari minority is intelligent and coherent, traits which do not add to its popularity among native-born Omanis. It is strong in the professions and in the police force.

The Shihuh of Oman's northern province Musandam are a wild and little-known tribe of fishermen and herdsmen, numbering not more than 15,000. They have two languages, one an Arabic dialect, and one a Persian dialect. They are darker than most Arabs and it is possible that they are the descendants of the original inhabitants of northern Oman, pushed into the mountains of the north by successive waves of invaders, just as the Celts in Britain were pushed to the fringes by invasions of Romans, Angles and Saxons.

Possibly the same might be said of the Bayasirah, a caste rather than a tribe or community. These are people found in central Oman and along the coast, and are regarded as socially inferior by Omanis. In the past, there were fairly strict rules about marrying into or out of the Bayasirah caste, but these seem to be relaxed today and in any case are somewhat ambiguous. There are various theories as to the origins of this caste, the most popular being that they descend from prisoners of war who were put to work at the menial tasks the true Omani would not touch himself. They are still a caste of menials and gardeners.

Another caste, but a very small one, is the group in Oman known as Zatut (singular: Zutti). These people could best be described as gypsies; they are tinkers, odd-job men, and are often employed to carry out circumcisions. They embrace Islam, call themselves Ibadhi, but have a dialect of their own and seldom marry outside their caste.

Finally, the pastoral people of the Qara mountains of Dhofar are radically different, being Hamitic rather than Semitic. They are not numerous; it would be surprising if they numbered more than 20,000 people. Their appearance and dress immediately illustrate the difference between them and the Omanis, and their language, Jebali, is not an Arabic dialect, although it has Arabic words in it. The men have a wild, unkempt appearance, and go bare-headed and bare-footed. Their women are unveiled and bold. Their animals are cattle, rather than the sheep and goats favoured by Omanis.

Oman, then, is a country which has no natural national cohesion, either ethnic or geographic. A shortage of the basic elements to support life, particularly water, has engendered at once a history of internal strife and an innate conservatism. This conservatism has been underlined by the tenets of a traditional and fatalistic religion, by geographic isolation and by the fragmented nature of the communities forming Oman. The lessons of history are clear; the society has been strongest when wise leadership could weld it together by the judicious use of capital earned in enterprises outside Oman, in particular trade. It has been weakest and most divisive when this capital was not available or was diverted to uses other than the underpinning of the nation.

Notes

1. E.C. Ross, (trans.), 'Annals of Oman', *Journal of the Asiatic Society of Bengal* (1874), pp.111-96
2. J.C. Wilkinson, 'The Organisation of the Falaj Irrigation System in Oman', School of Geography Research Paper No. 10, University of Oxford, 1974.
3. G.P. Badger, (trans.), 'The History of the Imams and Sayyids of Oman', Hakluyt Society, London, 1871.
4. Ibid.
5. Quoted in Sir A.T. Wilson, *The Persian Gulf*, London, 1928.
6. Ibid.
7. Badger, op. cit.
8. Ibid.
9. Ibid.
10. Ibid.
11. For an account of the Omani civil war see D. Hawley, *The Trucial States*, London, 1970.
12. J.B. Kelly, *Great Britain and the Persian Gulf, 1793-1880*, London, 1968.
13. Quoted in Kelly, op. cit.
14. Quoted in I. Skeet, *Muscat & Oman*, London, 1974.

3 THE GOVERNMENT OF SULTAN SA'ID BIN TAIMUR, 1932-1970

> 'All the states, all the dominions under whose authority men have lived in the past and live now have been and are either republics or principalities. Principalities are hereditary, with their prince's family long established as rulers, . . .'

As the thirteenth hereditary ruler of a family which had ruled Oman since the 1740s, Sultan Sa'id bin Taimur had much in common with the princes who ruled the city states of Italy in the late fifteenth and early sixteenth centuries. Educated at a school for princes in India, he succeeded his father Sultan Taimur bin Faisal in 1932, when he himself was aged twenty-one. His father had abdicated, having become tired and disillusioned with the apparent impossibility of governing Oman because of the stranglehold of debt.

Sultan Sa'id's first objective was to eliminate the debts he had inherited. Once this most significant and laudable goal had been achieved, his twin aims were to avoid further debts by the most parsimonious financial management and to stay in power. He managed to rule for some 38 years, and in doing so revealed a mastery of statecraft and an indifference to public opinion worthy of the most dedicated disciple of Machiavelli. Like the princes of Italy, Sultan Sa'id relied increasingly on mercenaries to sustain his position, and, as happened so often in the time of Machiavelli, his betrayal by his mercenary officers ultimately caused his downfall.

For the first 24 years of his reign, Sultan Sa'id was 'Sultan of Muscat'. His authority ran only along the coast from Muscat to Sohar and Shinas, in the port of Sur, in Dhofar, and in the Musandam peninsula. An Imam ruled in Nizwa the region known as 'Oman', the mountain valleys and foothills which formed the heartland of the country. The Treaty of Seeb defined the relationship between the two authorities in a way adequate for the needs of a society which had had, up to 1955, very little contact with the wider world.

Sultan Sa'id's government was unique, unlike any form of government previously experienced in Oman and the Arab world, and quite unlike the rule of those Indian princes whose style the Sultan seemed to be trying to emulate. One way in which it is possible to begin to understand this government is through his own 'word'. 'The Word of of Sultan Sa'id bin Taimur, Sultan of Muscat and Oman, about the history of the financial position of the Sultanate in the past and hopes for the future, after the export of oil' was drafted by the Sultan, after much prodding by European advisers, and published in January 1968 after the first oil exports began in August of the previous year. 'The Word', a much-quoted and interesting document, is reproduced in Appendix 1.

A number of points should be borne in mind. Sultan Sa'id drafted the document himself, almost certainly wholly from memory. For an Arab ruler to publish such a document at that time was certainly unusual; as far as is known, Sa'id had never previously addressed any such word to his people collectively. Naturally, therefore, he would wish himself to appear in as favourable a light as possible, as the wise father of his people, beyond questioning or criticism. He makes much of the financial plight of Oman, quoting this as the main reason for inactivity in the past. He tells of the loan from the government of British India in 1920 to pay off his father's debts, but he neglects to mention the *quid pro quo* that went with this loan: peace with the tribes of the interior and an effective split of the country in two pieces, Muscat ruled by his father, and Oman ruled by the Iman. Nor does he mention that this situation continued until 1956.

He suggests that the only government revenue at the time was from customs duties, with a small payment from oil companies beginning in 1937. He neglects to mention the Canning Award payments which continued until 1956 of 40,000 Maria Theresa dollars which probably went into his privy purse, together with a certain share of the oil company payments. He is critical of some of his father's officials, especially Bertram Thomas. He neglects to mention that his father would take on commitments and spend money before checking with his Financial Adviser and treasury officials to be sure that money was available. This habit, and a habit of never being sure which was the privy purse and which was the exchequer, ultimately became a contributory cause to the abdication of his father.

Sultan Sa'id's own achievement in balancing the budget and keeping out of debt within a short period of his coming to power should not be underestimated. He was immeasurably better educated than his father and any previous Sultan. He had been to school in Baghdad in the days of the British Mandate of Iraq, and from that school he had gone on to the school for princes in India as mentioned above. He was literate, spoke excellent English as well as his native Arabic, and had a knowledge of Urdu and Hindi. His examples were the independent princes of British India. He did not attempt to copy them in terms of personal display or extravagance, for he was a most frugal man and lived a simple life. He had been educated away from his people, and kept away from them during his whole life. His closest acquaintance was an Indian merchant with a large business in Muscat with whom Sa'id conducted much business to their mutual profit. Other acquaintances were British officers and advisers with whom in general he had an excellent social relationship.

By living a simple and frugal life himself, by refusing to pay subventions, subsidies and bribes to the many beseechers and suppliants crowding his Muscat palace, by spending more and more of his time away from Muscat in his Salalah palace where people could not easily come to see him, he was able to reduce expenditure. Money was spent on his army, the Muscat Levies, a somewhat irregular force of Beluch mercenaries with British officers, poorly organised and ill-equipped. Their role was more that of a royal guard than a force for national defence, and their enemies were more likely to be the Sultan's own people than any outsider.

His civil list covered the salaries of a few *walis* (regional governors), each of whom would have a few soldiers and a clerk on his staff, the customs department, and a few officials and clerks of the central government. Later innovations were a Minister of the Interior, who kept a day-to-day check on the *walis,* a Personal Adviser (British) and a Military Secretary (also British). He appointed a Development Secretary in 1958, but this man's salary was paid by the British government, as was the cost of the staff of the Development Department set up at the same time. When oil revenues began in 1967, he appointed an expatriate Secretary for Financial Affairs and Secretary for Petroleum Affairs, both British, the former a retired Indian civil servant, and the latter a retired army officer.

A further source of government revenue was the *zakat,* a religious tax on production, and also the *waqf,* a religious endowment and charity. These funds were intended principally for the upkeep of mosques and the salaries of *qadhis,* the religious judges.

The day-to-day impact of the Sultan's government on the average Omani was not great. In the average village of the coastal regions (it must be remembered that for the first 24 years of Sultan Sa'id's reign, he had no jurisdiction over the tribes of the interior and that there was an Imam guiding the faithful from Nizwa) there was very little crime. If a man had a grievance with a neighbour over property, or land boundaries, or failure to make an agreed payment, he would first complain to the headman of his village, or the paramount sheikh of his tribe (often the same individual). If the matter concerned a member of the same tribe, every effort would be made to settle the dispute by a consensus among the members of the tribe which would be ratified as a decision of the sheikh.

If the dispute was with a member of a different tribe, then the nearest *wali,* as representative of the Sultan, would have to decide the issue. Again, the general pattern was to find a consensus, the plaintiff and respondent each having the right to argue his case in front of a tribal gathering chaired by the *wali*. If the *wali* could see that a consensus was possible, he would announce this decision and the *qadhi,* sitting beside the *wali,* would record the decision. The *qadhi*'s advice would be sought on any matter requiring a precise interpretation of the Koran.

Both *wali* and *qadhi* would almost invariably not be native of the district in which they were administering justice. Most *walis* were relatives of the Sultan, or at least of his tribe. The choice of *walis* was a matter of some delicacy; many tribes have a long history of feuding with other tribes, and a *wali* has to be seen to be independent and not open to political pressures. Thus members of the Sultan's own family were often chosen as *walis,* for their family and tribal loyalty would be to him and thus they would be less tempted to cause more trouble by taking the wrong side in a dispute.

Matters incapable of resolution at village or township level by a *wali* and *qadhi* would be referred to Muscat to the Minister of the Interior, another relative of the Sultan. If he could not give a ruling himself, he would refer the matter to the Sultan, whose word was final. There was no right of appeal. This whole process could take months, or even years.

For a dweller in Muscat or Matrah, who would be more likely to be a member of a minority group, Indian, or Khoja, or Beluch, than Omani, the community concerned would try to resolve any disputes between its members itself. Cases which could not be so decided, or which were so serious that the community feared to decide itself, or which involved members of another community, would be heard in front of a chief *qadhi* and other senior *qadhis* in Muscat. If a decision was not possible at this level, it would be referred to either the Governor of Muscat (a close relative of the Sultan) or the *wadi* of Matrah, a Palestinian close to the Sultan. Really serious matters could be referred to the Sultan himself. Again, the whole process could take an inordinate length of time.

Cash payments to influence a decision by judges were a way of life.

The normal pattern was for a judge to say to the plaintiff; 'and how many witnesses do you have?', a polite way of asking how much money he was prepared to pay into court. A similar question would be put to the respondent. The man with the greatest number of 'witnesses' stood a good chance of winning his case. Rules of evidence followed the Koran, with the word of a man carrying much more weight than that of a woman or a slave. In Muscat during Sultan Sa'id's reign, there were no slaves in the strict sense of the word, but there were many dusky descendants of slaves who were family retainers and who were regarded for purposes of evidence as slaves. The injustices and inequalities of the system worried many expatriates, but were taken as a matter of course by the Omanis as part of an unchanged way of life. There is a recorded instance of a senior European adviser saying to Sultan Sa'id: 'Sir, your qadhis are corrupt!' The answer was: 'Yes, I know they take bribes, but if I stopped them taking bribes, I would have to pay them more.'[1]

Thus in the field of the everyday administration of justice Sa'id's government worked well enough; by the standards of Arabia the people of Oman were no worse off than anyone else. Sa'id's subjects and their cousins under the rule of the Imam had roughly the same rights, and the system was about the same in the neighbouring Trucial States. The Omanis were better off than people living in Saudi Arabia, where public executions, stoning, and the cutting off of the right hands of people accused of stealing occured every Friday. The death penalty was very rare in Oman, and stoning and the cutting off of hands were not practised. Sultan Sa'id threw some of his enemies into gaol and forgot about them. They stayed imprisoned without trial for years. But his cruelty in this respect was nothing compared to the torturing and sadistic, brutal judicial murders of the Imams Yehia and Ahmad of Yemen.

Sultan Sa'id was less effective in maintaining internal security in the lands under his control, but again no less effective than the Imam or his neighbours in the Gulf States. It was not wise for women and children to stray far from their home village looking for firewood or tending flocks. They risked being kidnapped and taken away to be sold in Buraimi as slaves. This continued until the civil war of 1956. After that, a greatly increased army ensured internal peace and security such as the country had not known for almost a century.

In the realm of the defence of the integrity of the state, Sultan Sa'id's effectiveness is arguable. He had little worry with external threats until the end of the Second World War brought a greatly increased interest in South-East Arabia by oil companies. International rivalries and undefined boundaries were an open invitation to intrigue. So it was that in 1949 the government of Saudi Arabia, prompted by the American oil companies active on its territories, claimed a large slice of land from its neighbours, Oman, Abu Dhabi and Qatar, land which was either believed to contain promising oil prospects or which would improve the ability of the oil companies in Saudi Arabia to export oil.

At the heart of the Saudi claim was the Buraimi oasis, which at that time was jointly administered by Oman and Abu Dhabi. Sultan Sa'id bin Taimur and the Ruler of Abu Dhabi requested the British government to negotiate on their behalf to try to settle the dispute. The British government was already involved in the dispute as it legally represented, by virtue of the Treaty of Maritime Peace and Prosperity of 4 May 1853, the then Trucial States, which included, of course, Abu Dhabi. The Ruler of Qatar had also accepted this Treaty on 3 November 1916, so he too was legally represented by the British government. Underlying the negotiations were the commercial interests of the Iraq Petroleum Company which, in spite of its international shareholding, was regarded as a British oil company, and Aramco, the American oil group which operated the main oil concession in Saudi Arabia.

The negotiations between the representatives of Britain and Saudi Arabia dragged on until the Saudis lost patience and sought to present the world with a *fait accompli* by sending a small force to occupy Buraimi on 31 August 1952. Sultan Sa'id accepted without hesitation his obligation to defend the territorial integrity of his people, and, finding common cause with the Imam, mobilised in a remarkably short time an army of 8,000 tribesmen at Sohar on the Gulf of Oman and within striking distance of Buraimi through the *wadi* al-Jizzi. Before he could mount his attack, however, the Sultan was dissuaded by the British government, responding to pressure from the United States government at Saudi instigation, from undertaking any military adventures, including marching against Buraimi. The Sultan accepted the British advice with reluctance, and his disappointed tribesmen dispersed and went home.

Seen with the hindsight of the best part of a quarter of a century, it seems that this advice from the British government to the Sultan was unwise. It certainly seemed to produce the result the Saudis wanted at the time. Had the Sultan, without any foreign aid, been seen by all to have been able to dispel the threat to Oman's territorial integrity by himself expelling the Saudis from Buraimi, he would have gained much stature in the eyes of his own people and the country would probably have been spared the civil war which broke out in 1955. This fresh internal Omani strife was caused in no small part by the dissatisfaction with the Buraimi débâcle by the Imam and his followers, who were encouraged in their challenge to the Sultan by Saudi promises, money and arms. Sultan Sa'id had lost face in front of his people, and having done so, the relationship between him and his subjects could never be the same again.

Following the Saudi seizure of Buraimi, and the turning back of the Sultan's efforts to recapture this village, the boundary problem was referred to an international arbitration tribunal. Again negotiations dragged on. An agreement was reached in August 1954 which permitted a Saudi police detachment to stay in Buraimi. This agreement was not acceptable to the people on the ground, and, to counter further intriguing, the British government, in a complete turn-about from its position of two years previously, encouraged the Sultan and the Ruler of Abu Dhabi to occupy Buraimi. This occupation was carried out on 26 October 1955 by the Trucial Oman Scouts, a British-officered military force based in Abu Dhabi.

During the period of the negotiations, the government of Saudi Arabia had attempted to strengthen its position by encouraging opposition in Oman to the rule of Sa'id bin Taimur. The death of the Imam Mohammed in May 1954 was followed by the election of Sheikh Ghalib bin 'Ali al-Hinai as the new Imam, an election which was opposed unsuccessfully by the Sultan. The power behind Ghalib was his brother Talib, at that time *wali* of Rostaq. The apparent imminence of oil discovery in Oman and hence the determination by both sides to control the prospective oilfields added fuel to the fires of jealousy and rivalry. Prodded by the Iraq Petroleum Company, which was drilling in the area, and led by two of its British employees, a small force of the Sultan's army took the town of 'Ibri from the Imam in October 1954.

The Imam's response was to declare the complete independence of the 'State of Oman', and to make application in its name to join the Arab League. An uneasy situation continued until the recapture of Buraimi a year later when the Sultan, relying on the presence of British troops in his country, occupied the whole country. The Imam, his brother Talib and their ally, Suleyman bin Himyar al-Nabbani, the self-styled 'king of the green mountain', escaped to Saudi Arabia, encouraged by the Saudi government. This was the end of the Imamate, and Sa'id from that moment onwards ruled over an undivided 'Muscat and Oman'.

It was an opportunity for him to weld together the country and lead it forward in a way that had not happened since the reign of Sultan Sa'id's great-great-grandfather, Sayyid Sa'id, who died in 1856. The British government withdrew its soldiers as soon as their task was completed, but would have been prepared to help Sa'id with advice and experts to heal the wounds of the civil war and build a new Oman. Considerable diplomatic pressure was put on the Sultan at this time by the British government. Whether he was still smarting at the British initiative which caused him such loss of face in 1952, or whether he wished to punish his enemies, or whether he wished to move in his own way but was too slow, is not clear. The fact is that nothing was done, and a new revolt led by the escaped leaders of the 1955-6 civil war broke out in 1957. Again the Sultan had to reveal to the world and to his own people his weakness and he was forced to request British assistance to suppress the revolt. Final victory did not come until January 1959 when a detachment of the British Special Air Service broke into the insurgents' position from the rear and dispersed them. Once again, the main plotters escaped.

Although his success brought in its wake an internal peace and security such as Oman had not witnessed for many years, and hence a strengthening of the Sultan's own position in one sense, it did nothing to win the hearts of his people. There had always been a great gap between him and his subjects. Alone among Arab rulers, he never encouraged the regular *majlis*, where any subject may come and air a grievance, where personal, tribal and national problems are discussed openly and freely. The rulers of the neighbouring Trucial States (now the United Arab Emirates) used, and still use, the *majlis* as a convenient sounding board of public opinion, as a finger on the pulse of their people, where all are welcome. The *majlis* is the natural tribal Arab equivalent of a constituent assembly. Its functions are advisory, only the ruler may make decisions, and legislation does not happen in a traditional Islamic tribal society. But the very fact of its existence gives the people a feeling of being represented, and gives them a path to their ruler. Had Sultan Sa'id been able to travel around his country, sit with his people, hear their grievances, explain to them himself the financial situation, explain the problems and priorities, he could almost certainly have won the untrammelled support of his people. Instead, he chose to isolate himself even more, and retreat permanently to his palace in Salalah, where he governed by radio-telephone. Thus his people saw him as a man who was apparently afraid to meet them, a man whom they knew to be cunning and vindictive, always ready to punish those who offended him, a ruler who appeared, rightly or wrongly, to be in the control of a foreign power, and who could apparently only settle his disputes with them, and keep them in check, by employing foreign armies.

Other Arab rulers, even the most conservative, equally despised the Sultan for his non-Arab attitudes and policies. He was referred to as 'that Indian', because of his education in British India, and because he had always looked to the Indian subcontinent in his own personal, diplomatic and commercial activities, at the expense of the Arab world. For his part, he regarded other Arabs as beneath his contempt. Thus politically he became completely isolated from his neighbours at the time when he had unified his country, his only friends being the British government, the Indian government and the maverick American oil man, Wendell Phillips.

Worse than this, his refusal to meet his own people and his isolation in Salalah caused him to be more and more detested by Omanis. The efforts of some of them to overthrow him had been defeated by the British Army, and now there was a largely Beluch mercenary army led by British officers maintaining law and order in the country and reporting the slightest infringement by radio-telephone to the despot in Salalah. There was little the Omani people could do to protest, save leave the country illegally, which they proceeded to do in their thousands.

The last twelve years of Sultan Sa'id's reign, and the development of his government, are overshadowed by the discovery of oil and hence the great pressure put on him to develop his country and spread the oil wealth among his people. In view of the reliance of the Sultan on the British presence to maintain his own position, and the fact that the management of the oil company, Petroleum Development (Oman) Ltd. (PDO), was British, it was British pressure on the Sultan over this time which gradually brought a change in his ways. This British military assistance to end the civil war, and to put down the subsequent revolt, had only been given on condition that he begin to develop his country. Thus development first became part of the official policy of the government of Oman, and a development organisation was established in the government structure, in 1958. In an exchange of letters with the British government, Sultan Sa'id agreed to accept British assistance in 'carrying out a civil development programme which will include the improvement of roads, medical and educational facilities, and an agricultural research programme.'[2]

Thus a study of the evolution of the government of Oman for the period 1958-70 becomes an analysis of the various attempts at establishing development institutions and the impact of these institutions on the overall body politic. Development is rather like marriage; most people have some experience of it but few have ever bothered to sit down and think through precisely what it means in terms of a given country in a given environment at a given time. Sultan Sa'id had thought enough about development in the context of Oman in the last years of his reign to know that he did not want it to happen. Taking the lid off the Pandora's box of his people's frustration would unleash forces which his anachronistic system of government could not control. Above all, he feared for his own personal security. He had seen his British friends lose India, he had heard of revolts against the establishment in other Arab countries led by young officers and students, he was aware of the murder of the Iraqi Royal Family by revolutionary groups. However, the British government gave him very little choice; if they were to give him the military assistance without which he could not survive, then a condition of this assistance was a modest development programme. The Sultan resented this pressure, and his resentment contributed significantly to the lack of success of the British-inspired development efforts.

Assailed in the United Nations about its intervention in Oman, the British government was in a dilemma. The Sultan had requested continuing military assistance and this was a request which found some echo of sympathy in British ears. First, the whole Persian Gulf region was regarded as something of a British preserve. Then the Sultan's government, with all its faults, was at least the sort of government which the British had dealt with in their colonial hey-day. It was almost identical with many of the petty Sultanates of the Aden protectorate. It was a government which would tend to favour British oil exploration and other commercial interests in the area, and on whose territory there was a base (on the island of Masirah) which the British Ministry of Defence regarded as a vital link in the communication chain to Singapore and Hong Kong. The preservation of a regional *status quo* through the support for similar régimes had long been a corner-stone of British policy, a policy which had its origins in the nineteenth century. Not to support Sa'id bin Taimur would be to question the basis for a British presence in the area encompassed by Aden and the Persian Gulf. The British government was not yet ready for such iconoclasm.[3]

However, following the humiliation of Suez in 1956 and continuing pressure in the United Nations, something had to be done to at least appear to wish to change some of the worst aspects of the Sultan's style of government. His request for military assistance was therefore agreed to, on condition that he accepted some development assistance as well. A new Development Department was established in Muscat, its first head being Colonel (now Sir) Hugh Boustead. Boustead was to report direct to the Sultan.

He had been proposed to the Sultan by the British government because of his achievements as British resident adviser in Mukalla in the Hadramaut region of the Aden protectorate from August 1949 to 1958. Here, with a very small budget, he had worked miracles of improvisation. In addition, he had met the Sultan on a number of occasions when the latter passed through Aden on his way to London. Boustead's background was such that the Sultan would be able to communicate with him. He spoke tolerable if at times rather strange Arabic, and had proved that he could work with tribesmen.

Boustead's Development Department had an annual budget of £250,000 from British government funds, and his detailed plans for expenditure had to be approved by both the Sultan and the British government. Although he made a significant start in setting up a development organisation and started the building of simple roads, set up two experimental farms and opened medical centres, Boustead was not happy in Oman. He wrote:

> Muscat was in a deplorable condition. This could only in part be blamed on local unrest which amounted to rebellion against the Sultan's rule. I had seen what could be done in the Hadhramaut and in Qu'aiti State in particular, with a revenue about one half of what the Sultan of Muscat drew in customs duties; yet here there were no medical services in the whole country. I made a tour soon after my arrival with an economic expert and a representative from the Development Division at the British Embassy in Beirut. The latter told the Sultan after the tour that, in twenty years' experience of most of the countries in the Middle East, he had never seen a people so poverty-stricken or so debilitated with disease capable of treatment and cure. This report led to the building of some twenty health centres and dispensaries throughout the Sultanate.

Although the rebel forces had been driven into the Jebel Akdar,

> a 10,000 foot mountain massif, irregular bands still penetrated the plain and shot up convoys. But their principal activity at this time was planting mines along the roads. The large plastic mines caused many casualties.
>
> It was not the most auspicious moment to inaugurate a brand new Development Department, the more so since the Sultan was, I felt, very half-hearted about plans for health, education, agriculture and so on. My first job was a road, something the Sultan was really keen about; but before I could start on anything, I had to organise the Department and find trained staff.[4]

Boustead stayed three years in Oman, from October 1958 until October 1961. His own title was 'Development Secretary'. When he left Oman he had built up a Development Department totalling 122 people. In addition to his own office (which consisted of an Assistant Development Secretary, an Accountant, and two clerks, all Indian, and a part-time Omani translator), there were sections concerned with roads, health, agriculture and education. The Department built simple earth roads where previously there had been none, built and staffed health centres where none had existed previously, established two experimental farms, one at Nizwa and one at Sohar, and built a new primary school in Matrah. Under Boustead, over the three-year period, £453,684 was spent on capital works and major items of equipment, and £250,750 on salaries, wages and general expenses. Boustead and the Chief Medical Officer were British, the school-teachers were Palestinian, other skilled and semi-skilled staff were Indian or Pakistani, and Omanis (generally of Beluch origin) were employed as drivers and labourers. No provision was made for training Omani staff, or helping them to acquire skills to improve themselves.[5]

Boustead was replaced by another Englishman, W.T. Clark, who stayed only a few months in Oman. The difficulties which Boustead had found in getting the Sultan to take an interest in the work of the Department multiplied under Clark. As his office was in Muscat, he had no direct link to the Sultan, and had to request audiences through others; the Sultan showed no willingness to see him. A Development Department existed in name, it did a little useful work, but it was not allowed to go further. Clark tried to organise a training scheme for Omanis but this was not approved, and he left.

He was replaced by another Englishman, Major D.N.R. Ogram, who was responsible for the Development Department from December 1962 until the subsidy from the British government was stopped at the end of March 1967, that is when oil revenues were expected. Ogram continued to be employed after this, but the Sultan was so incensed with the British decision to withhold payment of the subsidy that his effectiveness was much reduced. During the period of his incumbency in the post of Development Secretary, Ogram could do little more than maintain what had been started. He built up the Department so that at the time of the ending of the subsidy payment, it had the approved establishments shown in Table 3.1.

Table 3.1: Numbers Employed in Department of Development, 1967

Development Secretary's office	39
Roads	64
Health	138
Agriculture	36
Education	16
TOTAL	293

In fact the strength was always some 20 per cent below this establishment, due to poor pay and other recruitment difficulties. Most of the staff were Indian or Pakistani, with the most menial tasks being left to Omanis (generally of Beluch origin).[6]

The policy of the Department in those years was summed up by Ogram:

> The most important principle as regards the modernisation of an underdeveloped country is that the rate of progress should not be too rapid. This is very especially true of Oman, because of its small population and shortage of skilled indigenous manpower capable of developing the very considerable resources of the country without technical aid from outside. Any large scale or haphazard influx of technicians or teachers would seriously damage the most valuable traditions of the country and at the same time would bring in political influences which would probably be undesirable and would certainly be unsettling. This is mentioned here, as it has been very much a guiding factor in all development throughout the period under review.[7]

The words are Ogram's but the sentiments are undoubtedly those of the Sultan.

The achievements were modest: over 600 km of graded tract suitable for four-wheeled drive vehicles only, nine health centres inadequately staffed and equipped, with very few medicines and drugs, one school for boys without a curriculum or textbooks or teaching aids, and the two experimental farms.

The impact of these farms on the Omani people living near them was slight, simply because the Indian staff who ran them were generally not of the best quality and had no incentive, indeed often had a considerable disincentive, to move out from the farm and its fences and win the confidence of the local people in a way that was significant. They lacked professional direction, programmes were amateurish and records of experiments were not kept. They grew sufficient food for their own staff and a few favoured expatriate government employees in Muscat. It is not easy for expatriates in a country such as Oman to maintain enthusiasm and energy; given a remarked reluctance on the part of the Sultan to support their endeavours, it is small wonder that the Development Secretary and his staff did not achieve more.

It may be asked why the British government, whose money it was, and which had decided to concern itself with the internal affairs of Oman in this way, was not more determined in ensuring that its development aid was not properly used. The counter-argument usually runs along the lines that strong arguments were not wise with the Sultan, that indeed they were generally counter-productive, and that to go further would lay them open to charges of meddling in the internal affairs of Oman. This explanation is difficult to accept. The Sultan had revealed his inability to maintain his own position without the support of the British government. Having pushed him into accepting development aid as part of the price of military support, it does not seem too unreasonable for the British government to have insisted that its money be used more effectively, and to have carried out some form of audit to ensure that Omanis were really benefiting. There were, of course, some benefits. The roads helped, save that no Omani would be permitted to buy a four-wheel drive vehicle. The school in Matrah helped, but its intake of a total of some 400 boys did not help the people of the interior. The health centres were an improvement, but they concentrated almost exclusively on simple cures for simple complaints; they had no preventative medicine or public health facilities. The greatest thing the

Brtish government could have done to back up its aid programme at that time would have been to insist that the Sultan removed the petty restrictions from his people, to let them travel as they pleased, to buy vehicles and trade. Gradually there would have been some economic spin-off from the development aid, gradually more people would have benefited. Again, had some insistence on providing training facilities for Omanis been given, the results would have been greater. But a great opportunity was lost.

Oil was discovered in commercial quantities in Oman in 1964 and the first exports began in August 1967. The Sultan began to move very slowly towards development. A Development Board was set up, a consultant architect asked to draw up a development plan for Muscat and Matrah, and an Indian Director of Public Works was appointed. Two more British expatriates were appointed, a Director of Development and a Secretary to the Development Board. The Development Secretary (Ogram) was also still employed. The Sultan was also persuaded to appoint management consultants to define the relationships between the various entities, to suggest establishments for them and to advise on working systems and methods. All this activity, little though it meant in terms of progress and benefit to the Omani people, placed a great burden on the Sultan's system of government. It is worth examining this system in detail (though it should be noted that what follows describes the situation in 1969 and 1970).

It will be recalled that the Sultan was in Salalah, without a secretary or clerical staff, and all the people reporting to him were in Muscat, over 800 km away. A select few would make an occasional journey to see him, a few others had access to a signal centre which would convey messages to him (with no guarantee of a reply), and two had radio-telephone terminals. Most of the officials in Muscat were expatriate.

As oil was producing for him revenues far greater than he had ever dreamed of, the Sultan naturally took a great interest in petroleum affairs. It is probable that concern with oil production and revenues occupied more of his time than any other single matter. So it followed that the Managing Director of Petroleum Development (Oman) Limited was a frequent visitor to Salalah; in fact, he made the journey in his own aircraft far more frequently than any of the Sultan's officials. The Sultan made all decisions on oil matters himself, without advice. He had an expatriate Secretary for Petroleum Affairs in Muscat, but this man, a retired major from the British Army, had no technical knowledge or expertise. His advice was never requested by the Sultan who had so little confidence in him that he was not even allowed to have a copy of the concessionary agreement with the oil company. The managing director of PDO was a man of considerable force of character and ability, as would be expected of a senior oil company executive. He had won the confidence of the Sultan, and his advice was sought on a number of other matters, including development and the recruitment of expatriate staff and consultants. The relationship even reached the stage of the Sultan asking the managing director to pass on messages to the Omani Minister of the Interior and the Omani Governor of the Capital when he returned to Muscat. Thus it happened that the most powerful man in the country after the Sultan was an expatriate who was not an employee of the government. It must be said that the managing director was also an accomplished diplomat; others were understandably jealous of his power and his good standing with the Sultan, but never to the point of making the system, strange as it was, inoperative.

Another expatriate who was highly regarded by the Sultan was the manager of the British Bank of the Middle East in Muscat. The BBME had had a monopoly in Oman from 1948 for twenty years and during this time had built up a close personal relationship with the Sultan. The resident manager in 1969 and 1970 was a man who had become a genuine and trusted friend to the Sultan. There was also at this time a Secretary for Financial Affairs in Muscat (who, incidentally, had been recruited for the Sultan by the managing director of PDO), an Englishman of the greatest integrity who had received his training in the Indian Civil Service and who had been at one stage Political Agent and Consul in Muscat. Like the Secretary for Petroleum Affairs, the advice of the Secretary for Financial Affairs was never sought by the Sultan; the manager of the BBME gave him all the financial and fiscal advice he needed. The Secretary for Financial Affairs simply wrote out cheques when ordered to do so and kept budgets, books and records. The bank manager's influence was almost as great as that of the managing director of PDO, but unlike the latter, the manager never involved himself in other than financial and monetary matters. A skilled and polished diplomat and courtier, he kept the friendship of the Sultan after the July 1970 *coup,* but at the same time built up a similar relationship with Sa'id's son, Qaboos, the new Sultan.

The only government employee who had anything like the influence of these two expatriates was a third expatriate, the Military Secretary. After his oil revenues and his money, national security was the major concern of the Sultan. The Military Secretary had been a major in the British Army and had been seconded to Oman prior to the 1955 civil war. He stayed on, resigned from the British Army, ultimately being promoted to brigadier by the Sultan. He was responsible for the administration and equipping of the Sultan's Armed Forces, and had a large budget (up to 50 per cent of the national revenue) for this purpose. He had the full confidence of the Sultan, and was one of the two expatriates to have direct access to a radio-telephone terminal to Salalah, which meant that he could, if he wished, call the Sultan rather than wait to be called. Command of fighting units was in the hands of regular British officers seconded to the Sultan's Armed Forces, but the Military Secretary was always regarded as senior to these officers. In addition to military advice, the Secretary also controlled the Sultan's internal intelligence and communication network. The Director of Intelligence was another British expatriate. Finally, the Secretary, through a small engineer unit under his command, was able to look after the physical security of the Salalah palace. He never lost the confidence of the Sultan, because he kept strictly to his own job, which he did well, and did not join the chorus of those who cried out for change. He resigned, on excellent terms with the Sultan, in February 1970, and was replaced by another retired British officer who had commanded the Sultan's Armed Forces several years previously. The second Military Secretary, who preferred to be titled 'Defence Secretary', never succeeded in building the close relationship with the Sultan that his predecessor had.

The other expatriate radio-telephone terminal holder was the Personal Adviser. This man, a retired major from the British Army and the Indian Civil Service, had been Consul-General in Muscat and had made a somewhat dramatic dash from Muscat to Sohar in 1952 with the British government's message to the Sultan requesting him not to attack the Saudi force in Buraimi. After his retirement from the Foreign Office, he offered to stay on in Oman to help the Sultan with the problems created by the British actions. Although he had access to the Sultan he never enjoyed the same degree of mutual trust as the Military Secretary and certainly never had the same relationship with his employer as did the managing director and the bank manager. His responsibilities as Personal Adviser were not clearly defined; it was understood that they amounted more or less to 'looking after the Muscat end' while the Sultan was in Salalah. As the Sultan spent all his time in Salalah, this meant that the Personal Adviser had considerable power in Muscat. He looked after the Muscat municipality and through his supervision this body performed fairly efficiently. He kept a watch on the expatriate community in Muscat and made sure that they obeyed the strict rules as to social behaviour and dress. He also gave the Sultan a certain amount of advice on foreign affairs when necessary.

Other government employees who reported direct to the Sultan and who occasionally made the journey to Salalah at his invitation were the *wali* of Matrah, Ismail Khalil al-Rassassi, a Palestinian who had been in Oman since 1928, A.C. Mukherjee, the Indian Director of Public Works, and Muhammad Lisan al-Haq, the Indian Director of Audit. All three were basically technicians, but Wali Ismail had a position of considerable authority.

The only two senior Omani government officials in Muscat who reported direct to the Sultan were Sayyid Ahmed bin Ibrahim Al Bu Sa'id, the Minister of the Interior, a distant cousin of the Sultan and a descendant of 'Azzan bin Qais, and Sayyid Shihab bin Faisal Al Bu Sa'id, the Governor of Muscat, an uncle of the Sultan. These officials would make an occasional journey to Salalah, and would correspond with the Sultan. They were trusted, they were not forceful or adventurous, and would no nothing to incur the Sultan's displeasure. Ahmed bin Ibrahim had a great knowledge of the tribes and politics of the interior of Oman.

Although not in Muscat, and not officially a member of the government, there was at this time one tribal leader in Oman for whom the Sultan had considerable respect. This was Sheikh Ahmad bin Mohammad al-Harthi, the *tamimah* of the al-Hirth, the tribe whose opposition to the Sultan's father and grandfather had caused rebellions in the late nineteenth and early twentieth centuries. Sheikh Ahmad had never formally bowed his knee to the Sultan, though he averred to be 'with the Sultan'. His word was law in the Sharqiyah, the easternmost part of the Oman mountains, and after an incident in which a British officer was shot and wounded, the Sultan had agreed that his Armed Forces would keep out of Sheikh Ahmad's tribal area. Sheikh Ahmad would occasionally visit Salalah by the long overland route, and on one of these visits, he and Sultan Sa'id agreed to heal their differences and to confirm their pact by betrothing the Sultan's only son, Qaboos, to Sheikh Ahmad's daughter. A formal engagement was announced, but the Sultan was deposed by his son before the marriage took place. The engagement was forgotton, and the marriage never occurred. After the change of government, Sheikh Ahmad became a political prisoner and was placed under house arrest in Muscat.

Finally, no part of the government, and allowed to meet very few people, was the Sultan's son, Qaboos. Born in Salalah of a Dhofari mother, Qaboos had been educated privately in Salalah, and was never allowed to mix with other children. The British government suggested to the Sultan that his son be found a place in Sandhurst, and this was done, Qaboos spending several months in private tuition in England before going on to Sandhurst. After Sandhurst, he spent a few months in Germany with a British regiment before returning to Salalah. Upon his return, his father place him under what amounted to house arrest. Although no formal order was given as far as is known, he was not allowed to leave Salalah, was not allowed visitors without his father's permission, and was not given any work to do. When the consultants whom the Sultan retained to advise on the setting up of development organisations requested that Qaboos might work with them as an Omani counterpart, they were met with an angry refusal. Qaboos was allowed to play no part in the government of the country and would be lucky if he saw his father once a year. His father permitted him occasional visits from expatriates in whom the Sultan had confidence; it was through this loophole that Qaboos was able to sound out support for his overthrow of his father.

There was no way for the Omani people to make their voice heard by the Sultan, unless it was to be quoted to him by spies. There was no formal or informal consultative assembly or council, no certain way of laying pleas before the Sultan. His spy network gave the Sultan a continuing close knowledge of the mood of the country; as this mood became more restive, his restrictions became harsher. An armed revolt against him had started in Dhofar in 1965, and in northern Oman many young men left the country illegally.

During this time, many such illegal emigrants found their way to Kuwait, where they could get a secondary education. For those who wanted to go on to a university or technical college there was little choice. If they approached the British Council for a place in a British educational establishment, they would be turned away unless they could get the Sultan's permission. There was no way for them to get this permission. If they applied to the United States, they were similarly turned away. If they applied to the Soviet Union, they were accepted, provided that they would learn Russian. Many did so. Others went to the German Democratic Republic.

Opposition to the government of Sultan Sa'id was growing, both in Oman and in neighbouring Arab countries. More and more the British government was made to realise that it had a responsibility for the situation in Oman. No change would be possible unless it was with the compliance of the British Army officers and Air Force officers seconded to the Sultan and having a form of allegiance to him. A change of government could only take place if these officers were ordered at least not to impede it. A popular front movement had been formed in Dhofar in 1965, and a second such front, the National Democratic Front for the Liberation of Oman and the Arabian Gulf (NDFLOAG) was formed in Iraq in 1969 from Omani students and embittered émigrés. It attracted support from many Omanis, both inside and outside Oman. A group of its activists, using weapons smuggled into the country, staged an attack on the army post at Izki on 12 June 1970. The attack was beaten off, and in the subsequent pursuit of the attacking party, all its members were either killed or captured. Information supplied by the prisoners led to the discovery of a house in Matrah filled with smuggled weapons and propaganda material, which in turn led to the arrest of many more members of NDFLOAG in July 1970, an action which temporarily stopped the movement in Oman, though it continued to flourish outside Oman.

The attack on the post at Izki was the catalyst that forced action. Qaboos, the Sultan's son, had for several months previously been very outspoken about his father to many of his expatriate visitors, so much so that a message had to be sent to him discreetly informing him that not all expatriates shared his views about his father. His views were reported to the British government, whose ambassadors in other Arab countries were doubtless reporting the feeling of the governments to which they were accredited that a change in Oman could only take place if the British government let it happen. The British Labour government, which had already announced that there would be a British withdrawal from the Persian Gulf at the end of 1971, was defeated in a general election on 18 June 1970. The Conservative government which followed it was less inhibited about dabbling in the affairs of other states. Both the Foreign Office and the Ministry of Defence were worried that an unstable situation in Oman could well prejudice the smooth withdrawal from the Gulf in the following year. Accordingly, the British government let it be known that its officers should not stand in the way of a change of government. A controlled change would be very much more acceptable than an uncontrolled change which might come about through a spontaneous outburst of the Omani people backed by a popular front movement.

Some of the seconded and contract officers in Oman went a stage further than this, and actively helped Qaboos organise the stroke against his father. Eventually on the afternoon of Thursday 23 July 1970, Sheikh Braik bin Hamud bin Hamid al-Ghafari, son of a sheikh who had been *wali* of Dhofar for many years, and a man of great moral courage, went into the palace in Salalah with a demand for the abdication of the Sultan. Sa'id, warned that something was not quite right by the odd behaviour of servants and by the unprecedented and uninvited appearance of Sheikh Braik, reached into his desk for a pistol and shot Sheikh Braik, wounding him. In the pandemonium which followed, there was much wild shooting but the only other casualties were the Sultan himself, who was wounded in his stomach and foot, and one of his servants, who was killed. Eventually, later that evening, the Sultan agreed to surrender, but on condition that it would be to a British officer. A British colonel, on secondment to the Sultan's Armed Forces, accepted the surrender and the Sultan subsequently signed a formal abdication document.

With the departure of the Sultan, all of the ramshackle administration was swept away, the British advisers (save the Defence Secretary, who played an important role in the planning and carrying out of the *coup*), the Omani Minister of the Interior and the Governor of the Capital. Anyone who had apparently been loyal to the old man went. But more than this, the old Sultan had not left any organisation of government, there were no institutions with their own momentum (apart from the army, of course, and that had its momentum from its British officers), no cadres of trained or experienced people, no structure, nothing to give stability to that which was to follow. The legacy Sa'id left his son, the effect from his cause, was a vacuum of power and of the means to govern which could not easily or readily be filled, and which had a fundamental influence on what was to follow.

Sultan Sa'id failed for a number of reasons. The habits of strict financial care and the refusal to incur debts, at once so necessary and so praiseworthy, with which he started his reign, became ingrained and rigid. When the export of oil began, and with it a great increase in the expectations of his people, the Sultan's mental attitudes had become inflexible. Having lost much face and respect in the eyes of his people through his overt need to employ mercenaries to defeat his enemies and to maintain internal security, having retreated to Salalah to avoid meeting his people, when the time came to change his policies, he was quite unable to do so. The rising tide of Arab nationalism reached Oman at about the same time that oil exports began, and the Sultan's style of government became more and more anachronistic. A lifetime of looking to British India rather than to the

Arab world could not easily be ignored, the exposed loneliness which the British departure from India in 1947 must have engendered in the Sultan contributed much to his wish to seek isolation and turn away from a world which could only lead to his downfall. His isolation and his insecurity, his conservatism and his fear for his own life, caused such a barrier between him and his people that Omanis came to believe that he was completely indifferent to their needs and their welfare.

Notes

1. Recounted to the author by a senior expatriate who wishes to remain anonymous. The incident occurred in the early part of 1969.
2. Treaty Series No. 28, 1958, Cmnd. 507.
3. For the difficulties experienced by the British government in maintaining a consistent policy in the Middle East, see E. Kedourie, *In the Anglo-Arab Labrynth,* Cambridge, 1975, and G. Troeller, *The Birth of Saudi Arabia,* London, 1976. Both relate to the period prior to 1939, but there is little to suggest that attitudes in the British Foreign Office and Ministry of Defence in the early 1950s were markedly different from those of the Foreign Office and the India Office before the war.
4. Col. Sir Hugh Boustead, *The Wind of Morning,* London, 1971.
5. Col. Sir Hugh Boustead, 'Review of Progress of the Development Department in the Sultanate of Muscat and Oman Covering the Period from October 1958 to October 1961', unpublished report in author's archives.
6. D.N.R. Ogram, 'A Review of the Work of the Development Department from December 1962 until March, 1968', unpublished report in author's archives.
7. Ibid.

PART II: SULTAN QABOOS AND THE NEW ORDER

4 THE EMERGENCE OF THE AUTHORITY OF SULTAN QABOOS

> 'It should be borne in mind that there is nothing more difficult to arrange, more doubtful of success, and more dangerous to carry through than initiating changes in a state's constitution.'

Although the *coup* ousting Sultan Sa'id bin Taimur took place on the afternoon and evening of Thursday 23 July 1970, it was not until the following Sunday that Omanis knew about the overthrow of the despot they had come to hate. Careful plans were made to ensure that the old Sultan was safely out of the country before the announcement was made. He was flown on an RAF aircraft to Bahrain and thence to London where he spent some time in a London clinic until his wounds healed.

Amongst the first acts of Sultan Qaboos was to summon the manager of the Muscat branch of the British Bank of the Middle East to Salalah to see him. No government employee had details of either the government's finances or those of the old Sultan. The manager had both; he had a few days previously left Muscat for his annual leave and had to fly back from London. He was able to reassure the new Sultan that the financial position of the Sultanate was sound. Similarly the managing director of Petroleum Development (Oman) Limited was an early visitor to Salalah, as was the Defence Secretary. The old Sultan's other senior expatriate advisers were out of the country on their annual summer leave. The timing of the *coup* had been carefully planned so that it would take place when these officials, who, conservative though they may have been, had the highest personal integrity and who would not have been partners to the plot to overthrow their employer, were in no position to cause trouble.

It must be stressed that the *coup*, although it was received with the wildest enthusiasm by the Omani people, was not in any sense a popular uprising. Very few Omanis had anything to do with its planning or its execution; such participation was the last thing the planners wished for. Had the *coup* been followed by demonstrations all over Oman demanding participation in the new government, the planners would have been seriously embarrassed. Indeed, all those involved in planning and staging the *coup* had given little thought in depth to what would, or should, happen after it. The position of the British government was simply that the old Sultan's arch-conservatism and intransigence was causing it no little embarrassment and was putting at risk the proposed withdrawal from the Persian Gulf at the end of 1971. Omani thinking had probably not gone much beyond a desire to be rid of the old Sultan and to grab a share of the oil revenues which everyone believed to be vastly greater than they were. So it happened that when the post-*coup* tumult and shouting had died, and the heady euphoria of the old Sultan's departure had abated, it came to be realised that Oman had no government, no plans for the future, no people able to take office and make clear and firm decisions.

The new Sultan, Qaboos, after the nightmare of his lonely childhood, and the unhappiness of his years at Sandhurst where the British habit of ragging had not done a great deal for his self-confidence, had been alone in Salalah for seven years, with only social visitors carefully (but not carefully enough) chosen and screened by his father. By temperament and experience, he was ill prepared to take a firm lead, to give orders with authority. He knew personally very few Omanis and not one who could be a trusted friend, save perhaps the courageous Sheikh Braik who was at that moment lying wounded in a British hospital outside Oman. Around him were British advisers and British officers, alternatively fawning and patronising. He was well aware that he owed his position to them, and that he could make no positive policy decision without their support, and, indeed, without their strength to ensure its implementation. He had no personal Omani friends or contacts in Muscat or among the tribes of northern Oman. The army, that is, his British advisers, controlled communications throughout the country, and, through Cable and Wireless Limited, between Oman and the outside world. He had escaped from one situation where he had no power into another. Little wonder that he was not immediately able to take command of the situation.

Understandably, he felt a great bitterness against his father. In an interview with a Lebanese journalist, Qaboos said of his father:

> He knew five languages, but he wasn't cultured. Knowledge is one thing and culture is something else. He adopted a policy and would not agree to give it up, because he believed that this policy was the best one. He was headstrong and bigoted. He didn't believe in change. His thinking went back to an age which is not this present age.

So he had to fall from power, and this is what happened.[1]

In the vacuum which followed the *coup*, government was in the hands of an expatriate committee, a self-styled 'Interim Advisory Council'. This council was chaired by a retired British colonel, the Defence Secretary, who kept the Sultan informed of its work. It was advisory in name only, and its members took a number of decisions in the Sultan's name, which they were enabled to do by his inevitable lack of confidence and strength at that time.

One of its first decisions was to invite the Sultan's uncle, Sayyid Tarik bin Taimur, a younger brother of the deposed Sultan, to return to Oman from the exile imposed by his brother to take up the post of Prime Minister. Sayyid Tarik was at that time living in Germany where he had a German wife. His mother was Circassian, (his father Sultan Taimur having sired five sons and a daughter, all by different wives) and he had been educated in Germany. He spoke excellent Arabic, Turkish, English and German, and travelled regularly to the Middle East and the Gulf region as a representative of one of the largest German construction groups. His portly figure and commanding personality had become almost a feature of Beirut night-club society, and he enjoyed company, cards and gambling. An intelligent and well-informed man, he had long been an outstanding critic of his elder brother and the methods of his government. Sayyid Tarik had acquired a reputation as a bold leader at the time of the Imam's uprising, but was effectively banished from the country in 1958 for being critical of his brother. He represented something of a rallying point for Omani opposition to Sultan Sa'id (one of many, including the Imam and various popular front movements). Those planning the *coup* feared him and thought that he would be more useful in the government, as well as being much safer, than if he stayed outside and continued to be a rallying point for dissenters.

There is a certain lack of clarity as to the sequence of events leading up to the invitation to Tarik, as there is about much that happened at this time. Few conversations were recorded, few meetings were minuted. Memory can play strange tricks, especially when what may have seemed a good idea at the time turned out to be at least unfortunate. It seems that Tarik was invited back personally by the Defence Secretary, and it is not certain whether he made the invitation before or after seeking the Sultan's permission. In any event, Sayyid Tarik accepted and returned to Oman to become Prime Minister. No one had thought through what his responsibilities should be in this post; no one had bothered to define and have agreed the relative responsibilities and authority of the Sultan as Head of State and the source of all authority, and Tarik, as the executive head of the government. Indeed, and fewer things reveal the incapacity of those responsible than this, even if these statements of respective responsibilities and authorities had been drawn up in impeccable Arabic and agreed, it would have made little difference, because there was nothing at that time in the history or tradition of Oman, nothing in the education or experience of either the Sultan or Sayyid Tarik, to permit them, and the whole Omani polity, to understand with clarity what the terms used meant. 'Executive head of the government' could be rendered into Arabic, but no one could hope to know what it meant to Oman, because there had never been such a post, and no one could envisage how it would work.

In any event, Sayyid Tarik returned to Oman and met his nephew the Sultan. Neither trusted the other, each was aware of the British presence, and neither trusted the British. The British advisers professed the best intentions, but such intentions are classic paving stones. It was agreed between nephew and uncle that the Sultan should retain under his own authority all matters relating to finance, to petroleum affairs and concessionary matters, and defence and internal security. Sayyid Tarik should concern himself with development in northern Oman. There was no clarity on relations with other states, each believing that he had this responsibility. As is the way of such meetings in Oman, great politeness is observed, the Sultan deferring to Tarik as his father's brother and an older man, Tarik deferring to the Sultan as his sovereign, each enquiring endlessly after the other's health, discussing family matters and local gossip. The Sultan would inform Tarik of his thoughts and the latter would politely agree, it being considered bad manners to ask questions or to discuss. Thus Tarik returned to Germany after his first brief visit to Oman with little idea of what was expected of him.

Whilst he was out of the country, and whilst the Sultan was still adapting himself to his new situation, the Interim Advisory Council, continuing its cavalier interpretation of its advisory functions, made a number of decisions which the Sultan from a position of weakness and ignorance of the issues involved, proceeded to ratify. The intention was to present Tarik, when he returned to Oman, with a number of *faits accomplis.* So the Council moved as quickly as it could, and a number of its actions proved to be, with hindsight, unwise and regrettable.

Among the decisions so listed must be quoted the one which resulted in a new town being built as an extension of Matrah in the dusty and land-locked Ruwi valley, an airless site, surrounded by rugged mountains, never visited by cooling sea breezes, and where there was very limited room for future expansion. The so-called 'Greater Matrah Development Plan' was rushed through in six weeks, with no thought given to alternative locations, with inadequate planning, no thought to likely water requirements and their source, or the likely cost, or the likely population growth. The only reason seems to be that it suited the convenience of the Defence Department which occupied part of the site and looked forward to the day when it could move all its expatriate staff out to a nearby headland with a magnificent view and cooling breezes from the sea. As a result of this decision, Oman is now saddled with an untidy and badly located new town development, a development which will dictate the shape of the whole capital area for probably many generations.

Another decision of the Interim Advisory Council was to recruit a new Secretary for Financial Affairs to replace the previous incumbent, who had been asked to resign and who was given a generous gratuity. The Muscat manager of the British Bank of the Middle East, who had an unrivalled knowledge of the country's finances and who was highly regarded and trusted by Sultan Qaboos, was offered the post. He wisely declined it, feeling that he could contribute more where he was than as a member of the government. Subsequent events proved him right in this assessment. The British government was then asked for assistance in recruiting a suitable man and proposed an ex-colonial servant, a qualified accountant, who had held a financial post in Zambia prior to that country's independence. He was immediately available, and his appointment was confirmed without reference to the Prime Minister. Sayyid Tarik, at a meeting with another expatriate adviser on 23 September 1970, said that the appointee seemed to have a wrong idea of what his position in Oman was going to be. The Prime Minister stated that, in his view, this man was not going to be a replica of his pre-*coup* predecessor, but was in Oman simply to advise on the financial situation.[2]

Sayyid Tarik was not consulted because the members of the Interim Advisory Council knew that the Sultan had said that his uncle was not to have access to financial matters. This was in keeping with his father's practice, which had been not to let any Omani have details of the country's income. Well over 95 per cent of revenue at this time came from oil, and as the oil concession was in the name of the Sultan, this too was kept from Omani eyes. The oil revenues were paid into the Sultan's account, and he in turn released a proportion to the exchequer. No Omani was supposed to know how much. In fairness to Sultan Qaboos, he ensured that almost all the revenue from oil went into the government's accounts, holding back for his privy purse a very modest amount of money. The argument of both Sultans for keeping this information secret was two-fold: first, no Omani could be trusted to keep his mouth shut or to refrain from helping himself if the opportunity presented itself, and second, the information was of so secret a nature that only the Sultan himself, the oil company managing director, the bank manager and the Secretary for Financial Affairs should know details. These arguments are demonstrably false, but it was not until 1975 that the Sultan agreed to appoint an Omani to have executive control of the country's finances.

A further decision of the Interim Advisory Council smacked of pure commercial colonialism. Sultan Sa'id had been persuaded to have some essential roads built in and around Salalah, and a contract had been awarded to a West German contractor. This contract was cancelled and the work awarded to a British contractor.

It is possible to have a certain sympathy with the members of this Council. They were hopelessly out of their depth and made the decisions they did in general with good faith. Their integrity was not questioned and it is extremely unlikely that any of them acquired any personal gain from these decisions. They did not represent the British government, they were simply individuals at the end of a long line of colonial administrators, doing what they thought was right. They were at fault for trying to rush decisions, they were at fault for not involving Omanis in their discussions, and they were politically naive in thinking that they could get away with what they did in the name of expediency. The decisions made in those first days gave rise to much adverse propaganda in the Arab world, and in Europe and the United States as well, that 'the British' were ruling Oman for their own commercial and political benefit and that both Qaboos and Tarik were 'British puppets'.

It certainly passed into popular Arab legend that Sayyid Tarik had been brought back to Oman by 'the British', a fact that did little to help build a stable and confident government in the months that followed. Tarik himself resented this aspersion, and was severely critical, with some justice, of the Sultan's British advisers. He often claimed that they took too much on to themselves: worse, they took actions which no one had asked them to take. The situation was not made any easier by the fact that there was no Omani representation in three vital areas, petroleum affairs, finance and defence. In each case, a British expatriate had direct access to the Sultan, and it was felt, rightly or wrongly, that the expatriates concerned were adept at persuading the Sultan to take decisions which might not be in the best interests of Oman. Even in the area of responsibility allotted to him, Sayyid Tarik found expatriate advisers putting pet schemes to the Sultan for approval and then coming to tell him that 'His Majesty has agreed this scheme'. Tarik's hands were further tied by the fact that he had no idea of national revenüe or financial reserves, no idea of the defence budget, and no idea of how much money was available for development projects. All of this he blamed on 'British advice and interference'. Not always the most discreet of men, his conversations with others were reported and given a certain publicity.

Thus Tarik was given a responsibility for a part of the government without being given, with this responsibility, any indication of major policy and strategy, without any concept of national priorities, and basically without authority. The situation was not helped by his own personality; he is a brilliant talker, but no executive. It was to be expected that he would have no staff and no organisation to begin with, but he can be criticised for letting this situation continue for as long as he was Prime Minister. In July 1971 he commissioned management consultants to look at the government structure and make recommendations for improvements. One of these recommendations was that the Prime Minister needed a small highly efficient secretariat, employing the best experts that money could buy, on the grounds that Oman could not afford to have less. This secretariat would be headed by a first-class administrator, as *chef de cabinet,* and would have planning experts to define and appraise projects, legal experts and draughtsmen to study contracts and to draft laws and decrees, a personnel specialist, and an archivist. There was nothing particularly original about this recommendation; it was a matter of common sense and was a completely apolitical recommendation, the implementation of which would have strengthened the Prime Minister's position immeasurably. He rejected the recommendation because the consultants tried to spell out at the same time the relationship between the Sultan and the Prime Minister and to define relative responsibilities and authorities. He did not approve of this, and said that he had not asked them to do so, quoting this as yet another example of 'the British' doing things no one asked them to. The result was that nothing was done, and when he resigned his office at the end of 1971, he still had no staff, not even anyone to type a letter for him, and devoted friends had the unenviable task of opening and actioning some hundreds of letters which had come for him and had been left untouched during his term of office. As Prime Minister, all he had to do was command, and he would have had at least a secretarial staff. He quarrelled with the one professional secretary he did have for a few weeks and when this man left, he was not replaced.

In spite of this fundamental organisational weakness, which, coupled with the ambiguities attached to his position, made him very much less effective than he could have been, and also meant that he could not fight from a position of strength when other influences became strong with the Sultan late in 1971, Tarik pressed ahead with development. He was fortunate that many projects had been started or were at a stage where they could be started with minimum fuss. He inherited the energetic secretary of his brother Sa'id's Development Board, a British expatriate who avoided politics and concentrated on achievement. Between the two, projects were launched and pushed forward. It could be argued that the projects were not appraised, that contracts were signed without adequate checking of the legal and financial provisions, that no heed was taken of priorities, that too much money was paid to the wrong people in commissions, and many more similar reactions to projects pushed in haste. Although there is some weight in these arguments, the fact is that Oman in 1970 and 1971 had such an enormous need for almost anything, roads, ports, airports, schools, hospitals, housing, that everything had priority. The fact of foreign contractors being in the country and employing Omani labour, the fact of each one of these contractors having an Omani agent who earned his commission, meant that cash was being pumped into the economy and that there were immediate benefits to a significant number of Omanis. There is an Arab saying that tribesmen think with their eyes, and this simple statement justified most of the projects that were launched under Sayyid Tarik. People could see that something was happening, that the dead days of Sultan Sa'id had gone forever. Although criticism of the government was not halted, the fact of some achievement strengthened the government and gave it the beginning of an answer to its critics.

The weakness of Tarik's administration, and how it let not only him down but the country as well, is well illustrated by the story of the fishery survey he thought he had authorised. The seas around Oman seem to the casual observer to be full of fish and it was felt by many people that this represented a resource which should be exploited. Proposals were made, and on 7 October 1970,[3] the

Prime Minister authorised a Canadian group to carry out a preliminary survey. A representative of the company visited Oman immediately afterwards, and Tarik confirmed a week later, on 14 October,[4] that he wished the survey to go ahead. He said at that time that he would confirm his instructions in writing. As far as is known he never did, and the survey did not start. He did not do so because he had no organisation to write a letter. This fact was recalled twelve months later, when an American group was commissioned by the Sultan himself to carry out the fishing survey.

Another decision which proved to be bad, simply because there was no expert to guide him, was made on the question of water well-drilling. As has already been said, water is the greatest constraint to development in Oman, the genuinely scarce resource. Oman is dry and barren land with a minimal annual rainfall. Yet all that the combined Omani and expatriate wisdom at the time could think of was that to find limitless water was only a question of drilling holes in the ground. Tarik endorsed this view, and on 25 November 1970[5] endorsed a proposition for a limited water well-drilling programme. What was needed was a national policy for water conservation and resource management. No one could see this need, and the programme approved probably did more harm than good, in that it tended to encourage waste and the belief that money spent on drilling would solve all the problems of scarce water. Instead, permanent damage to natural ground-water reservoirs was caused by encouraging indiscriminate drilling and pumping, and consequent salt water intrusion. Although it is easy to blame Tarik for not insisting that more care be taken, it is only fair to add that all other Omanis shared, and continue to share, his belief that water is only a question of drilling in the right place. There is no awareness that the priceless heritage of water resources can be destroyed within a very few years and that, once this is done, there is no way to replace the destroyed natural ground-water reservoirs.

Tarik saw the need for planning and asked his advisers to draw up a five-year plan. This instruction was conveyed on 18 November 1970,[6] in the form of a single sentence. No one asked for, nor were they given, any indication of national priorities, any guidance on objectives, any awareness of what the government expected, any indication of what sort of society the plan was supposed to underpin. The only long-term guidance given was that the advisers were to include, in the fourth year of the plan, provision for surveys to be carried out in Nizwa with the aim of moving the capital there. This is yet another illustration of

Tarik's strength and his weaknesses. His strength was that he could see that a new capital in Nizwa could create a feeling of national unity and dispel all the old 'Muscat and Oman' mentality. His weakness was that he was unable to define any other policy guidelines, and above all, to ensure that a plan was produced. His advisers were even more at fault in that they did not press him for this policy guidance, and even more, that they did not even attempt the simplest draft planning document.

It could be argued that Tarik alone could not give the necessary top policy guidelines to his advisers so that they could begin to draw up a meaningful plan. This is begging the question. What was needed was for Tarik and the Sultan to sit down together, with a five-year projection of annual revenue. This the oil company could have prepared for them within a few minutes. It would have been the simplest exercise to say then, for example, so much will be required for national defence, so much for the civil government, so much for building financial reserves, and a residue for development. Further, it could have been indicated what development priorities were. Was it more important to have roads rather than schools, for example, or hospitals and public health services before television? The fact that this was not done can be blamed partly on the advisers in Oman at the time, who could have made the basic principles of planning known to their employers, and partly on the nature of traditional Arab society as a whole. When everything comes from God, and when God can take away what has been given, it is almost a blasphemy to think about making provision for future generations. A 'plan' tends to become merely a list of projects, without priorities, without detailed analysis and appraisal. In any event, all this is slightly academic, for no attempt was made to draw up a plan, and Tarik had no organisation to follow up and to insist that his instructions be carried out.

On the other hand, Tarik realised, when no one else did, that Oman's natural gas resources were an asset to be used. These resources are modest, but have a certain value, and could have been exploited, in spite of the fact that they lie some 300 km from the coast at Muscat. The gas resource could not be used without the construction of an expensive pipeline. The oil company was not encouraging, and Tarik's initiative lapsed, again because, although a man of ideas, he had no organisation to define, appraise and follow up projects. Had he been firm, and insisted, it is possible that he would have put Oman into a very much more favourable position in future years than at present seems possible. The oil price increases of October 1973 and January

1974 changed the economics of natural gas completely, and what was previously a marginal resource became a competitive one. By then, sadly, resources had been committed to non-income-generating projects and weapon systems, and there was no money for a project which would have assured future income for a number of years.

There can be no doubt that Tarik's greatest achievement for Oman was in the diplomatic field. Sultan Sa'id had maintained no diplomatic relations with other states. A British purchasing agent in London acted as honorary Oman consul. Britain and India maintained consulates in Oman. A US consular agent from Dhahran in Saudi Arabia would visit Oman once or twice a year. Apart from that, the wider world did not exist. Sultan Qaboos and Sayyid Tarik tried immediately to establish diplomatic relations with other Arab states and with other leading nations. Largely through Tarik's personal efforts, Oman became respectable in the Arab world, and was admitted to the Arab League in 1971 against the opposition of Iraq and the People's Democratic Republic of Yemen. This was followed by membership of the United Nations in October 1971.

During the period of Tarik's Prime Ministership, other ministers were set up. The most successful was the Ministry of Health, under a qualified Omani doctor who had studied in Karachi and London. This man was a close personal friend of Sayyid Tarik and the Prime Minister's support permitted him to make dramatic steps in launching a health service. He had the good fortune also to have an able Zanzibari Omani as an administrator and an experienced Dutch doctor recruited by the Netherlands government as Director of Medical Services. Other ministries covered education, the economy and labour. The diversification of authority, and the creation of ministries, a novel innovation in Oman at that time, was seen to pay a certain dividend on 1 September 1971, when Omani labourers working for foreign contractors staged a strike, protesting against the increasing number of foreign semi-skilled workers in the country, mostly Indian and Pakistani. The main target for their criticism, and the target of the professional agitators trained outside Oman was not the Sultan, not the Prime Minister, but the Minister of Labour. This was a minor, but significant, milestone in creating in Oman an awareness that the Sultan and the government were not necessarily always the same entity.

Sayyid Tarik spent much of the year 1971 outside Oman pleading Oman's case with other Arab nations as well as in the United Nations. Also, no small proportion of his time was taken up with personal matters. His absence meant that he had no organised presence in Muscat to keep business moving and answer expatriate trouble-makers who drew a certain pleasure from pointing out to the Sultan the fact of his uncle's absence from the country. Relations between the Sultan and his Prime Minister were still not blessed by maximum mutual trust, the lack of clarity on respective responsibilities in the field of foreign affairs resulted in ambiguity and confusion, and in addition to the ill will towards Tarik displayed by certain British advisers, the Sultan was now hearing other voices who were also critical.

An understanding of the final break and of Tarik's resignation as Prime Minister requires some background. The American oil business broker, Wendell Phillips, had met Sultan Sa'id bin Taimur in the late 1940s, when Phillips had had to leave his archaeological work in Yemen at very short notice. Phillips had great charm and the two men had a firm friendship. This resulted in Phillips acquiring an oil concession in Dhofar, a concession which he sold to US interests. Some oil was found, but of a quality and in a location which made successful commercial exploitation impossible at that time. Phillips had met Qaboos, and regarded himself as having a 'special relationship' with the new Sultan. Immediately after the *coup* in July 1970, Phillips, doubtless jealous of his commercial interests (he had a 5 per cent share in an offshore concession being managed by Wintershall AG, a West German oil company) and not trusting, with considerable justice, the British advisers in Oman to argue his case, tried to come to Oman. He reached Dubai, but was refused entry to Oman by British officers. It was not until February 1971 that he was eventually able to come to Oman and meet Sultan Qaboos again. His persistence was rewarded, and he was awarded another offshore oil concession, the so-called Ras Minji concession. In view of the importance of what followed, the following letter is quoted in full:

Salalah
March 7, 1971

From. Qaboos bin Sa'id
Sultan of Oman

To. Dr Wendell Phillips

Greetings,

With reference to our conversation regarding the offshore areas of Our Sultanate from the Ras al Hadd to Ras Minji, We are pleased

> to grant you an Oil Concession for the area as defined hereunder, allowing you a period of four months from April 1, 1971 to submit to Us proposed arrangements which will be subject to Our approval. The area shall be:
>
> > 'From a point at Ras al Hadd where the parallel of lattitude [sic] 22°30′ intersects the coastline, eastwards to a point on the continental shelf at a depth of 2000 feet, thence southwards following the 2000 foot isobar [sic] to the intersection of the meridian of longitude 59°15′, thence southwards to Ras Minji, following a line three nautical miles from the coastline, excluding therefrom the territorial waters but including the islands of Masira and Jazirat Shaghaf and their territorial waters and the continental shelf to a depth of 2000 feet.'
>
> Sultan of Oman

Phillips (who, it should be stressed, has nothing to do with the Philips Oil Company) gave his new concession a certain publicity on his return to the United States. In the United States, both the State Department and the Central Intelligence Agency were in any case concerned about the possible implications of the British withdrawal from the Gulf scheduled for the end of 1971. This coupled with Sayyid Tarik's efforts at the United Nations and with other Arab nations, drew many eyes to this erstwhile scarcely known corner of South Eastern Arabia. It was considered by others that British interests tended to regard Oman as an exclusive British commercial preserve, and further, it was considered, rightly or wrongly, that British military assistance against the insurgency in Dhofar was not as effective as it might have been, given the imagined rich commercial pickings available to British interests. This over-simplification can be challenged without too much difficulty, yet it was a point of view held stubbornly by many Arab, US, French and German individuals and organisations up until the end of 1974.

The Sultan himself was aware that as long as he was seen by others to have such a great British involvement in his country, he would find it difficult to counter the 'British puppet' argument put about by his enemies, and to demonstrate to the world that he had reversed his father's, grandfather's and great-grandfather's policy of looking to Britain and the Indian subcontinent at the expense of the Arab world. It was no secret to perceptive visitors that Qaboos, although wishing to retain British military support, wanted to open the doors of Oman to international interests in other fields. Among these perceptive visitors was a Libyan whom Sayyid Tarik had engaged as an adviser in foreign affairs, a man who had been close to the deposed King Idriss and who had extensive contacts. This man suggested to the Sultan that, during his summer holiday in London in 1971, he might like to meet a Libyan Ibadhi. The result was a lunch attended by the Sultan in London, at which the Libyan Ibadhi, Yehia Omar and a close business associate, Ghassar Shakr, a Saudi of Ottoman origin, were presented to the Sultan. The lunch was highly successful, and had great consequences for the future of Oman. The Sultan's new friends were both men of great personal charm and formidable ability. They were as well connected in the Arab world as they were in the United States. They were both the type of men intelligence agencies like to use as local agents; both were well thought of by US services and the Libyan had done some work for British services prior to the deposition of King Idriss. They conveyed to the Sultan the idea that they could help him politically, in presenting him to the world as an independent Arab ruler, diplomatically, in ensuring that he personally met every Arab ruler, financially, in being able to open to door to money from Saudi Arabia, and in the intelligence and surveillance field, where they could introduce him to a service which could do much more for him than the British were prepared to do, particularly when it came to keeping an eye on possible challengers to the Sultan outside Oman. Their reward would be in straight cash payments, and in the commissions that they would earn from commercial firms introduced to the Sultan. It is probable that very little was said to the Sultan at the time about the means of remuneration and its likely future total.

Although the Sultan's two new friends were tough and ruthless individuals, who profited in no small way through their association with Oman, and who made many enemies, it must be confessed that they were collectively far more effective than all the non-Arab advisers taken together. Where others talked, they acted. Certainly, the Sultan gave them his full confidence, and they never failed to get him what he wanted. They were invited to visit the Sultan in Oman in September 1971, and flew in a private aircraft direct to Salalah, after the Sultan's return to Oman from his European holiday. One piece of advice that they gave him was that he was not getting enough from Wendell Phillips, who stood to gain a considerable amount of money at Oman's expense. Accordingly, on 12 September 1971, the Sultan issued an instruction that Wendell Phillips should be cabled immediately 'advising him of the withdrawal of our offer of an oil concession in the southern off-shore areas of our Sultanate'. The Sultan said that he considered that Phillips had ample time to fulfil his obligations imposed on him as a concessionaire as laid down in the letter of 7 March 1971, and he (the Sultan) was of the opinion that Phillips was not able to comply with the terms of the letter despite an extension of time.[7]

Phillips was taken completely by surprise; he thought that his personal relationship with the Sultan was enough and did not realise (as many other also did not) that the world was beginning to change, and that other voices were being heard in Oman, tough political and commercial voices which would not tolerate amateurish prevarication. Phillips threatened legal action; through his new friends, the Sultan met Robert B. Anderson, an ex-Secretary of the US Treasury under President Eisenhower. Anderson proposed an ex-Treasury colleague of his to be the Sultan's legal representative. Before this man could take up the case, President Nixon offered him another assignment, and Anderson's people had to look again, finding a New York lawyer to take the case. This man was able to convince Phillips that he had no case, after much wrangling and negotiating. Subsequently part of the Ras Minji concession was taken up by an international consortium led by the Sun Oil Company.

Another deal arranged by his new friends on the Sultan's behalf was a fishery survey to be carried out by a consortium of US companies. This caused much ink to flow in the British press about US involvement in the Indian Ocean. It was alleged that a fishery survey was a cover for a CIA operation aimed at keeping an eye on Russian submarines in the Indian Ocean, an allegation which the apparent lack of fisheries experience of the people engaged on the survey did much to foster. In fact, these rumours were no more than low-grade gossip evocative of similar rumours at the time of the 'Great Game' a century beforehand, but they found their way to Sayyid Tarik, along with much other gossip about the Sultan's new friends. Tarik found out about the new arrangements, like everyone else, by hearsay and newspaper report.

Tarik felt slighted and somewhat ridiculous. His efforts throughout 1971 to get precise information about financial and defence matters had foundered on the lack of co-operation of the Sultan's British advisers. He considered that 'the British' were undermining his position, and that the Sultan's flirtation with US business interests and intelligence and surveillance services was to a large extent aimed at him. Rightly or wrongly, he believed at that time that the Sultan was having him watched. He went to Germany in December 1971 to spend Christmas with his family, and, after his departure from Oman, a letter of resignation was delivered to the Sultan in Salalah. The experiment with a Prime Minister had failed. Tarik and the Sultan were subsequently reconciled and uncle and nephew developed a close relationship which was cemented in March 1976 by the marriage of the Sultan to one of Tarik's daughters.

The experiment with a Prime Minister failed, as it was bound to. Quite apart from the personalities of nephew and uncle, and the machinations of expatriate advisers, it must be repeated that there was nothing in the tradition or history or experience of the Omani people to permit them to understand the division of authority between a ruler as head of state and a prime minister as the executive head of government. Other Sultans had employed a *wazir*, i.e. a minister, who was more of a secretary, who danced constant attendance, but who made no decisions that mattered himself. Tarik was not the man to be *wazir*, and in any case, saw the Sultan on comparatively infrequent occasions. Oman was not ready for a firmly structured government, the Sultan was not ready to begin to give up any power that mattered, and Tarik was not prepared to accept a simple administrative and representational role. Possibly the experiment might have worked had the personalities been different, but the fact is that they were not different. There was no one else in Oman in 1970 or 1971 who could have commanded sufficient popular support to be Head of State, nor was there anyone else in Oman at that time who could have been considered as chief executive of the government, someone who would have enjoyed the Sultan's confidence and at the same time commanded sufficient popular respect. As it was, it did not take people long to realise that all was not well at that time between uncle and nephew, and hence to play one off against the other for the sake of narrow petty advantage. Included in those who did this were some expatriate advisers who should have known better.

Two hypothetical questions need to be considered briefly. First, at the time of the *coup*, given the Sultan's inexperience and lack of self-confidence, what should have been done to ensure effective government, and, second, what post should have been offered to Sayyid Tarik?

Although the British advisers in Oman at the time of the *coup* would not have welcomed such a step, it seems, admittedly with hindsight, that the best solution to the problem at the time would have been to secure the services of a small team from an Arab government. The obvious choice is Egypt. Had it been possible to put together such a team, and there would have been considerable difficulties in choosing four or five top-class men who would be energetic and able, but who would have been prepared to be completely apolitical, then the development of government in Oman would almost certainly have been a less haphazard affair than it was.

As far as Sayyid Tarik is concerned, the only post possible would have been as Senior Adviser to the Sultan. Tarik is as wise an adviser as he is a bad executive. With Tarik as adviser, with the Sultan as executive head of the government, and with a small Cabinet of Arab professionals, Oman would have avoided many of the mistakes which will have to be lived with for a long time. No matter how able and dedicated non-Arab senior advisers might have been, they were politically wrong. This was revealed for all the world to see at the time of the oil price increases of 1973 and 1974, when there was something of a confrontation between Arabs and non-Arabs.

There is one fundamental issue which was never seriously considered by Sayyid Tarik himself, by the Sultan, or by those reponsible for putting both in the positions they held in 1970 and 1971. This is the question of popular representation in the government of Oman. Other Arab states cast in the traditional mould had at least the tribal *majlis*. Kuwait had an elected Parliament, and Bahrain was moving towards an elective assembly. Abu Dhabi, upon its full independence at the end of 1971, set up a small advisory assembly. Sayyid Tarik talked loftily about Oman becoming a constitutional monarchy, but neither he nor his nephew the Sultan was ever serious in thinking about the need to involve their subjects in government. The Sultan said to a Lebanese journalist:

> It was not possible to follow the Western tradition of democratic systems. We are not yet ready to embark upon this stage. We have no constitution. We have no chamber of deputies.[8]

He did not add, though he might have, that he would have fought tooth and nail to avoid the establishment of any popularly elected constituent assembly. He always liked to believe that he was the only decision-maker in Oman. Any other organisation with power would constitute a threat to his personal security, and therefore could never be countenanced.

The failure of the experiment with a prime minister had its positive sides. Tarik's departure left Sultan Qaboos in undisputed control of Oman. More than this, through the efforts of his two new Arab advisers, the Sultan was slowly becoming recognised as an Arab ruler by the heads of other Arab states. Tarik's efforts to have Oman elected as a full member of the Arab League and of the United Nations had contributed significantly to this recognition, but his new advisors could give the Sultan personal introductions to the President of Egypt and the kings of Saudi Arabia and Jordan. They could offer him alternative sources of funds, intelligence, surveillance facilities, and development experts to reduce his hitherto exclusive reliance on British sources for these services.

The result was twofold. First, there ensued a complete reversal of the Sultan's father's policy of looking to the Indian sub continent for all those services which the British government could not provide. Oman looked to the Arab world as it had never previously done throughout its history. Fifteen centuries' isolation was abandoned.

Second, the Sultan was seen to be his own man. Although the propaganda epithet 'British puppet' continued to be used by his enemies, his authority was now undisputed in his own land. No longer could British advisers tell him what to do in all fields. He listened to his British officers on all military matters, not hesitating to have those whom he did not trust, including the Defence Secretary who had helped him oust his father, removed. On political and development matters, the British influence was eclipsed. The Sultan ruled.

Notes

1. *Al-Watan*, Muscat, 6 April 1972.
2. Minutes of meetings with the Prime Minister compiled by Director of Planning and Development, author's archives.
3. Ibid.
4. Ibid.
5. Ibid.
6. Ibid.
7. Letter from HM Sultan Qaboos to Secretary for Financial Affairs dated 12 September 1975, author's archives.
8. *Al-Watan*, Muscat, 6 April 1972.

5 THE CIVIL WAR IN DHOFAR

'Nothing brings a prince more prestige than great campaigns . . .

Part of Sultan Qaboos' legacy from his father was a guerrilla war in the province of the new Sultan's birth, Dhofar. His own military training and deep interest in martial matters, coupled with the immediate need to fight a determined opposition to his regime, himself personally and his inherited style of government, made the struggle in Dhofar of the greatest concern to the Sultan. His preoccupation with this struggle, which escalated as he ordered firmer military measures, caused other matters, such as the political and administrative development of his government, his own relationship with his people, and the economic development of Oman, to attract an inadequate amount of his thinking and policy-making time. It is worth looking at the province of Dhofar, its relationship with Oman, the nature of the guerrilla war and the Sultan's concern with combating the threat which this war presented in detail.

Historically, little is known of this remote and poor area of the Arabian peninsula. Marco Polo described Dhofar in about AD 1285:

> Dhofar is a great and noble and fine city and lies 500 miles to the north-east of Esher. The people are Saracens and have a Count for their Chief, who is subject to the Soldan of Aden, for this city still belongs to the province of Aden. It stands upon the sea and has a very good haven, so that there is a great traffic in shipping, and the merchants take hence great numbers of Arab horses to that market, making a great profit thereby. The city has under it many other towns and villages. Much white incense is produced here, and I will tell you how it grows. The trees are small, like fir trees, they are notched with a knife in several places and from these notches the incense is exuded. Sometimes it also flows without any notch; that is by reason of the great heat of the sun there.[1]

It should be noted that ancient writers used the word 'Dhofar' to describe a city which was possibly situated at the site marked today by the ruins at Baleed, outside the modern town Salalah. Otherwise, the ancient city may have been at Sumhuran, near Taqah, a few miles to the east along the coast from Salalah. The use of the word 'Dhofar' to describe the whole region appears to have come into use during the eighteenth and nineteenth centuries. Also, although incense still grows in Dhofar, and is used locally, it has not for many years been important in the economy of the region.

Apart from Marco Polo's brief words, and other even more sketchy travellers' tales, historical references to Dhofar are few. Its people had no literature, and left no records, save a few monuments and tombs. Accounts of the society well into the twentieth century suggest a situation approaching anarchy. The people of Dhofar had little racial homogeneity, and were split into a number of tribal communities, with two main groups, the Bait Kathir of the plain around Salalah, who are traders and gardeners, and the Qara, or Jebali, people of the mountains, who are pastoralists and tend to be nomadic. There are also significant numbers of people of African origin in Salalah, and north of the mountains, nomadic 'Bedu' Arab tribes. The resources of the land are feeble, and the various groups have had to fight amongst themselves for a living share of the little Dhofar can offer them. It seems that throughout the history of Dhofar, fights and blood fueds between its peoples were the norm. This strife was not confined to the major racial or tribal groupings; within each tribe there were sub-tribes and clans, each jealous of its puny rights, all quick to take offence and seek revenge.

In 1931, Bertram Thomas wrote:

> The people, composed of warlike and rival tribes, have always found law and order irksome. They love unfettered personal liberty more than life, and glory in their hereditary wars. The alternative of an extraneously imposed authority has in the past been acceptable to them only by force . . . [2]

It was at the request of one faction in a characteristic Dhofari tribal war that Sayyid Sa'id bin Sultan sent soldiers from Muscat to Dhofar in 1829. This expedition soon returned home, but the ruler in Muscat left his interest in Dhofar in the place of his soldiers and from that moment, he and his successors regarded the region as their personal property. In 1880, again following a request from a warring faction for assistance, Sultan Turki bin Sa'id sent more soldiers and a regional governor (*wali*) to Salalah. There has been an Omani presence in Dhofar ever since, but until 1970, the country was regarded still as a personal property of the Sultan, rather than as part of Oman. The authority of the various Sultans scarce went beyond the confines of the long (about 70 km) and narrow plain of which Salalah is the economic centre. Their hold in the mountains was at the best tenuous.

Sultan Sa'id bin Taimur elected to live his whole life in Salalah from 1958. Apart from a few visits to London, made with great secrecy via Aden and with the courtesy of the British Royal Air Force, he never left Dhofar. Indeed, for most of the time, he did not even leave his rambling palace on the shore in Salalah. He was never seen in Muscat and governed the country by radio-telephone. Dhofar was something apart, his own private garden; whatever modest revenue could be collected from customs revenues and taxes was his own money, and was not paid into the treasury in Muscat. The inhabitants, numbering probably never more than 50,000 people, and possibly even fewer, were either completely subservient to his will, or else they were regarded as 'disobedient', to be 'punished' should they ever come into his power. The Sultan had some of the traits of a harsh Victorian nanny, save that his punishments tended ultimately to be fatal, in that those people who were not left to rot in prison would find their water wells destroyed and hence the essential staff of their life broken. Gradually, the tribal warfare, so long part of the history of Dhofar, became organised opposition to the rule of the Sultan.

Inevitably, once what had been mere tribal strife took on something of the form of an organised opposition, political elements crept into this opposition. Following the final defeat of the Imam's revolt in northern Oman in 1959, he ceased to be a rallying point around which the opposition to Sultan Sa'id could gather. Revolutionary movements which had their foundations in the ideological dogma of Marxist-Leninist or Maoist dialectic gradually became the motivating force of opposition to a ruler who would make no concession to the present. Oppressive though his rule was in northern Oman, it was his own presence and hence the feeling of personal oppression which fanned the spark of open revolt in Dhofar. In 1964, a small party of armed and determined revolutionaries, trained in Iraq, entered Dhofar. These men had been recruited from young Dhofaris who had fled from their homes following the Sultan's insensitive attempts to subjugate them. On 14 August 1964, a military vehicle from the Sultan's Armed Forces ran over a mine, which left one soldier killed and another wounded. Further incidents followed the Sultan's vengeful reprisals, mining and isolated attacks building up in the classic guerrilla warfare pattern. The Sultan imprisoned more tribesmen and destroyed more water wells: The establishment of a formal revolutionary movement, the Dhofar Liberation Front, was then an almost inevitable consequence. This formal movement was born at a meeting of the insurgent groups fighting against the oppression of Sultan Sa'id in the mountains of Dhofar on 9 June 1965. The Popular Front movement which inherited the struggle in Dhofar commemorated this date in subsequent years as the anniversary of the revolution.

The meeting of the insurgents on 9 June 1965 was elevated in status and called the First Congress. It issued a proclamation calling for the

> liberating of this country [i.e. Dhofar] from the rule of the despotic Al Bu Said Sultan whose dynasty has been identified with the hordes of the British imperialist occupation . . . This people [i.e. the Dhofaris] has long and bitterly suffered from dispersion, unemployment, poverty, illiteracy and disease . . .[3]

This proclamation is interesting in that it stresses the very limited aims of the Dhofar Liberation Front, that is, the liberation of Dhofar from the rule of the Sultan. The reference to the 'British imperialist occupation' is inevitable; any revolutionary document issued during the 1960s and early 1970s which did not use these hackneyed phrases would seem strange. The reference in the Omani and Dhofari context is also understandable. To the simple and unsophisticated tribesman who saw an oppressive and often cruel ruler kept in power by an army of Beluch mercenaries led by British officers, the propaganda of the professional revolutionaries would be in keeping with his own experience.

Had Sultan Sa'id had the political wisdom to counter this formal opposition to his rule in Dhofar with imagination and with reforms, the history of the next ten years may well have been very different. The proclamation of 9 June 1965 was the product of an economic and social frustration inflamed by a mindless political oppression. The answer to the proclamation was not an alternative programme with proposals for reform, or economic assistance, or even a constructive idea, but simply the use of even greater force. Nothing could be calculated to sustain a fledgling revolutionary movement more than this.

The initial stages of the Dhofar Liberation Front's war against Sultan Sa'id took the form of a simple, almost classic guerrilla operation with mining, ambushes and stand-off attacks. Then, on 28 April 1966, an attempt was made on the life of the Sultan. His bodyguard, in which there were many Dhofaris, fired at him from a distance of a few feet while he was inspecting them, and, quite inexplicably, missed their target, managing only to wound their Pakistani guard commander. The Dhofar Liberation Front claimed responsibility for the attempt. Some reports suggested that the Sultan was himself wounded in the attempt, but he was not, and his first action was in keeping with the complex and often contradictory character of the man. He immediately drove to the nearby camp of his Armed Forces at Umm al-Ghawarif and said to a British Officer in an apologetic tone: 'We seem to be having a little trouble down at the palace and I wonder if you would be so good as to come down.'[4]

There was nothing apologetic about his subsequent reaction, however. He never left his palace again as long as he ruled, but his command went out and the reprisals against the Dhofar Liberation Front were savage. Whether the Front would have survived or not is questionable had they not received great moral support, as well as arms and supplies, from the dissident forces at that time fighting the British government in Aden and its two protectorates. The British withdrawal from Aden at the end of 1967 was seen as a victory for popular liberation movements, and encouraged the movement in Dhofar, which had a certain understandable difficulty in distinguishing the difference between the British support for the Sultans of the Aden Protectorates with their support for the Sultan of Oman.

The nature of the fighting in the Aden protectorates and the background to the ideological support this conflict had among Arab nationalist and revolutionary movements are related to the development of formal opposition movements in Oman and are worth considering briefly. Aden had been occupied by forces sent from India by the British East India Company in January 1839. The city of Aden and its immediate hinterland was administered by the government of British India until 1937, when supervision of its affairs was transferred to the Colonial Office in London. The British presence had spread throughout what is now the Peoples' Democratic Republic of Yemen in the years following the occupation of Aden, and the area so concerned was divided into two 'Protectorates'. Each of the two Protectorates, East and West, had close ties with the government of British India, and then, from 1927, with the British government itself through the Colonial Office in London. Although thus legally not a colony, the distinction between colonial and protected status meant little to an unsophisticated and naturally independent people. Understandable resentment at the presence of an alien regime, no matter how benign and constructive it might have wished to appear, grew. This discontent was stimulated by two upheavals in the hitherto accepted balance of power in the Middle

East. First was the humilitating diplomatic defeat of the Anglo-French-Israeli military adventure along the Suez Canal in 1956, which encouraged ever-increasing anti-British propaganda emanating from Cairo and spreading throughout the Arab world.

The second upheaval was the revolution in neighbouring North Yemen, when, on 26 September 1962, the Imamate was overthrown and a nationalist and republican government established. Although the Imam Ahmad of North Yemen had given a certain amount of support and encouragement to the rebels in South Yemen, his own régime was so backward and anachronistic that he could never hope to inspire the faith and the ideology that a successful revolutionary movement requires. His death and the overthrow of his successor gave much encouragement to the movement to drive out foreign influences from the two Aden protectorates and from Aden itself.

Following the fall of the traditional régime in North Yemen, and in spite of the untidy civil war which continued in that country for a number of years, it became something of a race between the British government, trying to move out of the area with honour, and the dissident nationalist forces, who wanted a 'liberation', with the revolutionary kudos which such a victory would give them. Southern Yemen became the scene of bitter fighting which continued between nationalist and Marxist-Leninist groups long after the British withdrawal in November 1967. An end was not found (it could hardly be called peace) for almost three years. This was the result of the victory of the Marxist-Leninist, or Popular Front, movement over the nationalist. The country was renamed the Peoples' Democratic Republic of Yemen (PDRY) and its government was well to the left of any other republican régime in the Arab world. The new government of PDRY sought to divert the attention of its own people from their economic plight by exporting revolution to Dhofar, to Oman and to the emerging states of the Persian Gulf.

Thus the Dhofar Liberation Front was able to sustain the attacks against it by Sultan Sa'id's forces, and to reorganise, re-equip and revitalise itself with support, arms and equipment and revolutionary ideology from PDRY. A long common frontier in wild country with few tracks permitted a constant trickle of supplies and agents, enough to sustain the Dhofar revolution and, indeed, to permit it to take the initiative against the Sultan. In September 1968 the Dhofar Liberation Front held its second congress in the mountains of central Dhofar, increased its aims and ambitions, and renamed itself the 'Peoples' Front for the Liberation of the Occupied Arabain Gulf'. Over the course of the next two years, the strength of the revolutionary forces grew as Sa'id bin Taimur became more reactionary and oppressive. His strategy – negative, repressive, punitive, unimaginative – was perhaps the greatest single source of strength to his enemies. Moderates in Oman and Dhofar, increasingly alienated by the Sultan's policies, were attracted to the extremist forces of change because these forces represented the only effective opposition to the Sultan. By the summer of 1970, the Sultan's Armed Forces (SAF), in spite of British equipment and British officers, were completely on the defensive, and the Sultan controlled little more than the town of Salalah, which was protected by a barbed-wire fence all round it and its airfield, the latter run and defended by the British Royal Air Force.

The traditional economy of Dhofar, based on the free movement of people and their cattle from the mountains to the coastal plain and back again, following the monsoonal grazing, had been effectively destroyed. The insurgents were not strong enough to stop patrolling by SAF, nor were they strong enough to launch a frontal attack on Salalah. Equally, SAF was not strong enough to achieve more than the defence of Salalah and send out patrols into the mountains. The insurgent forces won much support for their cause in the republican Arab countries, the so-called 'progressive' states, especially Iraq, being in the forefront of those assisting the Omani opposition. Switching the initiative to northern Oman and organising the attack on the post at Izki (Chapter 3) was the catalyst which forced action by the forces which up to that time had supported Sultan Sa'id and resulted in the *coup* of 23 July 1970 and the replacement of the former ruler by his son Qaboos.

It was not to be expected that this change alone would suffice to stop the insurgency in Dhofar and cause the opponents of Sultan Sa'id to drop their newly acquired ideology in favour of a belief in Sultan Qaboos. The new ruler of Oman initially regarded himself as part of the opposition movement to his father and set out to counter the insurgency in a new strategy which contained five separate elements: the offer of a general amnesty to all those of his subjects who had opposed his father, the ending of the archaic status of Dhofar and its formal incorporation into Oman as the 'southern province', effective military opposition to those rebels who did not accept the amnesty offer, a vigorous nation-wide programme of development, and a diplomatic initiative aimed first at having Oman recognised as a genuine Arab state with its own legal form of government, and second at isolating the Peoples' Democratic Republic of Yemen from the support, tacit or actual, it was receiving from other Arab states. All five elements of the overall strategy were successful, and by mid-1976 the formal opposition to the government of Sultan Qaboos seemed to have been rendered powerless. The revolutionary ideology of the dissidents had been dispersed by petrodollars from Oman's own oil revenues plus considerable sums of money from Saudi Arabia and Abu Dhabi, just as those angry tribesmen who attacked the Sultan's great-grandfather and grandfather in Muscat in the late nineteenth and early twentieth century had been bought off with substantial sums of money. Before considering the permanence of this rout of the opposition to the government of the Sultan of Oman, it is worth considering each of the five elements of the strategy which led to the defeat, or at least the eclipse, of the revolutionary forces.

A general amnesty was offered soon after Sultan Qaboos deposed his father. Any Dhofari fighting with or allied to the rebel cause was promised good treatment if he surrendered to the government. He would get a cash grant, which would be increased if he brought his weapons with him. After a period of screening, the surrendered man would be re-armed and re-equipped and become a member of a tribal militia, the *firqat.* He would then, as a member of a *firqat,* return to the mountains of Dhofar, if possible to his old tribal area, where he would act as part of an internal security and peace-keeping force. He would be encouraged to bring his family with him, and a government shop, school and clinic would be opened in his area. The successful implementation of the amnesty and resettlement programme took time, and there were many problems, yet almost 2,000 erstwhile rebels surrendered and were incorporated in the forces fighting against their former revolutionary masters. Resettlement of the areas of the Dhofar mountains denuded of their population because of the guerrilla war went on at the same time. The amnesty offer was formally renewed in March 1976 following the cease-fire agreement negotiated between the governments of the Peoples' Democratic Republic of Yemen and Oman which came into operation on 11 March.

The formal incorporation of the province of Dhofar into the Sultanate of Oman has proved to be of great importance to Dhofaris. No longer regarded as living in the private garden of the Sultan, the colonial status of Dhofaris *vis-à-vis* the Sultan of Oman has been completely destroyed. Although there is no racial, national or tribal bond between most Dhofaris and most Omanis, Dhofaris under the patronage of the Sultan himself, who was born in Dhofar of a Dhofari mother, have taken what some may regard as a disproportionate share in the government of Oman. In mid-1975, four out of a total of fourteen Omani ministers were regarded by their fellows as Dhofari, though two of these four were born in Dhofar of Dhofari mothers, with in one case a Beluch father and in the other an Omani father. The Omani ministers knew that their Dhofari colleagues would have the Sultan's unswerving support. The population of Dhofar does not exceed 50,000 people, and is probably less; the population of Oman would be about 400,000 people.[5] Certainly, any complaint that Dhofaris had that they were second-class citizens to Omanis had been firmly removed five years after the ousting of Sultan Sa'id. Whether the bond of political equality will prove stronger than the historic racial and national differences is a question for the future.

A detailed account of the military operations in Dhofar is outside the scope of this book, but a brief summary is required because the guerrilla war in the mountains of Dhofar dominated all other thinking on the part of Sultan Qaboos from the date of his accession to power until the cease-fire in early 1976. During this time, the conflict was never regarded by a majority of Omanis as a national struggle. It was 'the Sultan's concern', or 'a British war'. Very few Omanis (as distinct from Dhofaris) cared about military crises or successes in battle of the Sultan's Armed Forces. For most of them, Dhofar was as remote and as inaccessible as the moon. Yet the armed struggle took up a significant proportion of the national income, and became the major preoccupation of the Sultan, so much so that his thinking on any other matter of government, the concept of a prime minister, the responsibilities of individual ministers, the question of any form of popular representation in an advisory or legislative assembly, questions relating to the future shape of the society, were either shelved or not focused upon, because of day-to-day involvement, in the fighting in Dhofar. It can be argued that this concentration was vital to the successful outcome of the struggle, and without the military success, the other four elements of the overall strategy would have been valueless. Again, whether or not the people of Oman have paid too high a price for their ruler's concern with military matters is a question that future generations will have to answer.

The Sultan's concern with the details of military operations led to a bolder strategy and a determination to carry the war to the enemy. Up to and including 1970, the Sultan's army had always retreated behind the barbed wire of Salalah, leaving the mountains and much of the plain to the rebels during the three months of the monsoonal fogs, mid-June to mid-September. Extremely poor visibility during this period had caused supply problems which had been regarded as insoluable. This three-month pause in operations had been of great value to the rebels, who were not worried as much by the poor visibility in a mountain area which was, after all, their homeland. The period of the monsoon thus became for the opposition a time of great activity, of resupply and reorganisation unhampered by threat of aerial observation and attack, of re-establishing their positions in villages from which they might have been driven by superior concentration of the Sultan's forces in the previous winter and spring.

However, in the monsoon period of 1971, the Sultan's forces, having built up their supply and radio communication positions during the previous months, and aided by the beginning of the flow of ex-rebels who had surrendered to them, occupied some posts in the mountains during the months of fog. This operation proved to be so successful that the scope was widened, and in an ambitious move which proved to have great significance for future operations, helicopter and air-lifted forces established a permanent fortified position astride the insurgents supply lines at Sarfait, a location on the top of a mountain some 8 km from the frontier with PDRY. Supplied by air, generally by helicopter, the fact of this position became a constant source of annoyance to the rebel forces. A regular bombardment of the position was maintained by Russian-built 85 mm guns located in Hauf, across the border in PDRY. The position drew a large volume of shells, rockets and mortar bombs on to itself, thus weakening the flow of supplies to rebel forces deeper into the mountains of Dhofar.

The rebel movement attempted to counter the success of the government forces by the direct involvement of its allies from the Peoples' Democratic Republic. An attack across the frontier on 5 and 6 May 1972 was countered by an air strike by Omani government aircraft against Hauf. This air attack was successful in that no further attacks were made from PDRY on Omani government positions, though PDRY militia units sometimes crossed the frontier to bolster the morale of rebel units.

A major victory, in terms of the scale of the operations, was won by the Sultan's forces on 19 July 1972 when the Front, in a desperate attempt to gain a victory to bolster the flagging morale of its adherents, attempted an attack under cover of the monsoonal fog on the town of Marbat, a few miles eastwards along the coast from Salalah. An estimated 200 of the best fighters the rebel movement could muster were assembled for this attack, but just as they launched their attack, the monsoon fog lifted, and the government forces, reinforced by helicopter, were able to inflict a heavy defeat on the attackers, killing, wounding or capturing about half their number. The rebel forces never recovered from this defeat and were never able to deploy sufficient forces to mount a similar attack elsewhere.

The Shah of Iran, an early ally recruited in Oman's diplomatic initiatives, had long been, and for that matter remains, deeply concerned about security in south-east Arabia, and particularly in the strait of Hormuz, through which all of Iran's oil exports must pass. The Shah has his own internal security problems and is regarded as a prime enemy by popular front movements in the Arab world. He responded to the situation in Oman by offering to send an Iranian battle group to take an active part in the fighting in the mountains of Dhofar. In December 1973, against light opposition from the insurgent forces, Iranian troops occupied the important road from Salalah to Thumrait, on the northern side of the Dhofar mountains. The Popular Front propaganda machine had attached great importance to this road, which was known to the insurgent forces as the 'red line', and vowed to win it back. This they were never able to do, and immediately following its occupation by the Sultan's allies, construction began of a modern black-top road from Salalah to Thumrait. Completion of this road represented a major step forward in the Sultan's position; he had restored the possibility of the free movement of people and their animals from the plain to the mountain and back again, thus opening the way to a recreation of an economic life for the people of Dhofar,

Over the course of the ensuing two and a half years, the military efforts of the Sultan's army consisted of building successive barriers across the insurgents' supply lines, making the position of those guerrillas caught on the eastern side of these barriers particularly difficult. A notable victory was won by the Sultan's forces and his Iranian allies following a period of much hard fighting at the end of December 1974 and the beginning of January 1975. Iranian forces striking south from a base established in the mountains were involved in a series of bloody battles which opened the way for the Sultan's forces to capture the village of Rakhyut, the last remaining settlement held by the Popular Front forces. Following this success, the Iranian forces constructed a line of fortifications, the 'Demavend Line', which interdicted all east-west movement by the guerrillas. As the barriers approached the frontier with PDRY, the insurgents began to lose their will to fight, and military operations ceased in March 1976 with a complete victory for the Sultan and his Iranian allies.

Long before this stage was reached, however, the forces backing the guerrilla operations in Dhofar had come to realise that there was no hope of victory for their cause coming from the military effort in Dhofar, and that the fight would have to be taken to northern Oman. On two occasions, in December 1972 and again in October 1974, large-scale attempts were made to organise sabotage and assassinations of key personnel in northern Oman. On each occasion, vigilance on the part of the Sultan's security services plus a not inconsiderable quota of luck caused the attempt to be discovered before any action was taken to implement the plans of the rebels. Arrests, trials, prison sentences and executions for the ringleaders in a tough and determined manner stopped any spread of the opposition, which in both cases was seen to have very little popular support.

A major factor contributing to this lack of support for the opposition cause was the success of the Sultan's efforts to develop Oman, the fourth element in his overall strategy to destroy the revolutionary movement. The accent of development in the first five years was on economic and social infrastructure projects. In a country where previously there had been practically no development, the sudden appearance of contractors' teams building roads, schools, hospitals, a major port and airport in Muscat, a small harbour and an improved airport in Salalah, houses, electricity supply, water supply and numerous small projects to people accustomed to thinking with their eyes, seemed like a miracle. The people of Oman, and of Dhofar, had for many years suffered from three tyrannies, the oppression of Sultan Sa'id, and with this political tyranny, the geographical and social tyrannies of distance and ignorance. In 1971, the first full fiscal year of Sultan Qaboos' reign, some 20 million Omani rials (just under $60 million) was spent on development. Five years later, in fiscal year 1975, the amount spent on development was 339.1 million Omani rials (almost $1,000 million).[6] The result of this was that the country had modern road, air and sea communication facilities with the world in a way that it had never known before. The journey from Muscat to Dubai, or to Abu Dhabi, which fifteen years previously would have taken two weeks on a camel, may now be completed in an air-conditioned car on a modern road in under four hours, or by air in 40 minutes. Five years previously, imported goods had to be unloaded from a ship on to a lighter and thence conveyed to a narrow concrete jetty. Losses and breakages were enormous. Now ships tie up to a modern jetty in a modern port and unload by crane direct on to the dock side. Five years previously, grieviously ill people could make a jolting journey of several days to Muscat on a camel or donkey for care in the one crowded hospital run by missionaries. Now, there is hardly an Omani who does not live within an hour's drive on a modern road to a small hospital or clinic. Five years previously, the only education possible for 99 per cent of the children was the *kutab*, or religious instruction, where the Koran was taught by rote. A few intelligent children would learn to read by this method, the majority would succeed merely in being able to quote endless verses of the Koran by heart. Now probably considerably more than half the boys of school age, and a significant proportion of the girls, have primary school places. This alone might not have been enough, but there is scarcely an Omani who has not got more money in his pocket than he could ever have dreamed of under the régime of Sultan Sa'id. There are, in 1976, far more jobs available than there are Omanis wishing to and willing to work to fill them, and wage rates are hence very high. Prices are also high, but there has been a dramatic rise in the living standards of a great majority of the Omani people. It is possibly a mere jeremiad to suggest that today's material welfare will almost certainly be at the expense of future generations, that Oman is consuming its own resources so fast that there will be little left for future generations. Most Omanis would not regard their new-found prosperity in this way; they are enjoying an almost immeasurably better way of life thanks to the development efforts of the government of Sultan Qaboos. It is very difficult for the Popular Front ideology, which flourishes best in a soil of poverty and envy, to make any progress against the tide of material prosperity enjoyed by the people of Oman. Of course, having once let its people taste the fruits the modern world can offer, the government of Oman will have an increasing challenge in the future to ensure that these undoubted benefits to all Omanis are maintained.

As for the Omanis, so for the Dhofaris. It is probable that the latter, and particularly those living in or near Salalah, have benefited even more than the average Omani. The combination of living in the birth-place of the Sultan, which continues to be his favoured residence and the permanent residence of his mother, the relative power of Dhofaris in the government of Oman, and the immediacy of the opposition's threat, has meant that a Dhofari population which cannot amount to more than 50,000 men, women and children has attracted a much higher *per capita* development expenditure than has the northern Oman population of about 400,000 people. Of a total of about 600 million Omani rials (about $1,750 million) spent on development over the five fiscal years 1971-5, almost one-quarter was spent in Dhofar on a small port, on roads, on modernising the airport, on the Thumrait air base, on schools and hospitals, on improved communications, housing, public buildings and a colour television service.

The province of Dhofar has its own specific development programme, something that northern Oman still did not have in the first part of 1976. This programme was very simple and had as its main objective the making of the southern province of Oman economically self-sufficient by 1980. It was approved by the Sultan at a meeting of the Supreme Council for Economic Planning and Development in Salalah on 18 October 1972. It was a simple document, designed to be published and broadcast and available to every Dhofari. It did not receive the publicity it deserved, basically because it was regarded as a product of expatriate thinking and hence not to be publicised. It is worth quoting in full:

> Dhofar Development Programme
>
> The objectives of the Dhofar Development Programme are to achieve the following by 1980:
>
> 1. To build a society in which all may live in peace and security and earn an economic livelihood;
> 2. To have launched a programme for the development of the Province's natural resources. This would include the provision of electricity and communications;
> 3. To build a modern land, sea and air communication network within the province and linking it with the rest of the Sultanate;
> 4. To make the Province financially independent, i.e. all civil government expenditure (this excludes Defence and Security) would be met from revenue generated in Dhofar;
> 5. To strengthen and spread the provincial and municipal administration within the Province and to train Dhofaris to assume full responsibility for it;
> 6. To provide primary school places for all boys between the ages of seven and twelve, and fifty percent of all girls of a similar age group;
> 7. To provide intermediate school places for fifty percent of the boys up to the age of fifteen;
> 8. To provide opportunities for adult education for those previously deprived;
> 9. To establish a technical training school tailored to the needs of the Province;
> 10. To provide adequate health services for the Province including campaigns to eradicate malnutrition and communicable disease;

11. To instil a pride in the community and a spirit of nation building.[7]

With hindsight this programme can be criticised, as indeed can any attempt to look into the future. In particular, its educational objectives seem modest, and the differentiation between boys and girls is unfortunate. All that can be said of it is that it was both realistic and attainable, given the resources then available, at the time it was drawn up, and that its implementation would have put Dhofar ahead of any part of Oman. Seen some four years later, the elements lagging in the implementation of the programme are those concerned with ensuring that an income is generated from the province's resources for the future. It has proved all too easy to spend money on projects which will make a demand on future revenues, it has proved very much less easy to identify and implement projects for harnessing the modest resources of Dhofar to ensure future income. Following the cease-fire of March 1976, the government of Saudi Arabia is reported to have promised a sum of $180 million for development in the mountain areas of Dhofar. Most of this amount will probably be spent on roads and on water well-drilling.

The diplomatic element in Oman's strategy to counter the opposition to its system of government has been particularly successful. It must be acknowledged that the Sultan's Libyan and Saudi advisers have had a great share in this success. They were jointly able to ensure that the Sultan was well received and listened to in both Saudi Arabia and Egypt. This diplomatic success has been greater with the more conservative régimes of the Arab world, Saudi Arabia, the United Arab Emirates and Jordan, than with the so-called 'progressive' régimes of Iraq, Syria, Libya and Algeria. A strong link has also been forged with Iran. This policy represents a complete turn-about from the policies of previous rulers of Oman who have always looked to the Indian subcontinent rather than the Arab world or to Iran. The common bond in the new policy is the wish to preserve the *status quo* in the Arabian peninsula and Persian Gulf, the common enemy the popular front movements which, with the support of Soviet, and sometimes Chinese, arms and money, seek to overthrow the anachronistic governments of the area. The fact of a popular front opposition to the government of the Sultan waging a guerrilla war on his territory gave the ruler of Oman a strong bargaining point in his diplomatic relations with his more powerful and more wealthy neighbours.

The diplomatic initiatives were wider than the immediate region of of the Arabian peninsula and Persian Gulf, however, and have brought Oman membership of the Arab League and the United Nations. Successful visits by the Sultan to France and the United States, as well as his regular private visits to Britain, were part of a pattern which included official visits made and returned to the Sultan's fellow heads of state in Egypt, Saudi Arabia and Jordan. The Sultan travelled to Iran on a state visit, and attended Arab summit conferences. A peace mission from the Arab League in 1974 and 1975 tried to find a solution to the war in Dhofar. Finally, in March 1976, following a Saudi initiative, and substantial cash payments to both sides, a cease-fire was agreed between Oman and PDRY. Although the diplomatic element was that one of the overall strategy which finally brought an end to the struggle in Oman, the diplomatic success could not have been achieved without the success, at least in the short term, which the other elements of the overall strategy had assured. These were the amnesty to insurgents who would lay down their arms, Dhofar as an integral part of Oman, the unchallenged military victory and development, assuring cash in people's pockets.

This clear military victory gave the Sultan much prestige in the eyes of his own people and of the world at large. The removal of the military and political threat to his government should have permitted the Sultan to concentrate more on other matters of national importance such as the involvement of his people in government, the husbanding of finances and resources, the strengthening of his civil government, and a re-examination of development priorities. There is still time for all of these things to happen. As of mid-1976, admittedly only a few months after the end of hostilities in Dhofar, the people of Oman have not been able to notice a relaxation in the style of their ruler. Three elements give cause for concern.

First, now that the Sultan has time to consider all of Oman as an entity, rather than concern himself specifically with the problems of Dhofar as a first priority, he is tending to extend the tough attitudes developed during the war to the whole of Oman. His efficient para-military policy force ensures that his authority in northern Oman is absolute. This is causing concern and some discontent among his people.

Second, instead of a reappraisal of development, development budgets are being cut to help pay for weapon systems. In spite of the great prosperity his people still enjoy, a halt in the provision of school places and the growth of an efficient medical service is noticed and criticised. The absence of a formal consultative assembly means that Omanis are generally ill-informed on government policies and priorities.

Thus gossip and rumour take over, and the Sultan himself is the subject of adverse publicity.

Finally, it was hoped by many people concerned with the future stability of Oman that, once the war in Dhofar had been brought to a successful conclusion, the Sultan would be able to dispense with a large number of his British officers. An informal suggestion to him from the British government was turned down and he let it be known that he wishes to retain his British officers. This is understandable in many ways; other Arab nations have suffered changes of governments arising from colonels' plots. Yet no matter how able, effective and loyal his expatriate officers are, their continued presence in Oman will gradually become counter-productive and cause resentment. The Sultan risks perpetuating the mistake of his father by maintaining an absolute form of government with a mercenary army.

The prestige that the Sultan has won because of the successful conclusion of the war in Dhofar has strengthened his position greatly. Had there been no guerrilla struggle to combat, it is unlikely that he would be in such a strong position today. The price of this prestige, this strength, has been the relative neglect of Oman at the expense of Dhofar. The Sultan and his ministers need to work out and publish a comprehensive policy document setting out national aspirations and priorities. Otherwise, the Popular Front movement, temporarily eclipsed in Oman but active in other countries, may again become a rallying point for dissent and opposition to the Sultan. Some of the Popular Front programmes are discussed in the next chapter.

Notes

1. *The Travels of Marco Polo*, Everyman Edition, London, 1967.
2. Bertram, Thomas, *Alarms and Excursions in Arabia*, London, 1931.
3. Quoted in F. Halliday, *Arabia without Sultans*, London, 1974.
4. Recounted to the author by a British officer present at the time.
5. See Chapter 1.
6. Central Bank of Oman.
7. Author's archives.

6 POLITICAL OPPOSITION: THE POPULAR FRONT FOR THE LIBERATION OF OMAN

> '. . .when a prince has the goodwill of the people he should not worry about conspiracies; but when the people are hostile and regard him with hatred, he should go in fear of everything and everyone.'

In 1976, there is no doubt about the victory of Sultan Qaboos over the guerrilla movement led by the Popular Front for the Liberation of Oman (the movement had dropped 'and the Arabian Gulf' from its title when it sought to win friends in the Gulf). It must be asked whether this victory is permanent? Has the Sultan gained such a victory over the opposition to his rule and to his system of government that he will never be seriously challenged again? Does the formidable international backing of the Popular Front movement accept its defeat in Oman?

It is strange and sad a fact of recent history that many rulers of states with a colonial past, who were so vociferous in the name of personal liberty in the days of their colonial masters, are the first to deny the right of their fellow citizens to criticise or question their actions once they have taken over the reins of power themselves. Oman was never a colony, in spite of its somewhat strange relationship with an ex-colonial power. The government of Sultan Sa'id was criticised, with justice, for denying any right of free political expression to the Omani people. The government of Sultan Qaboos, although having removed most of the petty restrictions which tied Omanis under his father's rule, has not yet moved towards granting the right of free expression of political views to its subjects. In this the Sultan is no different to many rulers of developing countries, nor is he very different in principle to his enemies in the People's Democratic Republic of Yemen or in Iraq. As with any absolutist régime, there is still opposition to his rule in Oman.

It has become part of revolutionary folklore to say that insurgency starts with little but a cause, and grows in strength, whilst those who fight insurgency in the name of established régimes start with a preponderance of material but no faith, and so ultimately decline into defeat. The American experience in Vietnam will long be the classic example of this dictum. The experience of the Sultan of Oman with his revolutionary opposition would appear to be the opposite. Yet any traditional régime is inevitably short of ideas and has to work very hard to engender a faith in its achievements which will be stronger than the heady wine of revolutionary dreams which are so attractive both to idealistic youth and to peoples suffering from poverty and deprivation. The traditional régimes of the Arabian peninsula, including Oman, cling on to the tenets of Islam, which, worthy though they be, are conservative and can be sterile; such régimes are anachronistic and are literally buying temporary stability with their oil wealth, just as their ancestors bought off troublesome tribes. The question to be asked is whether or not the régimes of the peninsula, all of whom are busy offering education to their sons and daughters in a way undreamed of even half a generation ago will be able to offer intellectual, political and economic satisfaction on the scale which their newly educated subjects will surely demand in a few years' time.

Before an answer can be found to such a question, it is necessary to look at the philosophy of the most serious opposition to the established order of things, the popular front movements. In Oman, or rather in Dhofar, this opposition crystallised itself into the Peoples' Front for the Liberation of the Occupied Arabian Gulf. Sultan Qaboos' seizure of power and the more energetic and imaginative steps he took to counter the opposition to his rule caused that opposition to reconsider its own strategy. PFLOAG and the National Democratic Front for the Liberation of Oman and the Arabian Gulf (NDFLOAG) widened their membership and appeal and joined forces in December 1971 to form a new group, the Peoples' Front for the Liberation of Oman and the Arabian Gulf. The third congress of the old PFLOAG had met in the mountains of Dhofar in June 1971 and agreed a lengthy new programme, which reads more as a classic revolutionary tract, and thus reflects the hold the academic professional revolutionaries, with their Marxist-Leninist or Maoist formal training, had taken on the Omani opposition. What had begun as a simple national struggle against an acknowledged tyrant had become transformed into the well-known ideological battle of words against the forces of 'imperialism'. The programme, with all its revolutionary dogma and dialectic, was formally agreed by the new PFLOAG at the time of its formation.[1]

There is no need to waste much time considering the inevitable references to British imperialism; popular front movements tend to make too much of this archaic jargon. The objectives of the Front are made very clear, however, and should be clearly understood:

> our determination to follow the path of protracted popular struggle,

> which is the only way to weaken the temporary superiority of the enemy . . . our determination with regard to the policy of armed struggle as a fundamental principle and a strategy, and the necessity to use violence throughout the area. . . .

The programme sets out clearly the Front's strategic thinking:

> Therefore it is important for the revolution to direct its energies towards those villages where the population is most under-developed, and to build up strong bases and revolutionary strongholds there.

The 'Tasks of the National Democratic Revolution' are set out under three main headings, the 'Local Dimension', the 'Arab Dimension' and the 'International Dimension'. Inevitably, the 'local dimension' is given priority and it is only this which need concern us here as relevant to a consideration of formal opposition programmes in Oman.

Of the 21 tasks listed under the 'local dimension', many are unexceptional and praiseworthy. Few would argue about the liberation of Oman from all forms of colonialism and the realisation of complete independence. As long as the executive command of the Sultan's Armed Forces is in the hands of a regular British general, as long as all fighting units are commanded by regular British officers, as long as there are some 450 British officers and other ranks serving in Oman, including a detachment of the SAS, and as long as an Iranian Brigade Group is deployed in Oman, rightly or wrongly the enemies of Oman will use these facts to give themselves a great propaganda advantage, and will have no great difficulty in making arguments to justify expressions like 'colonialism' and 'imperialism'. Indeed, just as long as the government of the Sultan lacks any vehicle for expression of the ideas of the people of Oman, let alone their will, it can be argued that the Omani people fall short of complete independence. The Sultan has absolute power, and there is nothing to stop him making decisions which will have a fundamental effect on the lives of his people without consulting them in any way.

Similarly, no one would argue about the paragraph in the Front's programme which talks of the eradication of slavery and the abolition of slave relationships. It might be argued against this that there are no slaves in Oman, which is strictly true. Yet the Sultan himself has several score 'retainers' who are descended from slaves and who are referred to in Oman in Arabic as *abeed*, that is, as slaves. Whether their relationship to their master is fully free or not is not the point; as long as these people are referred to in Oman as 'slaves' by the society of which they form part, the political enemies of the Sultan have a powerful argument against him.

Yet other points of the PFLOAG programme border on the absurd and betray the authors' unheeding obsession with the dogma of their Russian or Chinese masters. To talk of 'the building of an independent national economy with an agricultural and heavy industrial base' is an echo of sickle and hammer and reveals an abysmal ignorance of conditions and the economic potential of Oman. The need to build an independent national economy is pressing, and the fact that the government of the Sultan is not taking energetic steps to lessen Oman's dependence on its oil reserves is one of the greatest single causes for criticism of the Sultan. Having said that, the natural resources of Oman could never sustain an independent economy with an agricultural and heavy industrial base. Ideologies born in the densely populated homes of the revolutionary movements of the twentieth century, countries with large peasant and worker populations, cannot be translated without deep thought into the idiom of countries with small populations where traditionally heavy manual work has been carried out by slaves and mercenaries. The implication of the Front's programme requires a large labouring class, and ignores the fact that Arabs generally, and certainly Omanis, have no industrial tradition. Omanis are by nature traders and merchants, with the profits of their enterprises being invested in a marginal agriculture. The water resources of Oman will never be able to sustain a labour-intensive agriculture other than at a subsistence level. If the opposition programme could recognise this, if it could seek to define economic opportunities, (run by state-owned enterprises if necessary) which could seek to make capital from Oman's strategic location astride international air and sea routes to develop service facilities for aircraft and ships, if it could encourage a revival in Oman's own maritime and trading tradition, if it could seek to define opportunities for Omanis to use their natural talents for the profit of the society as a whole, it would be on much stronger ground. It is a profound weakness of contemporary revolutionary movements that they cannot escape the conservatism of their ideological masters. Many who call for change, who are strong in pointing out the need for change, cannot accept the unbending and often completely irrelevant dialectic which the arch-promoters of change in the modern world dare to call revolutionary ideology.

Weak and uncomprehending though it be on economic grounds, the PFLOAG programme cannot be faulted when it talks of 'the liberation of women from all forms of political, social and family oppression'. No matter what the strengths and virtues of Islam are, and they are many, the 'political, social and family oppression' of women must rank as one of its shames. Oman, being isolated and even more conservative than some other Islamic countries, has always downgraded its women, and the popular front movements, with all their faults, have tried to treat women as equals. Many of their most active recruits are women.

Again, the PFLOAG programme is not to be criticised when it sets out to ensure 'the eradication of social injustice and the provision of a decent living for every citizen', or 'the combating of moral, administrative and political corruption'. Indeed this last task would be a particularly appropriate one to be adopted with great firmness by the government of Sultan Qaboos; corruption in previously very poor countries which suddenly become rich is almost inevitable. In Oman little is done to discourage corruption in high places and fortunes have been made at the expense of the government, or rather, the people of Oman.

In spite of these sensible concepts, the PFLOAG programme must have caused its unsophisticated readers some puzzlement when it refers to the need to bring about 'the ending of exploitation by the comprador class'.*

Apparently the Front found this programme unsatisfactory itself, because Aden radio, over the period October-December 1974, broadcast a new set of policy intentions for the opposition to the government of Sultan Qaboos. By this time the clumsy 'Peoples' Front for the Liberation of Oman and the Arabian Gulf' had been shortened to leave out all reference to the Arabian Gulf. It had been realised that the old-style title alienated those people in the governments of states like Kuwait who were prepared to help it but who felt somewhat inhibited by the clarity of its aims as set out in its title. So the Front became merely PFLO, and with the help of its friends in Aden drew up a new programme, the so called 'National Act Programme'. A translation of this document is included in Appendix 2.

This programme has the inevitable predictability of all popular front movement propaganda tracts. No one would be surprised at its references to 'the British' and to 'imperialists'. Calls to nationalise foreign banks and insurance companies are so much a part of such documents that no comment is called for. Yet again, a careful study of

* Comprador: The *Concise Oxford Dictionary* says: '*n.* Chinese chief agent of foreign business-house; (fig.) agent of a foreign power'.

the programme reveals the abysmal ignorance of its drafters to the conditions prevailing in Oman. No matter what good sense may appear in such programmes, and it must be agreed that very often there is much to commend in contemporary revolutionary programmes, it becomes difficult to take them too seriously when the authors sacrifice truth for jargon, and worse, when the obsessive use of jargon phrases renders quite sensible points absurd. A novelty in this programme compared to earlier documents in Oman, but one which has become an obligatory feature of new-style Arab popular front tracts, is the promise to 'align with the Palestinian revolution and offer all potential aid to enable them to return to their country and abolish the Zionist state'.

If one is prepared to leave out the jargon and the inevitable references, there is much of interest, much that is thought-provoking, in this 'National Act Programme'. For example, its second objective:

> Establish a national democratic rule by the following methods:
> a. Abolish tribal and hereditary rule;
> b. Establish a popular democratic republic;
> c. Establish a peoples' electoral legislature
> and a progressive constitution.

Doubtless this means that Oman should establish a form of government like that of its neighbour, the Peoples' Democratic Republic of Yemen. To do so would be merely to replace one moderate absolutist government with another, far more ruthless, absolutist government. Yet the fact of hereditary rule and the absence of any form of elected legislature are together fundamental weaknesses in the present form of government in Oman. Any reform of government in Oman must face up to these facts. No matter what abilities and strengths a hereditary ruler might possess, and of course the fact of inheritance of a right to rule does not imply the inheritance of fitness to do so, the hereditary system related to an absolutist form of government is anachronistic and can not be expected to survive. An awareness of this fact in Oman, and the beginning of a public debate on alternatives, should not be taken as a criticism of the Sultan, but rather as an illustration of his own and his people's political maturity in that the will to think about future problems exists and is encouraged. It must be confessed that the chances of such thinking taking place, let alone being encouraged, in an open public debate in Oman are slight.

Similar thoughts apply to the tribal structure in Oman. Tribalism is deep-rooted in the history and tradition of the people of Oman, and by perpetuating petty rivalries and jealousies acts as a serious brake to political and social progress. On this point, however, there is a contradiction in the revolutionary programme; Article 12 calls for the protection of minority rights. There would be many tribes in Oman who would quote this passage in defence of the preservation of the *status quo.*

The third article of the programme calls for, *inter alia,* freedom of the press and free expression of opinion. Oman at the present time has government-controlled television, radio and press. People are free to praise the Sultan and his government, a certain amount of political argument is permitted, but expression of views strongly critical of the Sultan or of his government would not be permitted. The fact that such dissenting opinion would not be permitted in the so-called peoples' democracies either does not eliminate the strength of this article as part of the programme for a serious opposition in Oman.

The programme's economic sectors call for the inevitable nationalisation of foreign interests, but the section on agriculture is generally well informed and sensible. It provides for the improvement of water supplies and irrigation, a matter of fundamental importance if Oman is to have any future at all. It also calls for the liberation of farmers from 'usurers and brokers' and for the establishment of an agricultural credit bank, again a matter of importance and topicality. Yet by implication it would seem to wish to proliferate the system of small farm units. Although this is understandable from both the social and ideological points of view of the farmers of the programme, it ignores the fact of urban drift which is so rapidly depopulating the rural areas of Oman, and it also ignores the need for significant capital investment in agriculture if this sector of the economy is ever to break away from its age-old subsistence methods.

The programme is on very strong ground when it talks of labour laws. It provides for trade unions, for the right to strike, and for worker representation in the management of enterprises. The government of Sultan Qaboos will not allow trade unions to be formed and although strikes take place, they are illegal and tend to be settled by the police or the army rather than by negotiation.

In general, the 'National Act Programme' is much more realistic and well informed than anything which preceded it. It reflects the awareness of the opposition to the general great material progress of the majority of the people of Oman. It is a pity that it omitted references to women's rights and to the stamping out of corruption, important parts of the programme which preceded it.

There is a great temptation to considerable cynicism when reviewing the stated objectives of revolutionary movements. The words are one thing, the reality in those countries where 'popular democracy' has taken over another. Also, sophisticated readers become bored with the stale and often meaningless ideological phrases without which no such programme seems to be complete. Yet these programmes, with all their faults, are the only expressions of alternative policies to those of the government of the Sultan which exist. It is possible to study and understand the policies of the opposition to the Sultan's rule and to try to learn from these policies, without accepting the alternative form of absolutist rule which the authors of these opposition policies require. Rulers of developing countries often have great difficulty in distinguishing between propounders of alternative policies to those of the ruler himself, and extremist political opposition, sworn to oust the ruler and those near to him. It is not surprising to find this situation in Oman; the Sultan is an absolute ruler in the sense that few other heads of state in neighbouring countries are. He can enforce his will by means of a comparatively powerful army led by foreign officers, and through a paramilitary police force, again in the control of a foreigner. Other rulers in the area are not so free to disregard the views of their subjects as is the Sultan. There is no effective means of questioning national decisions and policies, no means of putting forward alternative policies for national debate, no vehicle for debating the national budget.

Iran has a national Parliament; this Parliament has not a great deal of power, but it does debate the national budget each year, and it does act as a sounding board for popular opinion. The United Arab Emirates has a national assembly, which is not afraid to criticise the government, and again which can debate the national budget. Bahrain and Kuwait have had popularly elected parliaments. Omanis are aware that their neighbours have this right. Sultan Qaboos insists that his people are not ready for democracy, in the same way that his father insisted that they were not ready for development.

It can be argued that all Omanis are so much better off under the government of Sultan Qaboos that any talk of popular representation in government is unnecessary. Omanis collectively, this argument would run, respect and trust him, he becomes more and more the father of his people, they are well content with the way things are and have no wish to experiment with forms of government which seem only to give trouble elsewhere. This argument would cite the Parliaments of Kuwait and Bahrain, and claim that both had become mere 'talking shops', of little constructive use and great embarrassment to the governments they were supposed to serve. Further, the example of the majority of the ex-colonial states in Africa could be cited; the colonial powers, at the time of their departure, generally tried to leave behind some form of popular democracy. In very few cases did this democracy survive. Finally, it might be argued that the Omani people are in general more concerned with money in their hands than they are with the niceties of popular representation in government. Under Sultan Qaboos, this argument runs, the Omani people have prospered as never before in their history, and therefore are not concerned with any other form of government.

All of these arguments have a certain validity, in spite of their obvious short-sightedness and cynicism. The conflict between governments who claim to 'know best' and the peoples they govern who demand to be consulted and informed about government policies before they are implemented is age-old, and at the heart of all political development. It is likely that, as long as the Sultan of Oman can continue to ensure that the dramatic rise in the standard of living of his people is at least maintained, and ideally increased still further, he may be able to survive without more than grumbled opposition to his policies. Pressures on him to change his thinking will develop as oil production begins to decline (1976 is likely to be a peak year) and as popular education and a knowledge of a greater world than Oman change the political awareness of his people.

There is no way for the government of Oman to continue development expenditure at the rates of the last five years. Even if some unforeseen minor oil discovery maintains production at existing levels, and price increases offset completely the effects of inflation, expenditure over the period 1971-5 has generated demands on future income to such an extent that deficits in annual budgets have become a permanent feature. These deficits are made up from borrowings from foreign banks and cash grants and credits from wealthy neighbours, particular Saudi Arabia and Abu Dhabi. Oman's neighbours clearly have an interest in ensuring political stability in that country. Whether they will always agree to do so is problematical. It is when the apparent infinite cornucopia of material benefits begins to falter that the Omani people may demand more say in their government.

At that time, they are likely to be rather more enlightened and politically aware than they have been up to the present time. The provision of popular education to a majority of children means that each year children with a few years' primary education, possessing little else but basic literacy and numeracy, will leave school unaware of the limitations of their education and demanding employment in keeping with their believed greater abilities. The village communities in which a majority of these children will have grown up will be unable to satisfy their demands for employment, and they will drift to the capital in search of dignified employment in keeping with their new status as educated citizens. Having no standards of comparison, and high expectations, these people risk being disappointed and disillusioned with the life the city can offer them. If patterns elsewhere are any guide, an underemployed, rootless urban proletariat will slowly develop. Such ground is a perfect nursery for revolutionary ideas.

The popular front movement failed to provide an effective opposition to the government of Sultan Qaboos. It must be said that its extremism and its incompetence was such that it deserved to be defeated. Although its programme had many useful ideas which could have been incorporated into the programme of a politically mature alternative to the extremist rule of the Sultan, victory for the Popular Front movement would have resulted in a harsh and negative extremism far worse than that of the Sultan, if the example of the Peoples' Democratic Republic of Yemen is taken as a guide.

Having removed this threat to his government, to himself, and to his friends and allies, Sultan Qaboos could demonstrate enormous political wisdom and maturity if he could announce a programme, no matter how long-term, for popular representation of his people in government, and for the drawing up of a series of national objectives, economic, political and social, for public debate. He should let it be known that alternative policies are to be encouraged, that popular debate of national issues is welcome. He should realise that he is perhaps the last paternalistic ruler in the history of political development in the world, and that no matter how much he tempers his absolutism with material progress for his people, the facts of history are against him.

Notes

1. Policy statement quoted in F. Halliday, *Arabia Without Sultans*, London, 1974.

7 THE DEVELOPMENT OF MINISTERIAL GOVERNMENT

> 'The choosing of ministers is a matter of no little importance for a prince; and their worth depends on the sagacity of the prince himself. The first opinion that is formed of a ruler's intelligence is based on the quality of the men he has around him. When they are competent and loyal, he can always be considered wise, because he has been able to recognise their competence and to keep them loyal. But when they are otherwise, the prince is always open to adverse criticism; because his first mistake has been in the choice of his ministers.'

The preoccupation of Sultan Qaboos with military matters and with the struggle against the extremist opposition to him personally and to his government meant that gradually he gave up more and more authority on non-military and non-security matters. In so far as he would have thought deeply about the matter at all, it is likely that he would have regarded the proposition for the appointment of a prime minister as fairly harmless as long as he, the Sultan, kept under his own strict control all matters relating to finance, defence and foreign affairs. Even though the experiment with a prime minister failed, a precedent of delegating some authority to ministers had been created. This trend was strengthened by the increasing weight of business in a modern government, a situation with which no Omani had had any experience.

The Sultan's uncle, Sayyid Tarik, during the period of his prime ministership, and with the Sultan's approval, had appointed a number of ministers. A first problem had been the Ministry of the Interior inherited from Sultan Sa'id. This was an organisation which had no real authority itself, presided over by Sayyid Ahmed bin Ibrahim, a descendant of 'Azzan bin Qais (see Chapter 2). Sayyid Ahmed, an old man well into his seventies, had an unrivalled knowledge of Oman, its tribes and groupings, and controlled the network of regional administration under about 40 *walis.* His authority was minimal, but his experience and wisdom were great and he had been an effective administrator for Sultan Sa'id. He was required to resign, and in his stead, two new ministers were appointed, a Minister of the Interior and a Minister of Justice. The dividing line was simple; the Minister of the Interior looked after *walis,* and the Minister of Justice the *qadhis,* or religious judges. It should be borne in mind that the Ministry of the Interior had never had any police nor internal security function. The army was wholly responsible for security within Oman, and the police force was controlled at that time by the Defence Department.

The choice of ministers for these ministries was sensitive. Given the tribal divisions and fragmentation in Oman, a minister concerned almost exclusively with tribal matters, as were these two, had to be seen to be above all factions. The solution to the problem was to appoint members of the Sultan's family. Sultan Qaboos' predecessors, Sultans Turki, Faisal and Taimur had been generous in the favours they had shown to ladies, and there is a large family of distant cousins. In Oman, only members of the Sultan's family use the title 'Sayyid'. In other Arab countries, Sayyid tends to mean 'mister', in Oman it means 'lord'. So it was to be expected that the Ministers of Interior and of Justice would be 'Sayyids'. As they were both dealing with traditional matters, the lack of a clear statement of their roles and responsibilities did not matter.

This lack of any sort of definition of responsibility or limits to authority mattered very much with other ministers. Appointments at this time included a Minister of Health, a Minister of Education, a Minister of Labour and a Minister of the Economy. The Minister of Health was most fortunate of the four, in that he was a qualified doctor himself, and had been employed by the Trucial States Development Council in Dubai, an organisation run by expatriates in the days prior to the creation of the United Arab Emirates. He knew what a medical service was supposed to do in detail, and he also had the services of a Dutch Director of Medical Services whose recruitment had been one of the last decisions of Sultan Sa'id prior to his forced abdication. A third member of the Ministry of Health team was a trained administrator, a Zanzibari Omani who had no knowledge of Oman, but who did know how to run an organisation. This team was able to launch a programme of hospital and clinic building and staff recruitment in a remarkably short time, and soon the Ministry of Health became an example of what could be achieved in Oman. The Minister of Health was helped greatly by his close relationship with Sayyid Tarik, the Prime Minister. Neither had any idea of how much money they could spend, but went ahead and spent. Although this complete lack of policy guidance and hence belief that there was enough money to pay all bills did not matter so much then, it helped create a cavalier attitude to finance which has caused the government of Oman grave problems since.

The Ministry of Education was not so fortunate. It took over responsibility for the three schools in Oman, one in Muscat, one in Mattrah, one in Salalah. It was completely without trained staff, without administration, without any concept of what it should do. The Minister was a comparatively sophisticated tribal leader who had spent some time outside Oman. It was not his fault that he knew nothing of education. He did not remain long as minister, and his successors continued to grapple with the problem of building up an education service suited to Oman's needs until eventually the Ministry of Education was strengthened by a World Bank technical assistance mission. Until that happened, the Ministry could not get much further than building schools and recruiting teachers from Egypt and Jordan.

The Ministry of Labour busied itself organising an employment exchange for Omanis and for issuing work permits to foreigners. As there rapidly became a superabundance of jobs for Omanis, the first part of the Ministry's task took little of its time, and it became soon merely an office to issue work permits. Eventually a labour law was drafted, largely at the insistence of Petroleum Development (Oman) Limited, the largest single employer of Omani labour in the country. The first Minister of Labour was a friend of Sayyid Tarik, and when the Prime Minister resigned, this minister was not long in following. He was eventually replaced by an Omani who had been employed for many years by the oil company and who knew a great deal about the mechanics of labour relations. He became effective, but eventually his conciliatory methods of settling disputes displeased the Sultan, and a trend began of using the police and the army to settle labour problems.

The Minister of the Economy was a cousin of Sultan Qaboos who had had a reputation of being something of a revolutionary in his youth. He was a man full of ideas, and with an awareness, rare in Oman, that alternative sources of revenue to complement and ultimately replace oil revenues should have a high priority in the government's planning. He was very active for a few months, ordering equipment and commissioning surveys. His enthusiasm alienated the Prime Minister and embarrassed the Sultan, and he was asked to resign, 'for reasons of health'. Of the projects he initiated, only an economic survey was completed. This proved to be of great benefit to future planners and administrators, because it was the first time that any data had been collected on the economy of Oman.

Early in 1972, after Sayyid Tarik's departure, the Sultan agreed to the creation of another ministry, a Ministry of Communications and Public Services, which took over responsibility for roads, airport and harbour construction, and for the increasing volume of building being sponsored by the government.

All of these ministries suffered from lack of a clearly defined role, lack of any form of statement of government policy and intention, lack of definition of the authority of ministers, particularly in financial matters, lack of trained and qualified professional and administrative staff, lack of leadership, lack of co-ordination. Given the legacy which the people of Oman had inherited from Sultan Sa'id bin Taimur, it is a wonder that so much was achieved in so short a time.

Under Sayyid Tarik, ministers never met together as a Cabinet, though there were occasions when they all met together informally. Financial sanction for capital projects was given either by the Sultan or by Sayyid Tarik. Neither bothered to consult the other, or the Secretary for Financial Affairs to ensure that money was available for projects they sanctioned. In those days, financial reserves were great enough to ensure that there was sufficient money available for all the projects at that time under discussion. Both the Sultan and the Prime Minister assumed that there was enough money; there is a theory, never proven, that Sayyid Tarik set out to spend as much money as he could on capital projects to force the Sultan to reveal to him the state of the country's finances.

All decisions concerning defence, the defence budget and the war in Dhofar were made by the Sultan in consultation with the Defence Secretary and the Brigadier commanding his armed forces at that time. A Minister of State for Foreign Affairs was appointed; all matters of importance were decided either by the Sultan or by Sayyid Tarik, not always with consultation between them.

Tarik's departure was a milestone in the development of government in Oman under Sultan Qaboos in that it forced the Sultan to take a much closer interest in government himself. The Minister of Health, Dr Asim Jamali, was appointed acting Prime Minister on Sayyid Tarik's departure, but he never could command sufficient support either from the Sultan himself or from other ministers, and the appointment was allowed to lapse without any formal announcement after a few weeks.

The Sultan began to meet his ministers formally himself, and the ministers became known collectively as the Council of Ministers. As a council, they met regularly, generally once a week, for the purpose of co-ordinating policy and for general discussion. The Sultan did not take the chair at every meeting of the Council of Ministers; often the Ministers would meet without him. When the Sultan did not attend, he let his ministers know that he would give overriding approval to any decision made at a Council of Ministers meeting at which he was not present, provided that such decision had been approved by all the ministers present unanimously. These meetings were completely unstructured, there was no formal agenda, no documents were circulated, no minutes or records of decisions were kept, rather in the manner of the British Cabinet prior to 1916. In the small community of Oman early in 1972, this lack of formality did not matter. Any decision of national importance would be published over the Sultan's signature in the official government gazette and thus would take the force of law. A fundamental weakness in the system, however, was that ministers made decisions without any idea of the financial implications of these decisions. Nor were they involved at all in matters of defence and security.

As far as capital projects were concerned, these also were rarely, if ever, discussed in the Council of Ministers. A minister would request the Sultan for 'a minute' after the conclusion of a meeting of the Council of Ministers, and in this time put to the Sultan a favoured scheme. In general, only the capital cost would be quoted. No one bothered to work out or to quote the future demands on revenue which the project would generate. If the idea made broad sense, and if the Sultan had confidence in that minister at that time (as in any court, individual ministers waxed and waned in favour), he would probably agree, and confirm his agreement with a signature. Sometimes he would ask for time to think, which would be a polite way of saying 'no' without hurting anyone's feelings or causing anyone to lose face. Armed with the Sultan's signature, the minister would go to the Secretary for Financial Affairs or his successors, to ensure that payments were made against the contract when required. No one would think to establish that funds were available before getting the Sultan's agreement, nor would the Sultan himself check with his finance experts to be sure that there was enough money for the project. As already stated, in those days there was always enough, a situation which changed radically three years later. Such projects were never appraised, nor was any attempt ever made to co-ordinate projects.

An early Cabinet decision made with the Sultan present, and aimed openly at foreign advisers, was made on 7 March 1972. Following Sayyid Tarik's departure from Oman, there was no one on the Omani side to check what was being done in the name of development. Although the expatriates concerned worked very hard, and were of the greatest personal integrity, the fact that they had a direct reporting line to the Sultan himself caused no little jealousy among Omanis. It was felt, without justice but perhaps understandably, that these expatriates were making decisions to suit themselves and that what they did was not always in the best interests of Oman. The decision of the Cabinet was to establish an 'Interim Planning Council', 'interim' because no one was prepared to take the responsibility of setting up a permanent council, with all that that would imply in terms of power. The decision was published in the official Omani government gazette over the signature of the Sultan's palace secretary. This decision is of great interest, and a translation is set out below:

> Subject *Establishment of Interim Planning Council*
>
> The Council of Ministers discussed at its meeting on Tuesday 7 March 1972 the possibility of the formation of an Interim Planning Council. His Majesty the Sultan approved the suggestion. The Council shall be composed of the following:
>
> 1. Sayyid Thuwaini bin Shihab – Chairman
> 2. Eng. Abdul Hafidh Salim Rajab – Member (Mechanical)
> 3. Eng. Barakat al-Lamki – Member (Electrical)
> 4. Eng. Saif bin Salim al-Maameri – Member
> 5. Eng. Salim Humaid al-Ghassani – Member (Road building)
> 6. Eng. Abbas Jaafar – Member (Civil Engineering)
> 7. Eng. Abdullah Hamdan al-Wohaibi – Member (Agriculture)
> 8. Eng. Salim Hassan Makki – Member (Petroleum)
> 9. Eng. Hassan I'sa Noor – Member (Mechanical)
> 10. Mr Ali Dawood – Member (Director of Commerce)
> 11. Mr Salim al-Ghaylani – Member (Director of Education)
> 12. Town Planning Adviser – Member
>
> As a result of this decision, the existing Tenders Committee is hereby cancelled. The Interim Planning Council will succeed it with the addition of the Secretary for Financial Affairs. The existing Planning Committee will report to the Interim Planning Council.
>
> (signed)
> Palace Secretary.

Both the Tenders Committee and the Planning Committee mentioned in this announcement were bodies dominated by expatriates, bodies moreover which had been set up without formal terms of reference agreed by the Sultan. Even if they had had the Sultan's seal of approval of their activities, there would have been nothing to stop him revoking their status without consultation simply by the issue of a decree setting up another body with similar functions. A great weakness in Omani government was that decrees would be signed by the Sultan without he himself, or anyone else, checking to ensure that the new decree was in accord with previous legislation. In a system of absolute government such as is practised in Oman, only a decree of the Sultan has force of law. Although the Sultan may delegate authority to others, and indeed does so, there can be no guarantee that this authority will not be withdrawn, either deliberately or accidentally without notice. The Sultan would sign almost anything which people he trusted put in front of him, without first asking two fundamental questions, first, does this decree contradict or render absurd or illegal any previously signed decree, and second, what are the financial implications of this decree? Attempts were made subsequently to ensure that anyone presenting a decree to the Sultan for signature would present with it a certificate from a legal adviser and a financial authority assuring him, as head of state, that the legal and financial aspects had been carefully checked, and that he could thus sign the decree with full confidence that he was not creating unfortunate precedents or committing the government to expenditure which would embarrass it. These attempts failed, largely because they resulted from expatriate initiatives, and also because the Sultan himself was not prepared to insist that the rules which he himself had agreed were to be followed.

Returning to the Interim Planning Council, the membership of this Council is of great interest. Sayyid Thuwaini bin Shihab bin Faisal, son of the Governor of Muscat under Sultan Sa'id bin Taimur and a distant cousin of Sultan Qaboos, had worked as a clerk in his father's office. He became Governor of the Capital after the change of government. He is a pleasant, amiable man, conscientious in the performance of his duties, but not regarded by anyone as a threat to the holder of any position of power in Oman. He tends to be something of a professional chairman, the Sultan indicating that Sayyid Thuwaini should preside over any meeting at which he himself cannot be or does not wish to be present.

Of the remaining members of the Council, no fewer than six of the other ten Omani members (the town planning adviser was never appointed), Abdul Hafidh Salim Rajab, Salim Humaid al-Ghassani, Abbas Jaafar, Abdullah Hamdan al-Wohaibi, Salim Hassan Makki and Hassan I'sa Noor, were educated either in the Soviet Union or in countries of the Eastern European bloc. This is understandable when it is recalled that it was extremely difficult for an Omani to get a technical or specialist higher education in any Western country under the rule of Sultan Sa'id bin Taimur. Both Abdul Hafidh Salim Rajab and Hassan I'sa Noor had Russian wives. It has never been seriously suggested that all or any individual one of these six Omanis has anything short of the maximum loyalty to Oman and to the Sultan. All worked hard, possibly harder than many of their colleagues, all were reasonably competent, again possibly with a higher average competence than most of their colleagues. Yet it could never be forgotten, given the history of the subversion attempts of communist-led countries in non-communist governments, that any one of these officials could have been ordered to return to his home country, to get himself a position of trust in the government and work hard and effectively until such time as alternative orders were given to him. No matter what system of government might ultimately be most appropriate for the people of Oman, any order to an Omani emanating from an authority in a Communist country could only be aimed at the overthrow of the Sultan.

Of the other members of the Council, Barakat al-Lamki and Saif bin Salim al-Maameri were Zanzibari-born Omanis who had never been in Oman in their lives prior to the 1970 *coup*. Ali Dawood was an Omani of Beluch origin who had worked in Bahrain for a number of years.

The Council was the first genuine Omani vehicle of government. The impetus for its creation came from its members. Neither the Sultan himself, or any of his foreign advisers, or members of his family, had had anything to do with its inception. Sayyid Thuwaini, as the not very strong chairman, was the only member of the Sultan's family represented. The strong man among its members was Abdul Hafidh Salim Rajab, a Dhofari of African origin who had a diploma in automative engineering from Kiev. Being Dhofari, he knew that he could count on much support from the Sultan. He had been made Minister of the Economy late in 1971 and also held the portfolio of Minister for Communications and Public Services. These two portfolios covered most of the development effort in Oman at that time.

It will be noted that the decree setting up the Council makes no mention of terms of reference, or of responsibilities or objectives. Its work rapidly became negative; it became inquisitorial, summoning all expatriates who had ever had anything to do with contracts before it, often late at night, and going through all details of every contract with a fine tooth-comb. This is understandable, if perhaps a little regrettable. Omani popular opinion was greatly against expatriate influence with the Sultan. In addition to this natural resentment, there was much jealousy and envy, and it was widely believed that expatriate advisers were making large sums of money for themselves out of the contracts they administered. When the most exhaustive scrutiny on the part of the Council failed to reveal evidence of malpractice on the part of those responsible for contract administration, the unfortunate expatriates concerned, instead of being exonerated, gained only a further reputation – one of diabolical cleverness.

Failing to find evidence of financial impropriety among expatriates, the Council turned on the one effective Omani ministry at that time, the Ministry of Health. The Minister had pushed on with an ambitious hospital and clinic building programme. Abdul Hafidh Salim Rajab started what became something of a personal vendetta against the Minister of Health. A man of strong personality, with a habit of speaking his mind loudly and firmly, he intimidates many of his colleagues and has become very adept at getting his own way. His natural Dhofari habit of mistrust and xenophobia has acquired a heavy veneer of Russian suspicion, and he has an almost pathological aversion to all things European, and especially things British. Although an able and effective minister, and a good organiser, his colleagues find him at times trying and difficult to work with.

The Interim Planning Council did no planning, and more and more it became regarded as the tool of Abdul Hafidh Salim Rajab. Its activities made the government of Oman look ridiculous. This would not have mattered so much, but in trying to tear down so much that had been painstakingly put together, it alienated much of that Omani support which had caused it to be set up. It was also guilty of serious maladministration, and after an incident in which two contractors were separately awarded the same contract, complaints were made to the Sultan.

His reaction was to establish yet another expatriate-dominated council. In September 1972 he signed a decree setting up the 'Supreme Council for Economic Planning and Development', this council to replace the Interim Planning Council, its membership to be the Sultan himself, as chairman, Sayyid Thuwaini bin Shihab, an Arab economic adviser and a non-Arab economic adviser. The advice given to the Sultan by his Arab advisers was that such a council should be set up as a board of management for Oman's development effort. The fact of the Sultan being chairman himself should remove all Omani jealousy and ensure that development decisions were made by the Sultan himself, with the benefit of professional advice. The terms of reference of the council were clear enough: it had to draw up a five-year development plan, it had to stimulate investment in Oman, encourage agriculture and fishing, develop close ties with international agencies offering multilateral and bilateral aid, and encourage in Oman a spirit of nation-building. The thinking behind the formation of this Supreme Council was sound, and the Council had some achievements to its name before it collapsed. Of the two non-Omani members, the Arab economic adviser had good academic qualifications, and excellent contacts in the United Nations. He had worked for the United Nations Development Programme in another Arab country before coming to Oman. The non-Arab economic adviser had been working in Oman and in other Arab countries in the area as a consultant before being invited to join the government of Oman in July 1972. He had led a team which had prepared an Economic Survey of Oman and which had presented its report to the government and to the World Bank in April 1972.

The Supreme Council agreed that a planning body should be set up as a matter of top priority. This body, known as 'The Centre for Economic Planning and Development', was rapidly established in the last quarter of 1972, and hired a number of Arab professional staff, as well as many Omani counterpart staff. It opened immediate relations with the United Nations Development Programme, and other UN aid-giving bodies, as well as the World Bank. Recognising that the Economic Survey presented earlier that year was, in the words of its authors, a 'first step', the Centre commissioned a number of resource surveys, principally water and minerals, and surveys of transportation and for popular housing. The water resource and transportation surveys were paid for by friendly governments as part of bilateral aid programmes.

In its determination to push on quickly and to establish a name for itself, the Centre was not as careful as it might have been with some of the contracts it negotiated. It had no legal adviser or contract specialist on its own staff, and was not adequately staffed with specialists with the experience necessary to ask sufficiently searching questions at the contract negotiation stage.

It created further trouble for itself by getting involved itself in details of contract administration, at the expense of its planning responsibilities. The thinking behind its formation had been that the Centre, as the executive body and secretariat of the Supreme Council for Economic Planning and Development, should be firstly a catalyst for development, and secondly a planning and co-ordinating body. It was never intended that the Centre should itself administer contracts; the original thinking was that, once a contract had been agreed in principle, the proposition behind it thoroughly appraised, once it had been established that the legal aspects of the proposed contract were in order, and finally that the financial commitments were clearly understood and that money was available, the responsible ministry would take over the contract and administer it to completion. The Centre itself would only look after those contracts for surveys and data collection, essential prerequisites to planning.

Although the Centre itself could be blamed for much of this involvement, there were other influences which forced it down the road of contract administration which ultimately caused its collapse. The Centre was to blame because it tried to do too much to quickly. It wanted not only to establish itself firmly, but also it wanted power and the publicity and kudos that major contract-signing ceremonies brought with them. Some of these contracts were wished on the Centre, however, by the Sultan himself, and by his two senior Arab advisers, neither of whom were ever seen publicly in Oman. As part of their remuneration, the Sultan permitted them to introduce contractors to the government who would be awarded contracts having a substantial commission element hidden in them. This commission went to the advisers. This meant that there were to be no more contracts put out to competitive tender, and that all contracts would henceforth be negotiated. As, apart from the Sultan himself, only the two economic advisers were aware of the arrangements, the result was that either of the two had to be involved in the negotiation of the contract with the nominated contractor.

Thus, the Omani public could see again the situation of foreigners being involved in contract administration. The fact that Arabs in general were involved rather than 'the British', did not soften the blow. If anything, this fact only increased the resentment and jealousy, because the Arab, non-Omani members of the Centre, as sophisticated northern Arabs, tended to look down on their Omani brothers, whom they regarded as 'camel drivers'. Ultimately, the Arab economic adviser aroused so much jealousy and ill-feeling among Omani ministers and officials that even the Sultan's patronage could not protect him and he left Oman in April 1973.

With his departure, the Centre collapsed, and much of the valuable work it had started was lost. The non-Arab economic adviser, who had not been a member of the Centre for Economic Planning and Development, stayed on. He was able to save some of the work of the Centre, but unfortunately such bitterness among the Omanis had been aroused that almost anything which had been originated by the Centre was automatically damned. At the head of those opposing the Centre and its work was Abdul Hafidh Salim Rajab, the power in the previous Interim Planning Council, who naturally resented the organisation which had supplanted the Council he had built up.

In summary it can be said that the experiment with the Supreme Council for Economic Planning and Development failed because it did not take sufficient heed of Omani sensibilities. In spite of the fact that the Sultan and his cousin were the Omani members of a four man council, and that thus it would be seen that the Council's decisions were Omani decisions, Omani ministers, officials and merchants became to resent more and more the fact that decisions were made affecting them without consultation or consideration. They could not criticise the Sultan, but the moment that one of the non-Omani members of the Council made a mistake, then there was a chorus of complaints to the Sultan.

The Centre, or rather, the rump of the Centre after all its non-Omani staff had been dismissed, was re-christened the General Development Organisation, an Omani was put in charge of it, and it became the Ministry for Development in November 1973. It never took the task of planning seriously, it insisted on keeping control of the administration of contracts, and became something of a 'dustbin' ministry, into which was put all the departments which did not easily or logically fit elsewhere. In November 1974, it was split up, becoming the Ministry of Public Works, and the Ministry of Petroleum, Minerals, Agriculture and Fisheries, these titles alone revealing what a loose collection of units had become caught up in it.

In March 1973, the expatriate Secretary for Financial Affairs left Oman and was not replaced. Part of his function was carried out by an Omani Director-General of Finance, part by the non-Arab economic adviser, and part by the Sultan's palace office (the Diwan). The Sultan regarded himself as Minister of Finance. Although he was not prepared to give up any control of finances, or to delegate any effective responsibility for the control of finances, he would not concern himself in the details of finance, so that financial control was always particularly weak.

The collapse of the Supreme Council for Economic Planning and Development was another milestone in the development of government in Oman. The Council was not formally dissolved, the Sultan's decree setting it up was never formally revoked. After the departure of the Arab economic adviser, no one ever proposed another meeting of the Council. Ministers felt that the Council's demise was a victory for them, and henceforth the Council of Ministers became a more coherent and self-confident body. Various attempts for it to have a permanent secretary failed. The co-ordinating function, the function of summoning meetings, the function of arranging for the recording and publishing of decisions, and having decrees signed by the Sultan and promulgated was in the hands of the Sultan's palace office. Most Arab countries have a similar office; in republics, like Egypt, there is a Ministry of Presidential Affairs, in traditional régimes, like Abu Dhabi, there is a Minister for Court Affairs. In Oman, the office is simply known as 'the Diwan' (i.e. 'department'), and this expression will be used henceforth in this book.

Sultan Sa'id bin Taimur, having little government machinery apart from himself, and being a particularly frugal man, had an Omani 'secretary', a distant cousin, Sayyid Hamid bin Hamoud, who looked after appointments and acted as a sort of office manager. By a feat of no little political dexterity, Sayyid Hamid managed to hold on to his job after the *coup* deposing Sultan Sa'id, and became an aide to Sultan Qaboos. As the new Sultan concerned himself very much more with the affairs of government and of his people than did his father, a need evolved for someone to handle documents and appointments for him. He had an expatriate private secretary, through whom he dealt with expatriates, but this channel was clearly not appropriate for Omanis. Gradually an office was built up, which looked after protocol, meetings with ministers, the day-to-day business of government which was the Sultan's affair rather than that of any minister, for example petitions and complaints, government personnel (the Sultan himself decides on all senior appointments), audit and similar functions of a general nature lying outside the scope of individual ministers. The Diwan became a great time-saver for the Sultan, as it could answer without reference to him literally hundreds of petty complaints and requests during the course of the average week. People wanting money to repair a house, to send a sick relative out of Oman for treatment, petty disputes, a mass of trivia which the absolute nature of his rule demanded that only the Sultan could handle. Had he tried to do so, he would have been inundated. Thus the Diwan became an effective buffer and filter between him and his people.

As it grew in practical importance, it also grew in power and political importance. Sayyid Hamid bin Hamoud became 'Minister in charge of the Sultan's Diwan'.[1] A man of no small political acumen, he often would take the chair at meetings of the Council of Ministers not attended by the Sultan. He was very careful never to convey to his ministerial colleagues any suggestion that he was other than their equal in status. He played the role of courtier extremely ably, and succeeded in being effective in the execution of his responsibilities without causing undue offence to his colleagues. In so far as it is accepted practice in the Arab world for a man to use his official position to enhance his private fortune, Sayyid Hamid is also a successful businessman, having got the Sultan to guarantee various loans for him from international bankers for his business ventures. He is also agent in Oman for certain foreign companies which have been astute enough to realise that an agent in such a position of authority and influence is likely to be a very useful agent indeed. It is stressed that this situation, which would be regarded as reprehensible in a Western government, is taken as a matter of course in Oman. It breaks no Omani law, nor does it offend Omani sensibilities. It may give rise to a certain jealousy, but a wise man ensures that anyone able to do him harm is able to share in the profits of the business ventures.

Meetings of the Council of Ministers in Oman are not very different to unstructured meetings in most societies. If the Sultan takes the chair, few ministers are prepared to speak up. This is yet another reason why Abdul Hafidh Salim Rajab succeeds; he does not hesitate to let his views be known forcefully in Cabinet. If none of his ministerial colleagues can think of a suitably strong reply, he tends to get his way by default. Other ministers enjoy periods of grace in the Sultan's eyes and periods of disfavour. During the former, they can, if they are careful, get decisions made covering the business of their ministry; if they are out of favour, they are wise to keep quiet. Individual ministers are in general particularly sensitive to their own and their colleagues' current standing with the Sultan.

Following the trials of Omanis arrested for sedition at the end of 1972, many were sentenced to death and the sentences were rapidly carried out. The action of the Sultan in ordering the death penalty was strongly criticised throughout the Arab world, and the Sultan was vehemently attacked by his ministers in a council meeting for this action. He defended himself vigorously, but was shaken by the apparent universal opposition to his decision, a situation without precedent in Oman. Whether his ministers would have succeeded in getting him to change his mind if they had protested as strongly before the executions had taken place is debatable, and in any case is an academic question. A second group of plotters was arrested in October 1974. This time, nothing was left to chance; all ministers were instructed to attend the public trial of the accused, and the death sentences were ratified by the Council of Ministers. In spite of the fact that the Sultan did not change his mind, the action of his ministers in challenging one of his decisions forced him to take more heed of their susceptibilities and eroded something of his absolutism.

These modest achievements in the evolution of ministerial government in Oman must be set against some of its failures. The failures are generally in the financial area, and this happened because there was no one up until mid-1975 in the Council of Ministers either informed enough or empowered to advise ministers on the financial implications of their decisions. Indeed, financial matters as such were never discussed. As mentioned earlier in this chapter, if a minister wanted to have a project approved, and if his personal standing with the Sultan was such that he believed that his request would not be turned down, he would request 'a minute' of the Sultan at the end of a ministerial meeting. Some became adept at judging the right moment to ask for this precious minute. The Sultan at such times was generally not interested in much detail; a brief indication of the main points of the scheme, an estimate of capital cost, and a quick 'agreed' scrawled on a document over the Sultan's signature would commit the nation to enormous expenditure. The most blatant example of this was a request for 'a minute' made by the Minister for Communications, Abdul Hafidh Salim Rajab, in March 1974. This minister also had responsibility for the capital area water supply. He believed, and he may have been right, that natural ground water supplies in and around the capital area were inadequate for the long-term needs of the growing population of Muscat and Matrah. He was also, correctly, concerned that the demand for electricity would outstrip the growth of the supply. From early 1972, the World Bank had been studying the electricity supply problem, and it had been indicated that the government of Oman could obtain a World Bank loan for the enlargement of its electrical generating capacity, this to include a programme for rural electrification. During the course of 1973, a survey of the long-term water demand of the capital area had also been commissioned. By early 1974, the government was reaching a stage where a decision based on a measured and carefully calculated projection of both electric power and water supplies could have been made, and a long-term plan worked out for the provision of both. Such a plan would have been a bankable proposition, and, if it had been too big for the World Bank to handle, it is likely that commercial financial resources could have been mobilised.

Disregarding all this, probably because it was being handled by expatriates, the minister got suppliers to put forward a combined desalination and power generation package proposition, with the necessary power supply grid and reticulation network. He secured the Sultan's approval of the scheme by saying that it would cost 'only' 20 million Omani rials (about $57 million) and that it would provide, *inter alia,* the Sultan's palace garden at Seeb with one million gallons of water a day. The Sultan was very proud of his beautiful palace garden; its consumption of water in the climate of Oman was prodigious. In fact, the total cost of the scheme came to over 100 million Omani rials (almost $300 million). The minister did not bother to find out whether money was available to cover the capital cost of the package; indeed, he said subsequently that he knew that if he had done so, those officials with responsibility for finances at the time would have done all they could to stop the scheme. Nor did he make any attempt to calculate the likely running costs of the scheme, nor was any allowance for depreciation or amortisation made. No part of the proposal was subject to an independent professional or technical appraisal, no checking with other suppliers was carried out to see if a better price could be obtained. Finally, the minister, in his brief presentation to the Sultan, promised that the scheme would be operating by 'National Day, 1975'. Schemes which the Sultan may declare open on the occasion of the annual National Day celebrations in November each year (the Sultan's birthday) have become part of a ruthless one-upmanship game played by Omani ministers. The upshot of a scheme which would provide water for his palace garden (no matter at what cost), and would be a National Day ceremony was enough for the Sultan. The scheme was agreed in a 'minute', without appraisal, without costing, without an independent check, without a legal appraisal of the contract. In fact, the desalination plant was opened on National Day, 1975, but was forced to close down temporarily shortly afterwards because of technical problems. Informal and incomplete calculations suggest that the power and water supplied through this package will cost about five times more than they might have cost. Naturally the contract price to the government of Oman would have included a substantial commission element.

The story of colour television in Oman is similar to that of the desalination plant. It seemed a good idea to have colour television in Oman for the 1974 National Day, so a technically very advanced system was installed on time, at a cost far greater than was necessary. Again, there was no appraisal of the scheme, or of possible alternatives. Above all, no one worked out the annual costs of television, especially of programmes, and little thought was given to the problems of maintenance and management. All because a decision had been made on an *ad hoc*, hurried, impulsive basis, in 'a minute'.

This, of course, is a very Arab way of doing things, and it can be argued that it doesn't really matter. This argument can carry a lot of weight, provided no one thinks very carefully about the future, in a so-called 'oil-rich' society, where money seems to be as freely available as air. It poses an interesting philosophical question as to the responsibilities of a government to the people it governs, and above all, to the children of the people it governs. It is easy for the Sultan to suggest, by implication, that he is most concerned about assuring his own security and popularity in the immediate future, and that he is prepared to sacrifice the future to the needs of his own position, the argument being that if he cannot do so, if he cannot ensure his stability today, there will be no future in any case for him and those near to him. He would argue further that if his ministers become wealthy through sharing the profits from contracts, they are thus indebted to him for their wealth and are less likely to challenge his position, just as in medieval Europe a monarch bought security by ensuring that the lords and knights whose loyalty he needed if he was to survive had the pick of the most valuable estates as the price of their loyalty. Loyalty as a duty would be regarded as a somewhat sentimental and pathetic idiosyncracy.

This is, of course, the mark of a system of government that has not developed, as is the system which permits ministers and others to enrich themselves through their official position. Any conscious efforts to modernise government in Oman, efforts that came from expatriates rather than Omanis, were aimed at creating institutions rather than building around individuals. This aspect of the development of government is considered in detail in the next chapter.

The Omani Council of Ministers gradually acquired an authority of its own, and could be expected to act on its own in the national interest whenever it met during the Sultan's absences from Oman. Such a situation would have been inconceivable under Sultan Sa'id. Yet more and more, save in the major fields of finance, defence and foreign affairs, government in Oman can and does continue without constant recourse to the Sultan. Even finance matters less, because of the system of annual published budgets and a gradual eroding of the Sultan's authority. Ministers have great individual authority within their ministries and also collectively acting in concert. They may not borrow large sums of money, or make treaties, or war, without the express agreement of the Sultan. Against that, the whole mass of routine government business, which, after all, is the face of the government which the average citizen sees and is most concerned with, is in the hands of ministers. The Sultan is not concerned with how they run their ministries. To that extent, he has moved away significantly from the stark absolutism of his father. Even if he wished, he could not take back that power without the strongest personal organisation about him to take on the weight of the work, and above all, to protect him from the undoubted popular outcry which would almost certainly follow.

Various attempts to codify the present situation have been made, without success, principally because the evolution of government remains such a dynamic force. What today may be capable of description in unambigious language will have changed tomorrow. Herein lies, of course, both the strength and the weakness of the system. Strength because it ensures flexibility when flexibility is a virtue, and because it permits a gradual but constant liberalising of the government and leads ultimately towards more popular representation in the making of decisions, weakness because the absence of checks and balances permits the Sultan to make instant, impulsive decisions without necessarily thinking them through, decisions which could be undermining the very fabric of Omani society.

One area where the Sultan continues to make detailed decisions himself is in that of defence, national security and internal security. To co-ordinate the activities of the various bodies concerned with these matters, and at the time of the resignation of the British Defence Secretary in June 1973, a National Defence Council was formed. Membership of this Council has remained fairly constant. The Sultan is chairman and the Council would not meet normally without him being present. To the end of 1975, Omani membership consisted of the Minister of State for Foreign Affairs ('Minister of State' implying a junior minister, with the Sultan himself having overall policy direction of Foreign Affairs), and the Deputy Defence Minister (the Sultan being Defence Minister). Early in 1975, the Governor of Dhofar province became a member of the National Defence Council, because most of the problems discussed in the council concerned the war in Dhofar. Other members were the British Major-General commanding the Sultan's Armed Forces, the British Director of Intelligence, the British Adviser on Security Affairs, the Economic Adviser and the Defence Department administrative staff. The Chief of Police, a Ceylonese who had lived most of his life in East Africa in the British Colonial Police and who carries a British passport, was also a member. This council was an advisory body, and its prime function was one of co-ordinating the defence and security effort. Its meetings were formal and structured, with documents being circulated prior to each meeting, a formal agenda and detailed minutes. Decisions were decisions of the Sultan. He could be persuaded to change his mind, but this was not frequent and in general members did not even bother to try. On one occasion, however, following a characteristic act of political terror by an extremist Palestinian group, the Sultan suggested to the council that he would like to ban all Palestinians from Oman. Almost with complete unanimity, the council members pointed out to him the political implications of such a decision and the matter was not pursued.

Another example of how decisions were made is that of the Thumrait air base in central Dhofar. During the course of his visit to Iran in March 1974, the Sultan had been promised by the Shah the use of a squadron of Iranian Phantom strike aircraft for use in attacking military targets inside the People's Democratic Republic of Yemen. The Iranians stipulated, of course, that a suitable base would have to be provided by the government of Oman. The Sultan ordered, at a meeting of the National Defence Council which took place shortly after his return from Iran, that a suitable air base incorporating a 4,000-metre runway be constructed at Thumrait, across the mountains from Salalah in central Dhofar. The original command was that the base was to be ready in four months; this was subsequently changed to be ready by the end of December 1974, regardless of cost. The target was met, the contractors engaged broke all previously known construction records, cement was flown in. By the end of 1974, the project had cost over 50 million Omani rials (about $145 million). The Iranian Air Force flew one sortie from the air base at the end of 1975, but it was also used by the Sultan's Air Force and provided an all-weather alternative to the airfield at Salalah which often could not be used during the period of the monsoon from June to September. Not one of the advisers present at that meeting of the National Defence Council queried that decision, or advised the Sultan against it. One reason was that the matter was presented to them without notice, and no one present had any idea of the size or the cost of air base at that time. Even if any individual present had had those details, there was no way of changing the Sultan's mind, apart from registering opposition, and possibly resigning on the issue. The Sultan had given his personal promise to the Shah of Iran that a base would be built to Iranian specifications, and hence there was no way for him to go back on his word, even if he had wished to.

The Thumrait decision aside, the National Defence Council was effective in that it did ensure co-operation and co-ordination of the national defence and internal security efforts, agreeing defence budgets and providing a forum for the airing of views on all aspects of national defence and security. This is not to praise it; simply as a committee of expatriate professionals, it should have functioned efficiently and did.

Another expatriate committee was less enduring, though its decisions were more in the public eye. Following the increase in the price of crude oil in October 1973 and again in January 1974, Oman moved from being a country with a modest oil revenue which could, if used wisely, meet all the needs of the nation and generate some income for the future, to being one of the 'oil-rich' nations. In Oman's case, this was probably unfortunate, because immediately everyone thought that the country had become as rich as its neighbours. No Omani could believe that the fact of multiplying Oman's oil revenues by a factor of five was any different to multiplying these revenues by an infinite factor. Everyone, including the Sultan himself, believed that this new wealth opened every door. No one was prepared to support the need for the strictest financial control, which everyone clearly understood when Oman's oil revenues were of the order of 60 million Omani rials. Now that the revenues approached 300 million rials, an unprecedented spending spree swept away all semblances of control.

A by-product of the oil price increases, which had been pased onto Oman by Petroleum Development (Oman) Limited, even though Oman was not a member of OPEC, was that Oman's resources of natural gas, which had marginal economic viability under the pre-October 1973 oil prices, had suddenly become a valuable economic resource which had potential for development. The problem was that the gas was situated about 300 km from the coast at Muscat and that, compared to competitive gas fields inside the Persian Gulf, which were on the coast, the profitability of the project would be less interesting. There were no resources of capital or management expertise inside Oman to permit this resource to be developed, nor did the government of Oman have access to markets for the gas or products manufactured from the gas. It seemed that the only way for this resource to be utilised was to locate a joint venture partner who would be prepared to share the capital cost of the project with the government of Oman, and who had the appropriate management expertise and access to markets.

This outline strategy was a product of expatriate thinking; Omani businessmen, and many leading businessmen were also ministers, preferred investment in projects which would have given them their money back within three years. Housing was the favourite venture, and rents could be charged to foreigners which would be high enough to cover the complete cost of the project within three years, the capital for the project having been borrowed from a commercial bank to start with. The profits of such ventures were almost invariably remitted to a foreign bank outside Oman, few businessmen having apparently sufficient confidence in the long-term future of Oman. Profits would rarely be ploughed back into a business; foreign banks in competition with each other for business were only too glad to lend money at competitive rates to permit businessmen to build even more properties for letting to foreigners. As long as the government was spending all of Oman's oil revenues on projects of one sort or another which required foreign contractors to work in Oman and bring in their own senior and middle-rank executive staff, all the property could be let, the high rentals being charged back to the government in the contract price for the project. As a means of redistributing income and creating a capitalist society, the system had many advantages. The whole essence of such a policy for redistribution of incomes is short-term, and the principle of getting profits out of the country as fast as possible augurs ill for the future of Oman. Such business thinking was clearly not going to invest private capital, or support the investment of government funds in a venture requiring a much longer period before a return could be earned on the investment, and a much more modest return on one's capital. Yet if this natural gas resource were not harnessed, Oman would probably not be able to earn income to cover the bare maintenance costs of the capital projects being completed at the present time.

Therefore, the Sultan's expatriate advisers had urged him to think very carefully about a policy for the harnessing of the natural gas. The Sultan's response was to appoint a council, the Natural Gas and Petroleum Council, with himself as chairman, and four members, all expatriate, two Arab (his senior Arab advisers) and two non-Arab. This council had sufficient business and professional expertise, and sufficient top-level contacts in international banking and business circles, to be able to have a natural gas project properly defined, and to interest possible joint venture partners in the project. The council was set up in April 1974, and by the end of that year had moved rapidly towards the finalising of an income-earning project which would ensure revenue for the government of Oman for a further forty years. The Sultan did not attend every meeting of the council, but careful and detailed minutes were kept of all meetings and discussions, and these minutes were taken to him, discussed with him, and invariably approved by him. Towards the end of 1974, a joint-venture partner had been found, leading international bankers were agreeable in principle to finance the project, and sufficient pipeline for the building of the essential link from the gas fields to the coast had been ordered and was being delivered to Oman. But at this point the characteristic, and understandable, jealousy of Omanis towards expatriates, and particularly of expatriates who seemed to be involved in the commitment of large sums of government money, and hence probably, in Omani eyes, earning high commissions, became so great that the Sultan was unable to resist pressure from his ministers to include several of them on the Natural Gas and Petroleum Council. The result was that the natural gas project died a slow death during the first six months of 1975, and the expatriate advisers ceased to be member of the council.

This case reveals a fundamental problem in the evolution of government in developing countries, for although it has many purely Omani features, it does reveal a situation which has been observed in most developing countries. Firstly, it is extremely difficult for rulers and ministers whose early years were spent in great poverty to accept that it is often a wise policy to invest today to assure future income for the community. Ministers have no difficulty with this principle in their private lives, but cannot divorce their personal ambitions from the long-term needs of the state. It would be naive to suggest that politicians in any country are motivated by other than self-interest, but in more developed societies, checks and balances in the machinery of government, plus an informed public opinion and a free press ensure that the innate self-interest is attuned to making a contribution to the greater national welfare, and also to ensuring that the society's resources are not squandered today at the expense of future generations.

Secondly, the lack of sophistication of ministers in developing countries, an inevitable and understandable lack, means that they will almost always have the greatest difficulty in understanding and communicating with foreign businessmen, particularly executives of large international corporations who have access to the most advanced techniques to assist them in making management decisions, and who have a self-confidence which permits them to make such decisions without the need for detailed and elaborate explanations. In other words, it is often extremely difficult for developing countries to engender an atmosphere of business confidence great enough to encourage foreign entrepreneurs to invest their money in joint-venture projects. There are exceptions, of course, one outstanding one being Sheikh Rashid, the ruler of Dubai.

The result is that it is rarely possible to encourage significant investment in developing countries, and thus the root cause of poverty, which is almost invariably a shortfall in investment, remains. The situation in Oman thus has large elements of tragedy in it. The country has, almost miraculously in the eyes of its people, access to a comparatively large income for a decidedly short period of time – perhaps not longer than twenty years. Used wisely to invest in income-generating projects, this income could ensure the future permanent prosperity of the community, perhaps not to the highest standards of Western industrialised societies, but certainly to a far higher standard than Omanis have enjoyed before. Yet Oman's oil revenues are being used rapidly on present consumption. Much of this benefits the society in terms of the economic and social infrastructure, but still more goes out of the country in payments for expensive weapon systems, in payments to contractors, and in high profits to a few Omani businessmen. Even the social and economic infrastructure, important though it is to Oman, is generating demands on future revenues for its upkeep and eventual replacement which those revenues, seen from mid-1976, may not be adequate to meet. Expatriates who worry about this and point it out to their Omani friends risk being strongly criticised for 'trying to stop us spending our money'. The argument that immediate expenditure ensures immediate satisfaction and hence immediate political stability is all that matters; the future is in the hands of Allah.

This trend has been multiplied by the recruitment of businessmen as ministers. Until the end of 1973, ministers were primarily ministers; if they used their official position to further personal schemes for self-enrichment, no one took it amiss or thought ill of them. In issue No.44 of the Omani *Official Gazette* dated 1 December 1973, there appears an announcement of great potential significance for the development of government in Oman. In a list of government changes the following was printed:

> To appoint Professor Qais Abdul Munaim Al-Zawawi Minister of State for Foreign Affairs.

Qais Zawawi was then a well-known Muscat businessman. The title 'Professor' in the *Official Gazette* is not understood; possibly it was meant to infer that the new Minister of State was an educated man, which he certainly was. Being a Muscati of Saudi origin who had been educated in India, and having no relationship with the family of the Sultan, the normal prefixes of honour, 'Sheikh' or 'Sayyid', would not have been appropriate. He had many profitable agencies, amongst these being the Mercedes agency in Oman. He was well connected in the Arab world, and his charm and excellent manners made him extremely popular with expatriates. His appointment as Minister of State for Foreign Affairs was welcomed on all sides. His business interests brought him an annual income many times in excess of the normal ministerial salary; to forgo this would have been a far higher sacrifice than he was prepared to make. For his part, the Sultan could not pay him significantly more than the normal ministerial salary without creating dangerous precedents. So it was agreed that he should not have to give up any of his business interests on joining the government.

He has an elder brother, Omar Zawawi, who is an even more astute businessman, and with whom Qais Zawawi is in partnership. The official position of one brother was of considerable value to the business interests of the other. Again, it must be stressed that this arrangement was made with the full approval of the Sultan, that it broke no Omani law or offended no Omani sensibility. The only people to complain were some of the business rivals of the Zawawi brothers, but even their complaints were muted, there being so much new business that all but the most stupid businessman could get his share of it.

The pressure on the members of the Natural Gas and Petroleum Council, and on the Sultan to widen the membership of this Council, came in part from the Zawawis. Here was apparently big business being conducted, and they had no part in it. They, along with many other Omanis, could not believe that the expatriates concerned were not making large sums of money from the negotiations. Certainly, had they, the Zawawis, being involved, they would have made money themselves, and they found it incomprehensible that others were not.

At the same time, pressure was put on the Sultan to at least share the authority to sanction capital expenditure and development expenditure. The results were far-reaching. In November 1974, at the time of the National Day celebrations, two more businessmen were brought into the government, and two new councils were created.

The businessmen were, first, an enterprising Muscati who had been born in Dhofar of a Beluch father and a Dhofari mother, Muhammad Zubair. He was regarded as a Dhofari, was an able and successful merchant, and was made Minister of Trade and Industry, a new portfolio. The second was a pure Dhofari, Sa'id Ahmed Shanferi, who had made a lot of money in Salalah as a contractor and agent. He collected the cumbersome-sounding portfolio, again a new one, of Petroleum, Minerals, Agriculture and Fisheries.

The new councils, both of them consisting of Omanis only, were a Finance Council, with the Sultan as chairman, Qais Zawawi as vice-chairman, and Omar Zawawi listed among the members, and a Development Council, again with the Sultan as chairman, and Qais

Zawawi as vice-chairman. A prominent member of the Development Council was the Minister of Communications, Abdul Hafidh Salim Rajab. All expatriate membership of the Natural Gas and Petroleum Council ceased, and the Minister for Petroleum, Minerals, Agriculture and Fisheries became vice-chairman of this council, again with the Sultan as chairman.

The establishment of these three councils put Omanis in charge of their own affairs in a way that had never been seen before. Although the Sultan was chairman of each of the three, he would not attend each meeting, and this meant that the vice-chairman had considerable authority. In the case of the Finance Council, he could sanction all expenditure on capital projects. Included in such projects were negotiated contracts with contractors for whom he or his brother were agents, and where the rate of commission exceeded 10 per cent. Again, this was with the full knowledge of the Sultan, and broke no Omani law. The Finance Council did impose an overall control over ministerial spending which had never existed before, and in doing so, took away a certain authority from the Sultan. The fact that this control was not always either wisely or prudently used does nothing to invalidate the point. The absolutism of the Sultan is being eroded in such a manner that he would find it extremely difficult to take back what he has given up. He still retains overall nominal control of finance, there is no finance ministry, and the Sultan continues to regard himself as Minister of Finance. Yet he has surrendered to the Finance Council a decision-making power which a few years ago would have been unthinkable in any hands but his own. Whether this diminution of his authority will in the long run benefit his people is not yet clear. Cynics would be forgiven for suggesting that the Sultan has been forced to give up some powers in an apparently painless way to people who are smarter than he is, and that his absolutism is being replaced by the absolutism of a profit-motivated oligarchy of businessmen who have ministerial authority.

As encouraging as this devolution of authority is, it must be remembered that it does not extend to the defence sector and here the Sultan still makes decisions without reference, even, in some cases, to his Defence Council. The outstanding example of this sort of decision, surely one of the most controversial he could ever have made, was his determination to acquire an integrated air defence system involving aircraft, missiles, radar and all necessary ground installations for the support of this system at a cost of some £300 million. Although other sources of supply were considered, the British government went to no little trouble to ensure that the British Aircraft Corporation would be the prime supplier of the equipment. Consideration of the thinking behind this decision of the Sultan and an understanding of his basic attitudes is an important prerequisite to an understanding of how his government does work and where the power lies.

It must be remembered that throughout the Arabian peninsula, and certainly in Oman, it has been regarded for generations as essential for a man to be armed; a man who does not carry a weapon, in Oman a rifle and a dagger, is not a man. His virility is in question. This attitude is beginning to change, particularly among town-bred people, and as popular education spreads. Still, however, it remains a most powerful influence. A boy at puberty is circumcised and given a rifle; both acts are important badges of his manhood.

Thus a strong tribe, as a collection of men, is a well-armed tribe, the respect by which it is held by other tribes being in direct proportion to the number of armed men it can parade. Taken to the next stage, a nation, as an amalgam of tribes, will only be respected in the world if it is seen to be militarily strong. This national trait is not only confined to the Arab states of the peninsula; most developing countries put expenditure on sophisticated weapon systems high on their list of national priorities. It is not done to enquire against whom these weapons might be used, nor with what effectiveness. The enormous wastage of modern battle, for example the Yom Kippur war or the most recent Indian-Pakistani conflict, is such that only major industrial economies could hope to make good the prodigious loss rate, when ammunition is expended like monsoonal rain, and expensive tanks and aircraft knocked out like so many clay pigeons. This factor is not considered; just as an unarmed man is not a man, an unarmed nation is not a nation.

Oman suffers doubly from this international game of keeping up appearances because the country could be said to be situated in a street with rich neighbours. Iran, the United Arab Emirates, Saudi Arabia, Kuwait, Iraq, all near to or bordering Oman, all with a very much higher and longer sustained expectation from oil revenues, are all profligate spenders on modern arms and advanced weapon systems. Oman has to be seen, at least in some Omani eyes, to be holding up its head in such a neighbourhood. If this argument should be thought trite, then the Sultan's reaction to the Shah's offer of Iranian Phantom aircraft provided that Oman could provide a base for them should be recalled; the Sultan could not let his rich and powerful neighbour and new friend see that he did not measure up to the standards of the rich man's club, and so the Thumrait air base went ahead, regardless of cost.

A third factor in the decision to order the air defence system is the Sultan's view of himself as a military expert. 'I am a military man and a Sandhurst graduate', he told a Lebanese journalist. His thinking is very much along military lines, and new weapons and systems have a certain fascination for him.

Finally, there was the need of Oman to counter the now apparently extinguished threat from the People's Democratic Republic of Yemen. At the time the air defence system was being considered and ordered, intelligence sources reported that PDRY was building advanced bases for its Russian military aircraft near to the Oman border and that Cuban pilots were in Aden. This did constitute a threat to Salalah, and the Sultan was understandably concerned about it. When he mentioned this problem to a visiting British minister, he was not pleased when his guest suggested a battery of light anti-aircraft guns as a reasonable deterrent to the possible threat from his neighbours. The end of hostilities in Dhofar has removed this threat, but the plans for an integrated air defence system were greatly in excess of what would have been reasonable to counter the possible threat from PDRY. Nor would it have had any relevance in the guerrilla war in Dhofar.

In April 1974, the Sultan asked those responsible for the recording of his finances to make provision for the purchase of Jaguar aircraft during 1974, and a figure of about £10 million was allocated. In June 1974, he asked for the financial implications of ordering Rapier guided missile equipment, then estimated at about £40 million, including radar and ground installation. He was informed on 26 June 1974 by hand-delivered letter that those responsible could 'not see a way to finance the Rapier equipment this year from our own resources'.

Those responsible for the national financial accounting at that time followed this warning to the Sultan with a proposal for his signature advising his ministers of the national financial situation in a brief form and stressing the need for keeping expenditure within the limits already agreed. The Sultan signed this decree which was issued to all ministers in July 1974. In view of what happened subsequently, it is repeated here:

> We praise God for all that has befallen us in this beloved country in the way of grace and prosperity after years of neglect and obscurity. With strong intent and faith in God and the efforts of all the loyal officials of the government we are once again moving towards the restoration of our beloved Oman's former glory. We must, however,

stop for a while after moving forward to ensure the appropriateness of the steps we have taken and that we have indeed made real achievements, so that if we have erred in any plan or project we should not continue to make such mistakes.

In view of the foregoing, we have decided:

1. The Government shall not undertake any further capital projects before January 1976, that is with the exception of projects already approved before the date of this decision and already in the process of implementation;
2. The Government shall plan capital projects for the year 1976 and present these plans to the Department of Finance;
3. The budget for 1974 will not be altered except with regard to salaries (as mentioned in the decision to that effect) which are increased by 15 percent, or by any further amendment in the event of any unforeseen rise in the cost of materials;
4. The 1975 budget for recurrent expenses will not exceed Rials Omani 62,500,000, that is to say an increase of 25 percent over the year 1974.

In order fully to appraise Government officials of our economic and financial position, we give below a schedule of income and expenditure, for the expenditure on development this year has trebled since last year, and the natural result of this increase has been development and construction.

In millions of Rials

	1973 Budget	1974 Budget Before Amendment	1974 Budget After Amendment	Proposed 1975 Budget
Total income	62.5	220.0	240.0	325.0
Expenditure				
Development	30.2	84.0	90.0	90.0
Recurrent Expenditure	18.8	49.3	50.0	62.5
Defence	42.0	58.5	100.0	125.0
Police*	.6	7.4	9.0	11.0
	91.6	199.2	249.0	288.5
Balance	–23.1	+20.8	–9.0	+36.5

[*Police – most police expenditure for 1973 was included in the budget for defence.]

The above-mentioned situation is one of the reasons for the issuing of this decision whilst the other reason, which is not the only one, is the problem of inflation and rising prices which the world is facing, and when the Government spends this enormous amount of money in the country it has an effect on prices and the cost of living.

In conclusion, we should like to remind everyone that these steps we have taken are only in the public interest and the service of our dear country, and with a view to ensuring that we do not blunder into error and that our financial position remains secure.

Trusting in God
(signed)
Qaboos bin Sa'id
Sultan of Oman

It should be noted that the figures quoted in this decree were the best available at that time. The final accounts for the year 1973 showed a total income of Omani rials 68.5 million, the difference between this figure and that shown in the Sultan's decree (62.5 million) being that between a final audited figure and a budgeted figure. Total expenditure for 1973 was Omani rials 92.9 million, compared with the budgeted figure shown in the decree of 91.6 million (Omani rials 1 = $US2.89524). The differences, important though they be, take nothing away from the validity and the intent of the Sultan's decree.

It should be recalled that Oman at that time had still fairly rudimentary financial accounting methods. It was seldom possible to be sure that all commitments made by the Sultan and his ministers had been accounted for. Also the technical accounting treatment of government investments was not uniform, so that all figures had to be viewed with a certain care. For example, it was not known at that time how heavily the government had been committed for the desalination plant complex mentioned earlier in this chapter; the figures in the 1974 budget assumed a total commitment for this project of some rials 20 million, when the figure should have been nearer rials 120 million.

Precise recording of government commitments is not easy in many countries (e.g. Britain), and in Oman the ultimate discovery of hitherto unrecorded commitments caused considerable embarrassment during the early part of 1975. It is stressed again that the lack of sophisticated accounting mechanisms would not have caused this embarrassment had the will to enforce the Sultan's decree existed.

Yet, in September 1974, only two months after signing this decree, the Sultan himself proposed to spend £200 million more on the air defence system. His Arab advisers assured him that they could find the money if his own people could not. He was determined to have these weapons and would listen to no voice suggesting that they were both beyond Oman's financial needs and irrelevant to Oman's military needs.

The Sultan's example was enough for his ministers, and in the six-month period October 1974-March 1975, further capital commitments were entered into. The following table shows the results of this spending spree.

Table 7.1: Oman's Revenue and Expenditure, 1971-5 (million rials)*

Revenue				Expenditure		
Year	Oil	Other	Total	Current	Development	Total
71	47.9	2.2	50.1	26.0	20.0	46.0
72	49.6	3.4	53.0	41.7	29.9	71.6
73	61.3	7.2	68.5	63.0	29.9	92.9
74	281.5	11.7	303.2	111.2	200.0	311.2
75	387.1	11.0	398.1	167.3	339.1	506.4

* The above figures exclude grants and loans. 'Current' expenditure includes defence and police expenditure, but excludes major capital items of defence expenditure such as the Thumrait air base.
Source: Central Bank of Oman.

The fact of no control other than the will of an impulsive man and the deviousness of one or two ministers with self-interest at heart is clearly illustrated by these figures. The stark absolutism of Sultan Sa'id has been greatly eased by Sultan Qaboos. Yet he remains an absolute ruler, sharing his power with a small group of businessmen. The efficiency of the government of Oman has increased each year since Sultan Qaboos came to power. A cash-flow crisis in 1974 caused foreign bankers some concern, but by 1976 confidence had been restored. Yet the structural weakness in the government of Oman remains. There is nothing to stop the Sultan and the business oligarchy around him continuing to commit the nation to demands on future income which this income will be inadequate to meet.

Postscript

Since the above was written, the following news item appeared in the *Financial Times* of 20 August 1976 under a headline 'Oman budget rises 20%':

Oman has increased its annual budget by nearly 160m. Omani rials for the current calendar year, bringing it to RO636m. compared with RO530m. in 1975, an increase of 20 percent.

Although the figures were drawn up several months ago and some were released provisionally in May, they have only just been finalised, approved by the ruler Sultan Qaboos and published in the fortnightly official gazette.

Estimated Government revenue for 1976 totals RO495m., showing a shortfall against planned expenditure of RO141m. However, this is being met in part by RO46m. in aid from other Arab countries and RO64m. worth of loans granted to the Government, leaving a deficit of RO31m.

According to published spending figures, defence and national security will account for RO274.5m., over RO23m. more than in the revised budget for 1975; civil expenditure will be RO289m. (RO237.3m. last year); the Government's participation in Petroleum Development (Oman) will be RO28m. (RO26.8m.); and loan repayments and interest RO44.5m. (RO15m.).

8 THE DEVELOPMENT OF THE INSTITUTIONS OF GOVERNMENT

'States are not maintained with words.'

As a counter to the absolutism of the traditional style of government in Oman, and to the development of a ministerial oligarchy motivated almost entirely by self-interest, a conscious effort was made, generally as a result of expatriate initiatives, to develop professional institutions of government which would have their own dynamics and which would be comparatively free of political pressures. Indeed, institution-building was placed among a list of five key tasks of the government of Oman, the other four being national security, the building of an economic infrastructure, the development of a social infrastructure, and the definition and realisation of income-generating projects.

Historically, as has been seen, the only institution of government in Oman was the Sultanate, which had grown out of the sheikhly and tribal system, and from which, as a sub-institution, had developed the supra-tribal regional governor (*wali*) network. This traditional institution had its own in-built stability, more as a matter of custom than anything else. It suffered from its unitary character and the consequent fickleness of its linchpin, the Sultan himself. An energetic Sultan could galvanise the institution of the Sultanate, a lazy, ineffectual, or solitary ruler could make it moribund. The whole society suffered, or prospered, simply on the weakness or strength of one individual. The ruler's personal foibles dictated the character and stability of the polity.

It became apparent to those thinking about the structure of government in Oman that, in the long term, the Sultan had to become less relevant. The nation needed its dignified and its efficient forms of government, it needed personalities, because it was a society that needed the focus of a strong personality to stimulate it and give it direction. It needed a Head of State who was recognised by all as the source of all authority, as the upholder of laws, and as the defender of the national integrity. Yet, given this need, it could not afford a system of government which was impulsive and unconsidered, where decisions of fundamental national importance concerning the management of resources were being made without anyone, least of all the society itself, being aware of the long-term consequences of these decisions. Long torn by internal strife, the society needed stable organisms of government so that when, in the inevitability of time, one ruler died or became ineffective, government could continue without a crisis which would shake the nation to its very fundamentals.

In the first proposals on structure of government which were presented to Sayyid Tarik when he was Prime Minister this need was borne in mind. The proposals called for the establishment of a professional civil service, and for a permanent Office of the Prime Minister. There was nothing startlingly original about these proposals; it seemed a matter of common sense that Oman should start immediately to build institutions which would have their own stability, and which would thus permit ministers (and prime ministers) to come and go without dangerous and inefficient gaps in continuity. This concept is so basic to Western government that it is not always easy for non-Omanis to comprehend a situation where there is no organised professional civil service and no ministerial organisation which is not personal to the individual minister. When a minister lost his job in Oman, generally the people closest to him in the ministry lost theirs also, and even the files of the outgoing minister would either be taken with him or destroyed.

Initially, after the change of government in July 1970, and the beginning of ministerial appointments which followed it, there were very few rules and examples to follow. Ministers were appointed by the Sultan or by the Prime Minister and left to engage their own staffs. There was an outline of a government salary scale, but this referred to clerks and drivers in the main and had no provision for professional and executive grades. Minister's friends were appointed as 'advisers', or 'directors', and if possible were given free accommodation and the free use of a government car. There was little attempt at standardisation and no attempt at professional job-grading. The Secretary for Financial Affairs gradually brought some order into the chaos, particularly in so far as junior clerical and administrative grades were concerned.

The recommendations to the Prime Minister on the creation of a civil service called for a small specialist department which would begin with job-grading and job evaluation, and which would lead on to co-ordinated training programmes, a civil service institute which would be responsible for clerical and administrative training in Oman, and a system of fellowships, using the multilateral and bilateral aid sources then available, for the training of higher echelon staff outside Oman. It was recognised that such a programme had to be long-term; in a situation where very few Omanis had had even a primary school education, there could be no dramatic strides and reliance would have to be placed on significant numbers of expatriates for a number of years. It was also recognised that training should be co-ordinated with the new education programmes, so that the output from the newly established schools could soon begin to play a useful part in government. It was realised too that for many years to come, government employment would be the major job opportunity open to school-leavers in Oman. Therefore it seemed of even greater importance to start a strong and professionally designed programme for training and building a civil service right from the start.

Unfortunately, the Prime Minister, while recognising the force of the arguments, did not see fit to order their implementation because he disagreed with other parts of the proposals put forward at that time dealing with his own relationship, as chief executive of the government, with the Sultan as head of state.

Eventually, in 1973, as part of the Sultan's Palace Secretariat, (the 'Diwan'), a Civil Service Department was set up, and a United Nations expert in personnel administration was seconded to the government of Oman to give the department professional backing. Progress was particularly slow, and the civil service department almost foundered in 1975 over the issue of a civil service law. Such a law was regarded as an essential prerequisite to the building of a strong, independent civil service. As of mid-1975, the law, which had seen several drafts, had not been approved by the Council of Ministers. The issue was whether ministers or the civil service department should have the authority to engage staff. Ministers argued that they should have the ultimate right to hire and fire staff, and that the civil service department should be merely a record-keeping and training unit. The department's experts argued that, to build up a strong and professional civil service, the department itself had to have the authority to engage and dismiss staff, and to be responsible for their professional qualifications and screening. The issue is clearly one which is fundamental to the future shape of government in Oman. Power in the hands of ministers over all their staff will perpetuate the oligarchic system, and mean that staff will tend to have a loyalty to the minister who employs them, rather than to the government as a whole. On the other hand, it is recognised that an independent civil service can be bureaucratic and negative; this danger can in part be guarded against by the greatest attention to the selection, training and development of top-grade civil servants. This condition requires in turn the highest professional expertise on the part of senior people in the civil service department itself. Oman has not yet found such experts.

Another of the recommendations to the Prime Minister at the end of

1971 concerned a small professional planning team as part of the Office of the Prime Minister. This recommendation was not accepted then, and neither the Interim Planning Council nor the Centre for Economic Planning and Development which followed made any serious attempt at planning, although the Centre would have done had it survived long enough.

Various World Bank Missions to Oman pointed out the need for a professional planning unit. The World Bank proposed, and the government of Oman accepted, a loan from the Bank of $3 million to cover the cost of setting up a planning team, plus teams in other key areas, highway planning and agriculture. The Kuwait Fund was prepared to participate in the project, but the government of Oman refused to accept assistance from Kuwait on the grounds that the government of Kuwait was helping the People's Democratic Republic of Yemen, in other words, Oman's enemies.

In recommending the project to its Executive Directors,the World Bank said, *inter alia:*

> The proposed technical assistance project is an essential first step in Oman's development. The country has begun to embark on a major development program, but still lacks the administrative machinery and expertise required to direct these development efforts. The assistance for economic planning would help devise the general framework and strategy for development. It would also help develop at an early stage in the project the essential data base needed for effective planning and economic policy making. Sector specialists would provide operational assistance to the agricultural sector, which employs about three quarters of the population and which will be the major focus of future development, and the transportation sector, which has received the major share of investment activity during the past three years, but lacks the institutional machinery needed to reap the benefits from this investment . . . Oman has embarked on a major investment program during the past three years, generated by its oil revenues. In the desire to move ahead quickly, before the essential expertise and administrative machinery had been fully established, the development effort has been unavoidably *ad hoc* and largely unco-ordinated. Investment decisions were made before establishing the general objectives of Oman's economic development and without serious attention to economic priorities or the financial implications of the projects undertaken.
>
> The result has been a rapidly expanding level of development

> expenditure, but without adequate direction, design or attention to the implications of such investment activity . . . Now that the Government has succeeded in stimulating economic growth, it recognises the need to administer this development, and guide its future direction. It wishes to replace the piecemeal studies, investigations and investment activity with a more rational program of development, geared to Oman's social and economic needs . . .[1]

The World Bank Technical Assistance project went ahead, and during the course of 1974, three teams of international experts began working in Oman, a planning team, a highway administration team in the Ministry of Communications, and an agricultural team in the Ministry of Agriculture, Fisheries, Petroleum and Minerals. All three teams found the going particularly difficult, as few Omanis saw the need for the expertise represented by each team. If success eventually blesses their work, each team will have made a genuine contribution to strengthening the government of Oman. The projects will each take a number of years to complete, and will be supervised by the World Bank.

A first fruit of this technical assistance project was a Development Law. Under an able Egyptian project leader, who was able in a short period of time to win the confidence of Omani ministers, the planning team, acting as a secretariat for the Development Council (see Chapter 7) drafted and had approved a Development Law. This is an interesting and valuable law which, if followed, could carry Oman forward into a period of economic viability. It is in marked contrast to 'the Word of Sultan Sa'id bin Taimur' and is set out in Appendix 3 of this book.

Following the publication of the Development Law early in 1975, the planning team set to work to try and encourage the preparation of a realistic development plan. In mid-1976 details were released of this plan which was awaiting final governmental approval. The plan suggests that total government expenditure over the five-year period 1976-80 will amount to Omani rials 950 million (about $2,750 million) and its basic aim is to relieve the dependence on oil and to diversify the economy. It calls for the development of an additional 20,000 hectares of land to be placed under cultivation (that is, increasing the present area of land under cultivation by about 55 per cent). It recognises that the major constraint to this development is the water supply, but then, surprisingly and controversially, goes on to make provision for 'heavy investment'[2] in maintenance of the existing *falaj* irrigation systems. The *falaj* systems require much hand labour for their maintenance and hand labour has become extremely expensive in Oman. Also, the *falaj* system moves water along open channels with large losses due to seepage and evaporation. There would seem to be a *prima facie* case for modern capital-intensive irrigation systems.

A second project loan was negotiated with the World Bank in the field of education. The tyranny of ignorance had been one of the major bars to effective development in Oman. Although much had been done by the government to build schools and employ teachers, the quality of education was poor. The World Bank commented:

> Following the present Sultan's accession to power in July 1970, a decision was made to modernise and expand education facilities at primary level. The demand for education quickly resulted in enrolments which outpaced the capacity of a system already lacking in qualified teachers, administrative and planning staff, instructional equipment and adequate facilities. Combined with outmoded curricula, these deficiencies have resulted in an education system of poor quality and with little relevance to the national needs. As there has been no teacher training institution thus far, the expansion of education has been possibly only by employing expatriate teachers with highly variable backgrounds, who teach different and often irrelevant programs, or unqualified Omanis with rote learning as their basic methodology. Sixty-eight percent of the teaching staff is unqualified and forty-four percent is expatriate. As trained local personnel hardly exists, Oman will have to continue to rely on expatriates for the next ten years to sustain the growth of primary and basic education – and probably twenty years in any other sector – until the pupils who entered the newly expanded primary system after 1970 have graduated in sufficient numbers from secondary and higher education.
>
> Yet the situation presents encouraging features. The Ministry of Education, itself hampered by insufficiently educated staff (only two staff members have university degrees and five have completed secondary education), is aware of the many problems besetting the present education system, and has set some broad educational goals to correct the situation. Financing of the related programmes to achieve these tasks is not likely to be difficult because of expected oil revenues and assistance from Oman's neighbouring countries. Expert guidance in the more refined formulation and implementation of these programmes will be a more serious constraint, one which this project would assist in alleviating.
>
> The most pressing needs of the education system are (i) to

> reorganise and strengthen the Ministry itself, (ii) to develop modern, practical curricula, methods and teaching materials, (iii) to train sufficient numbers of Omani teachers to replace unqualified and expatriate teachers, and (iv) to initiate the types of training to produce the numbers and kinds of trained personnel required for the nation's economy.[3]

The Bank proposed, and the government of Oman accepted, a project which would provide for the construction and equipping of Oman's first primary teacher training institute; this institute would become a national education centre. It would also provide for two so-called 'accelerated schools' aimed at giving basic literacy and numeracy to the 14- to 19-year old illiterates, plus a trade skill. Finally the project includes Oman's first agricultural secondary school, which would be set up under a joint arrangement between the World Bank, the British Ministry of Overseas Development, and the government of Oman.

A team leader for the project arrived in Oman late in 1974, and it was launched with full backing and co-operation from Oman's then Minister for Education, Sayyid Faisal bin 'Ali, a distant cousin of the Sultan, who returned to Oman in 1974 after a period during which he was Oman's Ambassador to the United States and to the United Nations. This is a project which spells hope for Oman. First, it is moving forward with the co-operation and understanding of the Omani authorities and stands a reasonable chance of being successful. Second, it will strengthen a ministry which is of the greatest importance in the building of a stable society in the future; a strong and professionally competent Ministry of Education is at once an example to other ministries and an investment of maximum importance in the nation's future. Finally, as long as the output of the education system is geared to the needs of the economy, the project will make a contribution to Oman's future economic welfare.

Another institution of importance for the future is the Central Bank of Oman. Set up with the assistance of the International Monetary Fund, the Central Bank has a legal foundation which would permit it to gradually bring some sense into the management of Oman's financial resources, and indeed, of the economy as a whole. It has sufficient independence in its charter to permit it to train and develop its own staff, to employ expatriate experts, and to co-operate with other central banks and with international banks. Again, the fact of the Central Bank of Oman is a sign of hope for the future; the Bank has the elements in its constitution to permit it to grow and become strong and self-confident, and hence to be able to exercise a role of the utmost importance. Its first Governor is the ex-Prime Minister, the Sultan's uncle, Sayyid Tarik.

Another element in the building of Omani institutions relates to a legal framework. A start was made over the five years 1971-5 to draft laws which a modern society needs, specifically a labour law and a commercial and business law. The weakness with these laws is that there is no independent judiciary to uphold and interpret them. The traditional Islamic judges, the *qadhis,* are unable to accept, for philosophic reasons, that there can be any other law but Koranic law. Thus they would not be competent or willing to act as a judiciary. Similarly they have great difficulty in accepting some of the provisions of a draft civil and criminal code.

The absence of an independent judiciary means that the Omani police, almost a paramilitary force, tends in many instances to be both law enforcement office, prosecutor and judge. If the police inform an Omani citizen that he has broken the law, then he has broken the law. It is difficult for him to appeal, because unless his alleged offence is covered by the traditional Koranic law, no means exists for him to appeal, and there is no court of appeal. He could in theory appeal to the Sultan, but the chief of police is very close to the Sultan and has responsibility for internal security in northern Oman. No appeal would be considered by the Sultan without seeking the opinion of the chief of police, and in general there would be no one to counter this advise and argue a legal ground for appeal.

Traffic offences and similar petty crimes are tried in front of the Governor of the Capital. The police prosecute, all people suspected tend to be put in prison before they are formally charged, bail is rare, and the police will tend to inform the Governor that the people they charge are guilty. An international company with its own experts and strong-minded management may be able to secure acquittals of its staff if it has convincing evidence of innocence, but the channel of appeal is direct to the police.

There is no concept of *habeus corpus,* and an Omani citizen, or, indeed, a foreigner, can be put in prison by the police without any formal charge being made. The police are in general well disciplined and there has been no serious abuse of their powers, although isolated instances have been known when junior officers have taken the law into their own hands and subjected people taken to a police station for questioning to a quite unnecessary degree of pressure and, in some cases, physical violence.

An undramatic but valuable step forward in developing institutions of government which have their own dynamic has been made in the field of local government. Muscat and Matrah have had a sort of municipal status for over twenty years, but the achievements and effectiveness of these municipalities were modest, being confined to elementary public cleansing. Following the change of government in July 1970, the municipalities were combined into one 'municipality of the capital'. Because of its close relationship with the government, and because the government was itself undertaking so much work and development in the capital area, the municipality was never certain of its responsibilities.

A municipal council was formed of nominated businessmen. As so often happens in all societies, the prominent few found themselves nominated for a large number of councils and committees, with the result that the time that could be devoted to any one council would be small, particularly in the case of men who had a thriving business to run. Gradually, membership changed to encourage younger business men, and gradually too, the responsibilities of the municipality became clearer. The capital area municipality has its own budget, and concentrates on public cleansing and rubbish disposal. Its achievements are still modest, but more people are getting experience in local government and a framework exists for sensible, if slow, development.

A municipality existed in Salalah from soon after the 1970 *coup*. Being smaller, and under the Sultan's direct eye, this municipality became effective in keeping the town clean and in supervising public markets. It also was the only municipality in Oman which elected its council by popular suffrage, albeit on a limited and strictly controlled basis. An attempt was made, from 1973 onwards, to set up municipalities in a number of other towns and villages in Oman, including Nizwa, Sohar, Sur and Sumail. For years people in these towns and villages had been used to sitting back and saying, 'Why doesn't the government do something for our town?', a relic of the days of Sa'id bin Taimur when nothing was ever done, and nothing ever permitted. With funds provided through a modest budget from the government, plus a small income from market stall-holders' licences and fees, and pushed by an energetic expatriate, people in these towns were challenged to 'do something' for their communities themselves. The results were in some cases dramatic; flies, breeding in the rubbish of generations, were a great curse in these small towns. The provision of public cleansing equipment and the organisation of a municipal rubbish dump were not acts of enormous weight, yet, carried out through a nominated municipal council with its own small staff, and using money provided in part by the central government and in part from locally generated funds, members of these small communities saw the vast difference a small effort could make. Again, slowly but inevitably, the self-confidence of communities which know that they can do much for themselves without looking always to the central government for assistance in even the most minor matters is being built up. The relationship of the new forms of government at regional level, the municipalities, with the old, the *wali* system, was carefully watched. In principle, the municipality would do nothing without the *wali's* approval. This proved to be an asset, though it was originally feared that it could act as a barrier to progress. Without exception, *walis* have welcomed the municipalities as both a way of integrating themselves into the community and of removing some of the criticism of 'things not being done' which otherwise was directed at them as representatives of the central government. The fact of the *wali*'s support gave the members of the municipal council enough confidence to make decisions. Achievements remain modest, but the experience with creating a local representative decision-making body which cuts across traditional tribal divisions and which is seen to be effective is a significant step forward in institution-building, and hence in the broadening and strengthening of the base of government in Oman.

There was one resounding failure in these expatriate endeavours to create institutions which would be above the pressures of day-to-day politics and which would ensure that policies for husbanding the nation's resources were thought through dispassionately. The Centre for Economic Planning and Development, with the approval of the Supreme Council for Economic Planning and Development chaired by the Sultan, had recognised the urgent need for water resource surveys.

Northern Oman was divided into three areas and the Salalah plain with its adjacent mountains in Dhofar was designated as a fourth. International teams, one Dutch, two British, and one French were appointed to carry out water resource surveys over a number of years. These surveys were paid for from funds provided by the government of Saudi Arabia and the British Ministry of Overseas Development. The surveys, which began in mid-1972, were initially to last three years. At the same time, through the Food and Agricultural Organisation of the United Nations, with funds supplied by the United Nations Development Programme, a National Water Resources Centre was established. The terms of reference of this centre included supervising the various teams carrying out the water resource surveys, and using the data provided to draw up a national water conservation and management policy. There was also a large element in the programme for the training of Omani staff.

The National Water Resources Centre and its Director, a Swiss, soon fell foul of vested interests in Oman. In the days before oil revenues gave a feeling of infinite riches, there had been no pressure to break the ingrained habits of centuries which ensured that water was not wasted. When Omanis began to receive benefits from the development programme, they tended to buy diesel pumps to replace the traditional animal powered methods of lifting water from wells, and also to supplement the flow from the older *falaj* system. The result was that much water was wasted, and many wells in coastal regions began to suffer from salt water intrusion as the sweet water table was lowered and sea water filtered through into the natural reservoirs of ground water. The preliminary results of the water resource surveys pointed this out, and pointed out also that permanent harm could be done to the natural reserves of water if action was not taken urgently to restrict the drilling of new wells and the indiscriminate use of powerful diesel pumps. The Director of the National Water Resources Centre did all he could to make ministers aware of the dangers, but in doing so made many enemies, as ministers were amongst the worst offenders. Large modern houses with gardens and swimming pools used much water.

The end came early in 1975, when results of surveys showed that the desalination plant was not the only solution to the water supply problems of the capital area, and suggested that careful professional management of the existing installations would result in a much higher water availability. This advise was considered unacceptable, the Director-General of the Food and Agricultural Organisation was asked to remove the Director of the National Water Resources Centre, and the three survey teams working in northern Oman were told to stop work and leave the country, even though all were at a stage were final reports were imminent. The general Omani comment was: 'We want water, not surveys and reports.' This would have been reasonable had Oman had very large resources of natural water. In the event, where rainfall is minimal and where natural resources of ground water are being depleted at a faster rate than they can be recharged, present policies of the government of Oman risk destroying or at least causing permanent damage to a resource which is fundamental for the future of the country.

Without exception, all the institution-building initiatives in Oman came from expatriate initiatives. The concept of a professional civil service, planning teams, strengthening the professional expertise of key ministries, laws and their codification, the need for an independent judiciary, the development of local government, the awareness of the need for water conservation, all of these concepts came from ideas and the determination to see them through from a few expatriates. It can be argued that expatriates, in pushing ideas against the feeling of the government of Oman, were at least guilty of an arrogant 'playing at God', and possibly even of disloyalty. This argument continues that only Omanis know what is good for Oman, and expatriates are employed only as technicians, to give advice related to their specific expertise when it is called for. There is force in this proposition, and many an expatriate adviser, in Oman as well as in other countries, has brought trouble upon himself by ignoring it. Certainly in Oman there was opposition to many of these expatriate initiatives merely for the reason that they were expatriate initiatives, irrrespective of whether Omani opinion considered the subject matter right or wrong. More than one worthy idea from an expatriate adviser was stifled at birth because of lack of care and sensitivity to Omani susceptibilities in putting it forward.

There is no easy answering argument. The obvious rejoinder of 'responsibility springing from a wider experience' leaves the proposer open to charges of 'colonialism' and obsession with 'the white man's burden'. As has already been pointed out elsewhere in this book, the argument that those in power today have a responsibility to future generations carries little weight in a society whose basic philosophy is fatalistic and which can regard a concern today about tomorrow's children as a blasphemous intervention with the divine will. Basically, only history can judge whether these expatriate initiatives in Oman will be of lasting long-term benefit to the society. And, of course, those in power today cannot be expected to support any move which is aimed at curtailing their power, no matter how subtly such moves be made.

No matter what their genesis, the moves towards creating professional and representative institutions in Oman do constitute a step away from absolutism, be it the absolutism of an individual or of a self-interested oligarchy. It is only when this absolutism has been tempered with stronger checks and balances, with an independent judiciary and a respect for the rule of law, with an effective popular consultative mechanism, that Oman's government can be said to have left the Middle Ages and becomes that of a genuine modern state.

Notes

1. Report and Recommendations to the Executive Directors, dated 15 February 1974.
2. *Middle East Economic Digest*, Vol.20, No.26, London, June 1976.
3. IBRD Appraisal Reported, dated 20 December 1973.

PART III: THE CHALLENGE OF THE FUTURE

9 THE DURABILITY OF THE GOVERNMENT OF SULTAN QABOOS

> '. . . men are won over by the present far more than by the past . . . the new prince will have a twofold glory, in having founded a new state and in having adorned and strengthened it with good laws, sound defences, reliable allies, and inspiring leadership . . .'

The Sultanate of Oman, in July 1976, is so different to that vestige of another age, 'Muscat and Oman', which Sultan Qaboos took from his father six years previously, that the Sultan in some ways can be thought to have founded a new state. Changes have been made, revolutionary in impact, which alter the fundamental structure of the society. A pattern of settlement dictated partly by extremely poor communications both within the country and between Oman and the outside world has had modern high-speed roads imposed upon it. Air travel has made journeys which would have taken most Omanis weeks or even months prior to 1970 now a matter of a few hours. The wider world, for so long both hidden from and forbidden to them, is now within free and simple reach. Foreigners, previously frowned upon, are now seen in every village and have become almost commonplace.

In the last years of his reign, Sultan Sa'id bin Taimur kept himself so much from his subjects that many thought him dead. Most Omanis will have seen Sultan Qaboos in the flesh, possibly only briefly as they stand by a roadside as his heavily escorted car flashes past, but undeniably and unforgettably. All will have heard frequently his deep and sonorous voice speaking to them on the radio on some matter of national importance, or on the occasion of the annual National Day celebrations, when he addresses the whole nation. Many will have seen him in his brilliant uniform on the Oman colour television service. His presence is felt in the land in a way incomprehensible in the days of his father.

The petty restrictions of the old days are forgotten. Every Omani has freedom to buy and sell, to make fortunes and to lose them, to build whatever sort of house he can afford, to educate his sons, and his daughters, to whatever standard he, or they, wish. And every Omani has the freedom to leave Oman and seek employment in other Arab states, should he, or she, wish to do so.

Any foreigner who had visited the country prior to 1970, and then not again until 1976, would be astonished by the differences. His first journey would have involved a perilous landing on a small airstrip surrounded by craggy mountain peaks, his trips around the country would have been by Land Rover on dusty and rough natural surface roads, his accommodation would have been as a guest in a private house. In 1976 he would have landed at a well-designed and constructed modern international airport, he would have been driven in an air-conditioned car on a well-made dual carriageway to a modern first-class hotel. He could see a great deal of the country on modern highways using his air-conditioned car. Before 1970 the traveller would have seen no sign of economic activity other than the ultra-modern oil installations and a pitiful, archaic agriculture. In 1976, especially in the Muscat area and in Salalah, he could be forgiven for thinking he found himself in the middle of a builder's yard, such is the level of construction activity going on on all sides. In his first visit, the traveller would have observed great poverty and need everywhere. In 1976 he sees, unless he is particularly observant and perceptive, only affluence.

Omanis know that their country is now, in every way, 'an Arab nation'. Oman is a member of the Arab league, and on their television sets they can see the Foreign Minister of Oman treated as an equal by the Foreign Ministers of other Arab nations at international meetings called to attempt to resolve various crises in the Arab world. Other Arab leaders visit Oman; the people of Oman will have been aware of the visits of King Khalid of Saudi Arabia, of King Hussein of Jordan, of President Sadat of Egypt, as well as ministers of many countries.

The Sultan is credited by his people with full responsibility for these dramatic and extraordinary changes in their status, way of life, welfare and general self-esteem. His personal impact is great, his personal achievement unarguable. The first pictures published of him shortly after his accession to power, taken by a not very skilful photographer, show a slight, shy young man of thirty in traditional robes with a large unkempt beard in the Ibadhi style. Now, coloured photographs by highly competent international photographers show a good-looking man in an elaborate and colourful military uniform, with a neatly trimmed beard, and an air of undoubted authority. These photographs are of a man who knows what he has done, knows that he proved to the world that he was not the tool of his British advisers, knows that he took Oman into the Arab world, thus making a complete turn-about in a policy followed by his family for over a century. This is the man who proved to the world that he was a stronger man than his uncle, Sayyid Tarik. This is the soldier who led one of the few successful anti-guerrilla wars of the last quarter-century. This is the Head of State fêted by the Shah of Iran, honoured by the President of France, decorated by the Queen of England, welcomed by the President of the United States. Indeed, one of the most striking developments in Oman over the six years since July 1970 has been the growth of the Sultan's self-confidence.

This 'brilliant renaissance' picture of Oman and its rulers, perfectly acceptable as a public relations image, is one much loved by Omanis themselves, other Arabs and many others who either visit Oman or have relations of one sort or another with Oman. Like all such facile generalities, it is not incorrect but can be dangerously misleading. Without in any way wishing to denigrate the achievements of Sultan Qaboos and his people during the first six years of his reign, it must be remembered that outside influences have undoubtedly caused more changes in Oman than have internal policy decisions made by the Sultan and executed by his people.

First among these outside influences must rank crude oil production. The consequent transient wealth, regarded by most Omanis who think about its origins as a divine gift, has permitted Sultan Qaboos in essence to buy his new state. He is not alone in this; most governments of major oil-producing nations in the Middle East could be said to have done the same thing. This is a novel concept in the history of political development.

Without the revenue from oil, none of what has been achieved in Oman in the first six years of the Sultan's reign could have been even started. However, Oman's oil production is about to decline steeply. By implication, the period of purchased achievement in Oman is drawing to an end; achievements in the future will depend more on the Sultan's personal leadership qualities, on his statecraft, resilience and diplomacy, than have those of his first years.

The other major outside influence has been the provision of military expertise and of soldiers by the Sultan's allies, specifically, Britain, Iran and Jordan. Without this military assistance, the war in Dhofar could never have been won, and almost certainly would have been lost. Competent leadership of front-line troops, plus an effective supply organisation built around aircraft and an SAS unit involved in critical engagements was the British contribution. The Iranian soldiers were involved in much hard fighting in December 1974 and January 1975, fighting which finally destroyed the guerrillas' determination. Jordanian units played little part in the actual fighting but their presence was important for the final victory. None of this could have happened without the Sultan's overall direction, and his diplomatic endeavours, of course. The point is not so much one of downgrading the Sultan's achievements as one of giving perspective to a picture of his government and his state. Now that the war in Dhofar has been won, and the Sultan has, with justice, received the congratulations of his people and of the world, the question to be asked is could he defeat a similar military challenge to his régime without seeking assistance from his allies? The Sultan himself appears to think that he could not. Although, in July 1976, he agreed that the British government should give up its base in Masira island, he is most reluctant to cease to employ senior British officers in executive positions in his armed forces.

In the field of development, it is not generally known (or perhaps is conveniently forgotten) that plans for the new harbour and airport near Muscat were drawn up by consultants during the reign of Sultan Sa'id bin Taimur. At the same time, plans for two hospitals had been completed, and work had begun. The first major road contract, from Matrah to Sohar, was being negotiated when Sultan Sa'id was ousted. The first girls' school was completed in 1970. All this meant that, when Sultan Qaboos came to power, so much ground work had been completed that dramatic development progress was seen in the first two years of his reign. Subsequently, motivation for the development programme came in no small measure from expatriate advisers.

Far more important than these qualifications to the achievements of the Sultan is the question of the durability of his government. If his government can survive, if Oman in, say, the year 2000 is a viable economy and a stable polity with 'good laws, sound defences, reliable allies, and inspiring leadership', then the reliance on oil, foreign soldiers and expatriate advisers will be seen by history as a transitory phase, worthy of little more than passing reference, and in no way qualifying the achievements of Sultan Qaboos and his people.

This happy state of affairs is attainable by the Sultan and his people, but it will not happen automatically, nor is it likely to happen if present policies are followed. The key element in any analysis of the durability of the government of the Sultan is the man himself, Qaboos bin Sa'id. People who knew Sultan Sa'id have no difficulty in recognising Sultan Qaboos as his son. Foreigners particularly feel the same charisma, the same apparent warmth and charm, the same generous hospitality. The difference is also apparent: the elder Sultan modelled himself on those Indian princes with whom he spent his formative years, whilst the younger attempts to follow the pattern of Sandhurst in the early 1960s.

Sultan Qaboos is proud of his military education. He said to a Lebanese journalist early in 1972: 'I hope that you are not forgetting that I am a military man and a Sandhurst graduate.'[1] This is a theme which he has repeated to many other visitors. He has an especial love of pageantry, ceremonial and the display of things military. He himself wears uniform well, and when he inspects parades of his armed forces or of his police, the smartest man in terms of dress and drill on parade is the Sultan himself. This is not to suggest that his soldiers and his policemen are not smart; on the contrary, their commanding officer's example is followed by all ranks.

Any visitor to Oman who is fortunate enough to be invited to functions such as the Sultan's annual garden party given on the occasion of his birthday in November cannot fail to be impressed by the careful and discreet protocol, the excellent domestic organisation of the royal palace, and the moving but simple ceremony accompanying the lowering of the Sultan's flag at dusk. Similarly, any such visitor who knows the British Army will recognise the genesis of the protocol, the organisation and the ceremonial.

This 'dignified' aspect of the Sultan's government, the aspect epitomised by the public image of Sultan Qaboos himself, is the one which most visitors see. They will be aware of the care with which all arrangements are handled if they come to Oman as a guest of the Sultan, and they will be charmed by their host's presence, warmth of personality and unfailing sense of hospitality. Everyone who is present when the Sultan addresses a public gathering of his people is impressed by the force and clarity of his delivery, and by the skill with which he projects his personality. Experienced and careful expatriate observers have suggested that the Sultan has the potential to develop into a formidable public orator. Certainly, in the public performance of his duties as Head of State, the Sultan has few peers.

Useful though skill in public relations may be to the ruler of a modern absolutist state, such skill is not enough to sutain the state on its own, nor will it ensure durability of the ruler's government. Aristotle, in the fifth book of *The Politics*, sets out the problems an absolute ruler has to face if he is to survive. No matter what public relations dressing may be given to the policies of the government of Oman at various times, the prime objective of the Sultan, in political terms, can be expressed in one word: 'survival'. The most formidable potential opposition to his rule, an opposition already defeated militarily but in no sense destroyed, an opposition backed by great powers and having a revolutionary ideology, is sworn to destroy him. His style of government must reflect this threat, just as it must reflect his own dynastic inheritance and a concept of law based on a conservative religious faith.

There is nothing new or startling about this. A similar basic situation is faced by other rulers in the area to a greater or less extent, and particularly by the Shah of Iran. Each ruler faces the problem in his own way. Sultan Qaboos uses a style of government which Aristotle would have had little difficulty in recognising. Artistotle contends that a ruler must have sufficient power to rule his subjects 'whether they like it or not', though he should always endeavour to 'act or appear to act in the character of a king'. The ruler should be seen to be the guardian of his people and should spend money to improve the city. When he must use force against his people, or punish them, he should seek to make such action seem like the punishments of a father. The ruler should be seen by his people to be religious. All this Sultan Qaboos is, and he has a great power over his people, 'whether they like it or not'.

The Sultan's basic political programme must therefore become one of maintaining this power over his people to ensure his own survival, ideally with their support, but if necessary in spite of their opposition. In short, he will need to demonstrate marked qualities of statecraft. Machiavelli, who knew his Aristotle, was concerned with political reality, with the need to ensure durability of government in an imperfect world. He recognised that politics is a matter of what people are and what they do do, not a matter of what people should be and should do. It might be argued that the Sultan should introduce a liberal democratic form of government with an elected legislature and all the trimmings of modern Western states. Maybe he should, but he is unlikely to do so. Given this improbability, how does his skill as the executive head of his own government rate? Will he be effective enough and strong enough to continue to govern his people whether they like it or not? It should be recalled that Aristotle was discussing rulers whom we call 'absolute rulers' and whom he referred to as 'tyrants'.

The first area where the Sultan's effectiveness as an executive, rather than his skill in display, should be examined is that in which he prides himself most, and in which his success will be crucial if he is to maintain his power, that is, as a military commander. His leadership has been exercised on three levels, day-to-day contact with the operational commander of his armed forces, longer-term co-ordination of all military and security matters through the National Defence Council (Chapter 7), and the strategic formulation of defence policy.

Concerning day-to-day matters, and the conduct of military operations, the Sultan left all detail to his operational commander during the Dhofar war. He expected to be kept fully advised on details and on all significant developments, and expected to have his authority sought for all major actions and actions having possible diplomatic or political implications. He was always accessible to his senior officers and gave clear and unambiguous decisions quickly. As his own self-confidence developed, he began to make regular visitors to fighting units during their periods of rest and impressed his soldiers by his familiarity with their weapons and with their operational problems.

As Chairman of the National Defence Council he is effective and business-like. He reads documents carefully before meetings and is invariably well-informed on all matters likely to be discussed. He takes an interest in the minutes of meetings and likes them to record all that was said at a specific meeting, not merely to be a record of decisions taken. If a meeting goes on too long, he tires rapidly and loses interest.

He has his own ideas on the likely shape of any future military threat to Oman and recognises that internal security must always have a high priority if his system of government is to prevail. His intelligence department is competent and his paramilitary police force is extremely well-armed and well-equipped. He recognises that his British officers are the brothers of those his father trusted and whose betrayal caused his father's fall. He is determined that this will not happen to him, and his police force, which has no British-born personnel in any position of authority, could act as an alternative to the army if the Sultan himself were threatened by the sort of *coup* which unseated his father.

He is aware that, at the present time, in spite of the presence of Russian aircraft and Cuban operational pilots in the People's Democratic Republic of Yemen, a serious military threat from that quarter is unlikely. The complete absence of roads and airfields capable of sustaining a major military operation in the 5th and 6th governates of PDRY, that is, in the administrative areas of that country which border Dhofar, would make even the mounting of raids difficult. Major construction work on roads or airfields in these governates could not be undertaken without being observed, thus giving Oman time to take counter-measures, both military and diplomatic. In any case, the economy of PDRY could not sustain more than support for the sort of guerrilla war that the Sultan defeated in Dhofar.

The Sultan considers that the most likely long-term military threat to Oman from external sources would come from the north, that is, from the area of the Gulf. The cause of such a threat might come from a confrontation between Iran and Iraq, or Iran and Saudi Arabia, or Saudi Arabia and Iraq, or groupings and alliances of states bordering the Gulf for control of that strategic waterway and its oilfields. Otherwise a military threat from the north might take the form of a popular front movement from, say, Abu Dhabi. Native-born Abu Dhabians are outnumbered by about five to one by other Arabs, and the Sultan's intelligence services have warned him that there are many members of extremist Palestinian groups in Abu Dhabi. His fear is that such a group, despairing of ever defeating Israel and regaining the homeland of its parents, might be tempted to take over Abu Dhabi and all its wealth as a Palestinian home from home, and from such a base launch attacks on all the anachronistic rulers of the Gulf area, and through them, their friends and allies in the Western industrialised nations. Oman's isolated province in the Musandam peninsula, commanding the Strait of Hormuz, would be a first target in any armed struggle in the Gulf. Whoever controls the Strait of Hormuz has the power to interdict all tanker movements in and out of the Gulf.

His ocean flank, that exposed to the Gulf of Oman and the Arabian sea, is not seen as a serious concern by the Sultan. He sees no threat from either India or Pakistan. The Russian presence in the Indian Ocean is a worry, but it is thought that this is likely to be balanced always by an American presence.

His appraisal of the likely military threats to his government is respected as realistic, but the same respect does not cover the realism of his plans to meet these threats. The background to the Sultan's purchase of an integrated air defence system built around Jaguar aircraft and Rapier surface-to-air guided missiles were set out in Chapter 7. The argument against this purchase is that whatever benefit it might give the Sultan in terms of prestige and power, the cost in terms of Oman's ability to pay is too high. Money spent on arms means less money spent on civil development and on projects to ensure future income. This in turn creates a potential domestic crisis in Oman and could add fuel to internal insurrectionary pressures.

Similarly lacking in realism is the Sultan's intent, or rather, hope, to double the strength of his army within five years. Neither the population of Oman nor its financial resources are great enough to build and sutain such an army.

The Sultan's clarity of thought on military matters is often clouded by an understandable concern for his own physical security. When it was reported to him in 1974 that 12 Palestinians and 12 Dhofaris were being trained in underwater sabotage at a special school in PDRY, his immediate reaction was to enquire about underwater radar. Part of the role allocated to the integrated air defence units is defence of the Sultan's palaces in Muscat and in Salalah. This is not intended as a reflection on his own physical courage. If it is accepted that the prime objective of his government is survival, then such concern is a logical consequence.

The Sultan has had no financial training, and appears to be as uninterested in financial affairs as he is interested in military affairs. In this he is very different to his father, who was obsessed with the details of financial control. The lack of training could be overcome rapidly if the will to become involved existed. As mentioned earlier in this book, Oman's crude oil production from existing fields will begin to fall in 1977, and will be approximately half its present level within five years. Figures published by the Central Bank of Oman showed a fiscal deficit in 1975 of over 100 million Omani rials (just under $350 million). In absolute terms, this is a paltry sum compared to the British government's fiscal deficit, of course, but such a comparison, often made in Oman, is meaningless. There is just no basis of rational comparison between the economies of a highly industrialised and diversified country with a large and skilled population and a one-commodity desert country with a small, largely illiterate population.

In terms of the economy of Oman, the fact of this deficit, met by borrowing from banks and by gifts and loans from Saudi Arabia and Abu Dhabi, and the fact that the major source of government income, indeed, for practical purposes, the only source of government income, will be so reduced in so short a time, means that Oman risks having serious financial problems with a very few years unless a bold and tough government fiscal policy is implemented urgently. As a top priority, this policy could be expected to have a strong bias towards income generation and a severe brake on expenditure that will create demands on future income. Evidence of such a policy, evidence that it existed and was being firmly implemented, would go a long way to making out a case ensuring the survival of the Sultan.

Yet that part of Oman's development programme given most importance by expatriate advisors, projects which will generate income in the future, is the part where progress is almost non-existent. It would be thought that these stark facts would be uppermost in the Sultan's mind, that he would be constantly pressing his ministers for action to both ensure that there is no waste in present expenditure and that every effort is being made to give priority to income-generating projects. The reality is quite the contrary: by the lavishness of his own personal expenditure (he is an extremely generous man to those around him), he creates the impression that there is no financial problem. By his refusal to stamp out the acceptance of 'commission' on contracts, which becomes akin to corruption, he is encouraging waste, not eliminating it.

Recent reports talk of a plan to invest some $200 million in agriculture over the space of the next five years.[2] This is encouraging, and is a step in the right direction. Against this, the failure to get a natural gas project moving (Chapter 7) should be borne in mind. There is now talk in Oman of reviving the natural gas project; it is to be hoped that the Sultan will instruct his ministers to push this project vigorously. It is to be hoped also that he will be firmer than he was with a cement factory project. This was first mooted in 1972, when Oman had a need for cement, and when there were no other plans for cement production in the area. A consortium of British and Swiss interests was prepared to invest several million dollars in Oman. The Sultan signed a decree drafted by his lawyers following detailed negotiation between the government of Oman and the consortium. Omani jealousies have consistently opposed this project. A decree signed by the Sultan one week would be countermanded by a conflicting document put to him by opponents of the scheme the following week, a document which he would sign without reference to those responsible for the execution of the cement project. This state of affairs continued until early 1976 when the consortium, having shown endless patience and having tried to meet every Omani objection to the scheme, finally gave up and withdrew from Oman. By this time rival cement projects in neighbouring countries had been launched. What could have been a money-saver and a foreign-exchange-saver for the government of Oman became something of a bad joke. It could have been a successful project had the Sultan been interested enough to see that it went through. Admittedly, if he followed the details of every project, he would rapidly be overcome by an impossible load of work. All he had to do was to appoint one man he trusted as project co-ordinator, and give him clear authority. Had he done so originally, Oman would now have a functioning cement plant supplying all of its own needs and possibly having an export surplus.

It is rare for nations to become bankrupt; doubtless Oman will always find ways to make ends meet, by borrowing or by soliciting large financial gifts from Abu Dhabi and Saudi Arabia. This has been the way out of financial difficulties up to the present time. The problem, a problem which it seems that the Sultan cannot see, is not so much that money will run out, but that his government will not be able to sustain the expectations of his people aroused by the heavy expenditures of the first six years of his reign.

The common experience of most developing countries is that the spread of popular education means urban drift and rural depopulation. The government of Oman is not yet taking strong enough steps to provide jobs for its new classes of partly educated citizens. They may join the army, or work for the government, or emigrate. As they become educated, they are less willing to accept menial and labouring employment. In the past this type of employment was for slaves; now it is for unskilled and semi-skilled contract workers from India and Pakistan. The effects of falling government expenditure on development will be cushioned from Omanis as long as this expatriate contract labour force exists. Ultimately, however, the trend is likely to mean that there will be serious unemployment among Omanis who no longer have their tribal structure to offer them social security and who have left their former gardens from which they could at least subsist. These are the people who cheer Sultan Qaboos today. Energetic action by the Sultan, which has to be followed through with the attention he normally gives only to military matters, can avoid these people coming to curse their ruler and to work for his overthrow.

Oman's financial situation is difficult, but by no means impossible. For several years, advice was given to the Sultan that the financial position was basically sound, providing the strictest financial discipline was maintained. The basic situation is now very much less sound, because this discipline has not yet been imposed, though controls are much better in 1976 than they were in 1974. Only the Sultan's will can enforce this discipline throughout the government of Oman. He has consistently refused to become acquainted with financial details; until he does, or until he gives someone else complete and unfettered financial authority and responsibility, the situation will deterioriate. This is a very real and immediate challenge to the durability of his government which no well-organised and executed flattery of foreigners will be adequate to counter. No chief executive can afford to let this challenge go unheeded, and hope to survive.

As with a lack of concern about managing his financial affairs, so with an indifference to husbanding natural resources. In the last chapter an account was given of the failure of attempts to set up a National Water Resources Centre, and to carry out comprehensive national water resource surveys which would lead to a national water conservation policy. The Sultan was made aware of the issues but took no action. If Oman runs out of money, there will always be someone who will find a way to bail the Sultan out. If Oman's water supply runs out, or is permanently damaged, there is no way back, there is no 'water bank' which could make up the deficit. The desalination plant near Muscat, and doubtless other desalination plants elsewhere if the money could be found to build and run them, could supply domestic water at a price. The state of the art of desalination is still far from a stage where fresh water from sea water can be produced in such quantities and at such a price to make its use for irrigation a vaiable proposition.

Blindness to these issues on the part of the Sultan is revealing both of his poor knowledge of the history and of the economy of his own country. The art of managing a limited water supply had to be learned the hard way by his forefathers. The preservation of this art sustained generations of his antecedents. Information is available to him on the finite nature of the existing water resource. No absolute ruler can afford to be so blind on such a fundamental issue.

Then there is the question of justice. Traditionally, as has been seen, Oman's laws are contained in the Koran. Upon this base new laws have been promulgated to cover situations not envisaged by the prophet Mohammad. In general, these laws are professionally and competently drafted and are relevant to the needs of Oman. When it comes, however, to the interpretation of these laws and the administration of justice, the medieval precept evolved to explain baronial departures from the laws of the church, 'necessity has no laws', prevails. This is inevitable when the administration of justice is in the hands of the police, who are at one and the same time takers-into-custody, prosecutors and judges. Basically, an offence has been committed when the chief of police decides that it has been committed, and a man is guilty when the chief of police decides that he is guilty. This is the way the Sultan wishes justice to be administered in Oman. Given that his objective is survival, and that he exercises power over his people 'whether they like it or not', this system is understandable, even if many people deplore it. Arguments that a powerful independent judiciary, well-trained and well-paid and assured of the Sultan's unfailing protection, would be able to administer justice in a way less offensive to public opinion have, to date, not found favour with the Sultan. He has not been able to see that the establishment of such a judiciary would serve to strengthen his position *vis-à-vis* his people, not weaken it.

His attitude to a popularly elected legislature, or even an advisory body, is the same. Expatriates can be criticised, with a certain justice, for their presumption in suggesting that they may sometimes know better than Omanis what is good for Oman. By the same token, the Sultan and those ministers close to him can be criticised for maintaining that the people of Oman are not ready to share the responsibility of governing Oman, and not even ready to be consulted on how they should be governed. The Sultan is always ready to criticise his father, Sa'id bin Taimur, for his refusal to see that times had changed. Sultan Sa'id told the author of this book in Salalah on 29 April 1969, that 'our people are not ready for development.' His people disagreed and danced in the streets fifteen months later when their ruler was deposed. Sultan Qaboos told a Lebanese journalist in 1972 that he considered that the Omani people were then not yet ready for democratic systems.[3] Four years later, there is no evidence to suggest that he has changed his mind.

The Sultan, and those who share his view, maintain that the Omani people have for so long been deprived and kept ignorant of the wider world that they will not be able to make any significant contribution to either governing themselves or even being able to advise on matters affecting their welfare and the future of their children. How the Sultan himself and those few ministers close to him overcame this hurdle themselves is not explained. Indeed, it seems that the Sultan has no wish to give up any power at all. In the interview with the Lebanese journalist already quoted, he said:

> The ruler can't be told 'you rule and do not govern', for I am the one responsible for the country, and hence for its finances and defence.

Over the last six years a number of fundamental matters have been decided by the Sultan himself, generally without much consultation, and almost invariably with reliance on the advice of expatriates if advice was sought at all. In the first days of his rule, Sultan Qaboos had very little personal authority, but by the time had had granted the interview to the Lebanese journalist quoted above, he was undisputed master in his own house. At any time he could have, had he wished, invited, say, 25 (the number does not matter – what would be important is that there be a small but representative group) senior and respected Omanis to attend him in his palace in Salalah or in Muscat for the purpose of seeking their views on matters of vital importance to the community. The group would have to be carefully chosen – it would have to preserve a balance between the Hinawi and Ghafiri factions of the tribes of Oman, it would have to include representatives of the merchant communities in Muscat and Mattrah, with their minority racial groups (Khoja and Beluch), it would have to include some

Dhofaris, but should not have included any member of the Sultan's own family. The selection of such a group would not have been a simple matter, a subtle balance would have had to have been preserved between members nominated by the Sultan and members representing a particular tribal group or minority interest. However, given the will to do so, it would certainly have been possible to call together such a group. There is ample precedent in Islam for such a consultative council (*majilis ash-Shura*).[4] Rules of procedure would not have been difficult, because of the historical precedents; the council's advice would have been sought and listened to, matters of national importance would be debated, the Sultan would reserve the right to make a decision contrary to the opinion of a majority of the members of the council, if he deemed it in the national interest to do so. The members of the council would be completely familiar with the system, because it would be simply their own tribal councils but on a larger scale. Many would be familiar with the councils of the individual rulers of the constituent states of the United Arab Emirates, Oman's near neighbours.

Had the Sultan called together such a consultative council, had he met the council, flanked by his ministers, and in the days when there was a Prime Minister, with the Prime Minister on his right hand, had he put to them the matter of great national importance on which he and his ministers sought the advice of their fellow citizens before making a decision, had foreign advisers been invited to put their advice to the council and then withdraw whilst the matter was debated, it is possible that Oman would have developed a significantly broader-based government which might have ensured the future prosperity and stability of the country to a far higher degree than at present seems possible. Opponents and cynics could argue that such a council would never open its collective mouth, or, if it did so, it would be only to tell the Sultan what it, the council, believed he wanted to hear. This may well have happened at the first few meetings, but gradually, as members of the council became better-informed on matters of national importance, as the groups and interests they represented felt the effect of government decisions, it is difficult to believe that its members would have remained a mere collection of sycophants.

Naturally, there can be no guarantee that such an advisory council would have ever asked sufficient searching questions ever to cause the Sultan to think again, but at least the people of Oman would have had an opportunity to hear about national policies at first hand and to make its collective view known to the Sultan and his ministers. The Sultan does not want such an advisory council because he is afraid that it would weaken his authority. Again, given his basic motivation, this is understandable, though it may be far from wise.[5]

Political analysis is concerned with prevailing states of affairs and policies, not with Utopias and ideals. The Sultan of Oman is very clear in his own mind as to what his fundamental objectives are. In this, he is no different to his father, or to other absolute rulers. He has sufficient power to sustain his position at the present time. This power, coupled with a charismatic public presence, can avoid him becoming the unpopular, and ultimately unsuccessful, ruler that his father was. Success for Sultan Qaboos, the durability of his government and hence his personal survival, depends on him solving the twin problems of finances and managing Oman's natural resources. With assured revenue he can give the great majority of his people sufficient material benefits to make them comparatively unconcerned about injustices and the narrow base of the Sultan's government. In any case, a safety-valve exists in that Omanis can always leave the country and find well-paid employment in the United Arab Emirates. With conservation of natural resources, particularly of water, Sultan Qaboos will ensure that life is possible for his people. Given a continuance of present policies, however, there would seem to be little hope that the Sultan of Oman can solve these two problems.

Notes

1. Quoted in *Al-Watan* newspaper, Muscat, 6 April 1972.
2. 'The Omani Economy – March into Deficit', *Financial Times,* London, 13 May 1976.
3. *Al-Watan,* Muscat, 6 April 1972.
4. See the Koran, XLII, 36, '. . .their affairs are subject to consultation among themselves.' Quoted in Majid Khadduri, *Political trends in the Arab world,* Baltimore, 1970.
5. A recent book by Arab authors Riad El-Rayyes and Dunia Nahas, *Guerrillas for Palestine,* London, 1976, stated: 'The stark truth is that most Arab régimes are as frightened of their own people in arms as they are of the Israelis'. This certainly applies to Sultan Qaboos.

10 OMAN AND ITS NEIGHBOURS

'. . . the one who adapts his policy to the times prospers, and likewise . . . the one whose policy clashes with the demands of the time does not.'

If Oman were an island, set in some far-off ocean, as remote from the politics of the modern world as its scattered villages were to a world that did not need oil, the effectiveness and durability of its government would concern no one but its own citizens. But Oman's neighbours and near neighbours, Iran, Iraq, Kuwait, Saudi Arabia, Qatar and the United Arab Emirates collectively supplied about 43 per cent of the non-Communist world's demand for oil in 1975. The picture can be seen more clearly from Table 10.1.

Table 10.1: World Oil Demand and Gulf Production, 1975 (million barrels per day)

Demand in 1975 (excludes Communist countries)	
United States	15.3
Western Europe	12.4
Japan	4.5
Other non-Communist countries	11.3
Total non-Communist world demand	43.5
Gulf Production in 1975	
Saudi Arabia	7.1
Iran	5.4
Iraq	2.2
Kuwait	2.1
United Arab Emirates	1.7
Qatar	0.4
Total Gulf production	18.9

Sources: Petroleum Economist, London, July 1976 for world demand; *The Economist,* London, 31 July 1976 for Gulf production.

Oman's rate of production in 1975 was about 360,000 barrels per day.

Almost all the oil produced in the Gulf is exported in tankers which have to traverse the Strait of Hormuz and the Gulf of Oman. Some of the oil produced is refined locally in Iran, in Bahrain and in Saudi Arabia, but most is exported as crude oil. The Trans Arabian Pipeline from Saudi Arabia to the Mediterranean and the pipeline from Kirkuk in Iraq to the same sea are now little used, and in any case their combined capacity could take only a fraction of Gulf production. Thus any government in Oman whose policies were aimed at disruption of the Western industrialised nations and which was either strong enough itself, or had strong allies, to sustain its action, could, by preventing tanker movements through the Strait of Hormuz, create a major international crisis.

This is one of the main reasons why the British government has been ready to give military support to Sultan Qaboos. It is the principle reason why the Shah of Iran, who controls the northern shore of the Strait of Hormuz, was ready to give decisive military assistance to the Sultan in the struggle in Dhofar against the People's Front for the Liberation of Oman. It is also the principle reason why Saudi Arabia in particular, Abu Dhabi, and to a small extent, Qatar, have been ready to offer financial support to Oman.

From an opposing point of view, the vulnerability of this crude oil artery must be part of the thinking of the Iraqi government and its Russian allies when they support the Popular Front for the liberation of Oman. Similarly, it is known that the extremist Palestinian groups, and particularly Dr George Habash's Popular Front for the Liberation of Palestine include the 'overthrow of the imperialist puppet régime in Oman' in their programmes. No matter what benefit, or what curse, a government calling itself the 'People's Democratic Republic of Oman' would bring to the Omani people, such a government could only mean trouble to the Western industrialised world and to most of the governments of the Gulf.

The Shah's 'White Revolution', whereby he is trying to make Iran a leading industrial power within a very few years, depends upon maximising oil production. With a population of some 33 million people and a strong tradition of craftsmanship among its people, Iran is the strongest military power bordering the Gulf littoral. The Shah is an absolute monarch and his system of government brooks no opposition. Iran has a popularly elected parliament, but only one legal political party, the Rastakhiz (Resurgence) party. It also has a highly efficient and ruthless secret police, Savak.

Economically, the Shah's policy has been to broaden the base of the

Iranian economy, using his oil revenues to develop his country and to husband his other natural resources so that when oil ceases to be important, Iran will have a viable mixed economy. This policy calls for strengthening traditional agriculture, and also for developing a heavy industrial base to the economy with steel, petro-chemicals and manufacturing sectors. The constraints to development have been the shortage of professional managers and supervisors and an overloaded transport sector, especially ports. Shipping and cargo congestion in Iran's ports is particularly bad. Time will remove both constraints and although it may not become the world's fifth industrial power by the 1990s, as the Shah hopes, Iran has all the elements to make it a viable and stable diversified economy.

At this stage, it will need export markets, and the obvious direction to look for such markets is among its neighbours bordering the Gulf. This long-term need is understood, and is probably one of the reasons why current Iranian foreign policy is concerned about improving relations with its Arab neighbours and near neighbours. This is a delicate area of diplomacy, seemingly at odds with Iran's massive military build-up and thinly disguised plans for hegemony in the area.

The Shah's government is effective. The ultimate test of durability of what he has achieved in Iran will come after his death. He was born in 1919 and is a vigorous and energetic man. As long as the Shah rules, the Sultan of Oman is likely to have a firm ally whose military assistance can be counted upon. Attempts by the government of Oman to get cash grants from Iran have not been successful and demands by Iran itself on its future oil revenues are such that it seems unlikely that such grants would ever be forthcoming.

Iran may be able to claim, with justice, that it is the leading military power in the Gulf area. The financial giant, both now and for at least until the end of this century, in the area is Saudi Arabia. With a population estimated to be rather more than six million and a revenue from oil in 1975 of $26.8 billion, Saudi Arabia has become the paymaster of the Arab world. Egypt, Syria and Jordan all look to Saudi Arabia for significant capital aid. This financial strength gives a commensurate political strength and influence. No conservative Arab state questions the leading role of Saudi Arabia, and even nations like Syria, with revolutionary political philosophies guiding its rulers, heed Saudi counsels because they cannot manage without Saudi money, especially for their arms purchases.

An analysis of the political structure of the Saudi state merits a book of its own. The Kingdom of Saudi Arabia, as the country has been known since 1932, was welded together by Ibn Sa'ud in the 1920s from a union of the tribes of the Nejd, the eastern part of the country adjoining the Gulf, and the Hejaz, adjoining the Red Sea. The country, in its strict adherence to the religious law of Islam, is even more conservative than Oman. Its government, by an oligarchical group drawn from a large ruling family, is as absolute as that of the Sultan, but with two important exceptions, the fact of a formal constitution and the fact of a high degree of professional competence among the members of the governing oligarchy.

The constitution, simple and conservative though it be, does provide for the setting up of consultative advisory councils. The membership of these councils is a nominated one, there being no provision for popular elections. Nominations for membership have either to be made by or approved by the king. Councils exist at national, provincial, tribal and village levels.

The ruling oligarchy is competent and efficient. No better example of this can be given than by citing the smooth enthronement of King Khalid and the consequent necessary reshaping of the government following the assassination of King Faisal in March 1975. The government is aware of its responsibilities for husbanding the resources of the nation.

As the largest single producer among the OPEC nations, and having by far the largest reserves of crude oil of any nation in the world (including the Soviet Union), Saudi Arabia has played a significant and responsible role in the politics of the international oil business. Increasingly the nation's productive capacity and reserves make it a leader among the OPEC nations, a role which other members, for example Iran and Iraq, have accepted with some reluctance.

The responsibility and consideration for the future shown with oil is repeated with the nation's water resources. In a similar basic situation to Oman, with a very low rainfall and modest resources of ground water in natural reservoirs, the government of Saudi Arabia has built up a highly competent team of Saudis and expatriates charged with measuring this resource, checking its rate of consumption and recharge, and monitoring reservoir performance.

Saudi Arabia's political development is in many ways unique. In previous centuries and, indeed, still in this century, absolutist governments maintained their position either by a policy of pure repression or a more subtle policy of exercising power over their subjects, 'whether they like it or not'. Success of this second policy required the sort of statecraft and stark awareness of the law of necessity which Machiavelli understood so well. The government of Saudi Arabia has a formidable understanding of the rules of statecraft. It also has, as no other absolutist government has ever had, the power to buy the allegiance of its citizens. It has the power to provide its citizens with a particularly high standard of living without the bane of almost all other governments, the need to tax them.

Future developments in Saudi Arabia are likely to be full of interest for political analysts. A society which has always known great poverty, its whole-hearted embracing of a particularly conservative form of Islam, a religion favouring a simple and spartan life, has given it great stability in the past. Its enormous new-found wealth has not been allowed to erode the basic religious laws. The late King Faisal led a most simple and ascetic life, and set an example to his people.

Now, with the investment of oil revenues partly in the development of the country, and with universal education available to all, boys and girls, a new class of citizen is developing. In most societies, modern education with its emphasis on science and travel have tended to erode traditional religious beliefs. Whether this will happen in Saudi Arabia, and whether today's students will accept as enough for their moral satisfaction the material benefits which their society offers them ten years from now is today an unanswerable question.

Saudi Arabia has been interested in Oman since Sultan Qaboos paid his first visit to the Kingdom in 1971. At this time, the Imam of Oman met the Sultan, and subsequently ceased to be any political threat to the latter's government. The government of Saudi Arabia has shown great understanding of the Sultan's position and has helped him diplomatically and financially, as well as offering help with specific development projects. A project being discussed currently (1976) is for an oil pipeline from a new oilfield being developed by the Saudis near the point where the frontiers of Oman, Saudi Arabia and the United Arab Emirates meet. This pipeline would traverse Oman and would make the Saudis less vulnerable to any irresponsible or hostile closing of the Strait of Hormuz.

The government of Saudi Arabia is effective in almost everything it touches, even if it is sometimes slow and bureaucratic. Oil production from Saudi fields can continue at least at present levels well beyond the end of the century. There would seem to be no reason why the government should not be as durable as it is effective. Given this, Saudi Arabia is likely to be the best friend Sultan Qaboos can have. His form of government is clearly understood in Saudi Arabia, his Sultanate occupies territory over which the Saudis have had ambitions in the past, and which they would be extremely unhappy to see in hostile hands at the present time. Saudi financial support to Oman has, so far, been without significant strings or conditions, though vague references have been made to the possible granting of territory should a pipeline bypassing the Strait of Hormuz ever be built. Territorial concessions, or a closer Saudi overseeing of the actions of the government of Oman might well be a condition for further significant financial assistance.

Oman's third northern neighbour, and closest neighbour in terms of day-to-day contacts, is the United Arab Emirates. A federation of the former Trucial States, the United Arab Emirates was formed on 2 December 1971 by the states of Abu Dhabi, Dubai, Sharjah, 'Ajman, Umm al Qaiwan and Fujairah. Ras al Khaimah joined the federation in February 1972. The territory of the Emirates runs from the southern border of Oman's Musandam province for some 600 km inside the Gulf. The Emirates also has some 80 km of coastline bordering the Gulf of Oman, thus dividing Oman from the Musandam peninsula.

The Emirates have developed very quickly in the five years of their federal existence. Population in 1976 is probably approaching 600,000, of whom about one-fifth would be native-born and the balance immigrants, generally from other Arab countries, especially Palestinians and Lebanese. The native born people of the Emirates were traders, fishermen, pearlers and nomads. In general they did not have the traditions of permanent settlement as did the tribes of Oman, an important difference between the peoples of the Emirates and their Omani neighbours. Oil revenues in 1975 (earned mostly by Abu Dhabi with Dubai making a comparatively small contribution) were $6.4 billion. Apart from oil, the Emirates have a thriving commerce based on Dubai, which has become in many ways the market of the lower Gulf. Although Dubai's oil production is similar to that of Oman, before oil exports began, Dubai, encouraged by its ruler, Sheikh Rashid bin Sa'id al Maktoum, had become a viable economic entity in its own right, basing its wealth on the activity which its citizens understood best, trade.

The United Arab Emirates has a formal constitution, agreed by the rulers of the members' states, and a federal government as well as the individual governments of the constituent states. The federal president is Sheikh Zayed bin Sultan al Nahayan, the ruler of Abu Dhabi. The constitution provides for a supreme council of the federation, consisting of the seven rulers of the states, and a national assembly of nominated members. This assembly has advisory powers only. It debates the annual budget of the Emirates, for example, and does not hesitate to criticise the government for delays in presenting the budget nor to ask for details of allocations and expenditure. The assembly's power is limited, but it does exist and is a vehicle for permitting the voice of the people to be heard. Also, each member state of the federation continues with the traditional ruler's council (*majlis*), an informal gathering which all male citizens of the state may attend if they wish to put petitions and requests to the ruler and request his ajudication in disputes.

The commercial spirit which reigns over the Emirates, and particularly over Dubai, is in contrast to the asceticism of Saudi Arabia. Thus the power of the traditional religion of the people as an element in political stability, of great importance in Saudi Arabia, is less important in the Emirates. Material values tend to have become more important than spiritual ones, and the political climate is such that every citizen is free to, indeed is encouraged to, make as much money as he can. Many have made fortunes and the curse of poverty has been almost completely removed from the Emirates.

An element of potential instability is the fact that native born citizens of the Emirates are in a minority, especially in the cities of Abu Dhabi and Dubai. Palestinian, Lebanese and some Egyptian families living permanently in the Emirates, their children born and educated there, can be expected to ask for a greater say in government than they have at the moment. This demand will be muted for as long as material benefits are available. More serious than this, however, is the threat presented by members of some of the more extreme Palestinian groups, whose dogmatic and ideological policies are at odds with the anachronistic traditional style of government of the rulers of the various states. These people cannot be bought off by material benefits and in the future may present a serious threat to the established order in the Emirates, a threat which could spread to Oman.

A more fundamental and more immediate threat to the stability of the United Arab Emirates lies in the Federal Constitution itself. The first constitution was termed an interim one, to be replaced by a permanent constitution within five years. This period of five years expires at the end of 1976. Abu Dhabi, which contributes more than 90 per cent of the federal budget, becomes more and more concerned about the political will of the other six members to stay together in a federal form. A federation of autonomous states, as the German Federal Republic, or Switzerland, or the United States, exists only when there is sufficient political will in the constituent states to give up no small amount of sovereignty. This the rulers of the individual states of the United Arab Emirates are not prepared to do, although they expect Abu Dhabi to pay for their own civil development programmes. It seems most unlikely that the Emirates can survive in their present form.

An as yet (mid-1976) unresolved problem which could spell political isolation for the Sultan and friction with the neighbours on whose support he depends is the question of his borders with Saudi Arabia and Abu Dhabi. In 1974 much publicity was given to the apparent final resolution of the border dispute between Abu Dhabi and Saudi Arabia which dated from the Buraimi confrontation (Chapter 3). The Sultan was represented at the discussions which preceded the agreement by his Saudi Adviser who, in the Sultan's name, accepted the proposed new boundaries on behalf of Oman. What was not appreciated at the time was that the map which formed the basis of the agreement was inaccurate, and that the effect of the agreement was to give away much Omani territory. The agreement has never been ratified, but nor has any amending agreement been negotiated. An uneasy and embarrassed silence is maintained by all parties on a problem which will not go away.

A suggestion often made in Oman, and in the Emirates, is that Oman and the Emirates should seek to find a formula to permit a political union of the two countries. This suggestion seems to be eminently sensible. Differences between the two peoples are minor when compared to their common characteristics. Many Omanis work in the Emirates, and the armed forces of the Emirates is recruited to a very large extent from Omanis. Oman has a modest oil revenue and dwindling reserves, and is a country with a hinterland. The Emirates have oil production more than four times greater than that of Oman, reserves of crude oil which would permit this production to be increased should world demand increase, and consists of a series of city states with no significant hinterland. In economic terms, a union of Oman and the Emriates would permit the creation of a balanced economy and could ensure, given wise policies and continuing firmness in their implementation, that when oil is exhausted, or ceases to be economically important, an economic structure will be left which will be viable.

There is already a close link between the two countries in economic matters. Dubai's general efficiency as a market and as a port, plus the existence of modern highways linking Oman and Dubai, has meant that much of Oman's imports come through Dubai. Sheikh Zayed of Abu Dhabi has paid for the roads linking Buraimi to Sohar through the *wadi* al-Jizzi, and from Buraimi to 'Ibri in northern Oman. People in the north-western corner of Oman, from al-Khaburah through to 'Ibri, tend to look to the Emirates for their commercial and economic needs rather than to Muscat and the currency of the Emirates circulates unofficially in this part of Oman. It is much easier for an Omani living in 'Ibri to go to Abu Dhabi than it is for him to go to Muscat.

A pipeline through Oman to the existing oil port at Mina al Fahal near Muscat would permit Abu Dhabi oil to be exported without going through the Strait of Hormuz. Control of this strategic waterway will always be important, but alternatives to it are clearly worth looking for. A unified strategy for possible petro-chemical plants, for the exploitation of natural gas resources, and for oil refineries should increase the viability of such projects, and hence bring greater economic benefits to the society.

The political barriers to a union between Oman and the Emirates are formidable. It seems extremely unlikely that Sultan Qaboos commands sufficient respect outside Oman to permit him to be an acceptable ruler over the politically much freer states of the Emirates. Equally no ruling family in the Emirates would have sufficient standing to be acceptable to the tribes of Oman. The only possible solution, one which may mean that a political union is several years into the future, is a republican one. An 'Arab Republic of Oman', stretching from southern Oman to Abu Dhabi, would have an ethnic, geographic and economic logic which ought to be able to engender a common political will in time. This political will can only be found when the anachronistic sheikhly structures and the system of dynastic succession has given way to representative forms of government. Dhofar is unlikely to have a place in such a republic, because its people are not Arab. Their comparatively small numbers might make assimilation into an Arab state a simple matter, but it cannot be taken for granted that this would be so. Dhofar may well remain a political problem in the area, in spite of Sultan Qaboos' military success. The problem of Dhofar aside, however, the 'demands of the time' must eventually lead towards a political union of Oman and the states forming the United Arab Emirates.

A political union of Oman and the Emirates would be carefully watched by Iran and by Saudi Arabia, and a republican form of government even more carefully watched. Skilful diplomacy would be required to ensure that the friendship of these allies was not lost. The long-term political organisation of the region is almost certain to be as a republic; an 'Arab Republic of Oman' is likely to be much more acceptable both to the people of Oman and the Emirates and to the world as a whole than a 'Peoples' Republic of Oman'.

BIBLIOGRAPHY

In addition to the works mentioned in the notes at the end of each chapter, the following books have been used extensively:—

Aitchison, C.V. (ed.), *Government of India Foreign Department – Collection of Treaties Relating to India and Neighbouring Countries,* Volume XII, 5th edition, Calcutta, 1932.

Busch, B.C., *Great Britain and the Persian Gulf,* University of California, 1967.

Holden, D., *Farewell to Arabia,* London, 1966.

Hopwood, D. (ed.), *The Arabian Peninsula: Society and Politics,* London, 1972.

Kelly, J.B., *Eastern Arabian Frontiers,* London, 1964.

Landen, R.G., *Oman since 1856,* Princeton, 1967.

Lorimer, J.C., *Gazeteer of the Persian Gulf, Oman and Central Arabia,* Calcutta, 1908/1915, republished London, 1970.

Miles, S.B., *The Countries and Tribes of the Persian Gulf,* London, 1919.

Thesiger, W., *Arabian Sands,* London, 1960.

APPENDIX 1: The word of Sultan Sa'id bin Taimur, Sultan of Muscat and Oman, about the history of the financial position of the Sultanate in the past and the hopes for the future, after the export of oil

We consider the first period to run from pre-1914 to 1920. The Government in the era of our grandfather, Sultan Faisal bin Turki, and in the era before him had only a simple way of despatching all the affairs of the country; no budget, no planning and no organisation. Improvisation was the basis of all that was done and said. This was the situation prevailing at that time in most Arab countries.

In 1913 (1331) our beloved father, Sultan Taimur bin Faisal, succeeded to the throne on the death of Sultan Faisal bin Turki. He inherited a legacy of many debts and a Government burdened with loans due to be repaid to the merchants of the country. This situation continued and the debts increased until 1920, when, realising it was not easy to rule the country with its finances in such a state of weakness and disorganisation, he determined to improve the State finances by introducing modern methods. Finally it was clear that his Government could make little progress until it was freed of its burden of debts which, as we have said, were to a number of merchants in the country. He realised that it would be best to negotiate one major loan which would enable him to liquidate the old debts and still leave a surplus which could be used to achieve the desired reforms. The only body able to meet his request was the Government of British India, which agreed to lend him the money necessary to free himself from his debts on the understanding that it would be repaid in 10 years. He decided at the same time to ask the Egyptian Government for officials to reorganise the Customs. The Egyptian Government agreed and sent him three Customs experts who set about their work with a will. He also engaged an English official, Mr. D.V. McCullum, to supervise the reorganisation of the Finance Department. Thereafter the finances of the Government slowly recovered; there were no deficits in the annual budgets and the loan instalments were paid off regularly. The English official engaged in 1920 stayed for only six months, however, and, in the absence of a successor, Sultan Taimur appointed Mohammed bin Ahmed al Ghashan, then Wali of Matrah, as his Minister responsible for financial affairs. This situation prevailed until the end of 1924, when there was a deficit due to the negligence of the responsible officer and the maladministration of the Treasury Officer, as a result of which the State finances were so shaken as to make it impossible to continue to repay the instalments of the loan at the proper time.

The second period begins in 1925 when, in view of the poor state of Government finances, Sultan Taimur bin Faisal decided to engage a new official to reorganise them. He selected an Englishman, Mr. Bertram Thomas, whom he appointed as Finance Minister, on a five-year contract, with a view to his improving the financial position of the Government. (Mr. Thomas was the first Westerner to cross the Empty Quarter, doing so from Dhofar to Qatar in 54 days.) At the outset he exerted considerable efforts which produced a measure of improvement in financial affairs but unfortunately this improvement was not maintained for more than three years, after which the financial situation again deteriorated and the Government ceased to repay the instalments of the loan. This was due to the maladministration of the official referred to in the previous period for he allowed Government spending to exceed the approved Budget. This led to a deficit and disorder in State finances. The balance of payments was upset and unpaid instalments of the loan, and other expenditure, piled up, constituting a new debt, additional to the balance of the previous one.

In 1930 an economic slump struck the world. This affected the trade balance, resulting in a sharp fall in Customs revenues, which were virtually the Government's only source of revenue. While great hopes were pinned on Mr. Thomas to repair what others had destroyed, he in fact brought the finances to ruin and left them in an even sorrier state.

Thereafter Sultan Taimur bin Faisal considered engaging a financial expert to put right what was wrong. In 1931 he engaged as his Financial Adviser, Mr. Hedgecock, an Englishman and a senior official of the Iraqi Finance Ministry, who immediately set to work with great vigour and determination to rescue the finances from the state they were in as a result of Bertram Thomas' maladministration. He reduced salaries and cut expenditure and was eventually able to put the financial records in order and to organise proper Budgets. We reveal no secrets if we say that at that time the Government's Budget was no more than Rps.700,000 (£50,000) from which the Sultanate had to pay the cost of the Government machine, repay the balance of the loan and meet various other items of expenditure, including the customary gifts and presents to the tribal Sheikhs and delegations, since, outwardly, the Government appeared very rich. Mr. Hedgecock deserves admiration and respect for what he did to reorganise the finances of the Sultanate. Unfortunately however he did not stay long, resigning for private reasons after 8 months.

At that time we were Prime Minister with oversight of the Sultanate's financial affairs. After the resignation of Mr. Hedgecock it was decided to appoint Mr. R.J. Alban, an Englishman, as Financial Adviser. And then, on 2 Shawal 1350 (11 February 1932), we succeeded to power upon the abdication, for reasons of health, of our beloved father, Sultan Taimur bin Faisal.

We gave our special attention to finance but found that because of the effects of economic pressure on world trade we were compelled to reduce expenditure in various sectors, our first economy being to halve the Sultan's Privy Purse. The reader may be surprised to learn that when we took over the reins of power the Sultanate's Treasury was completely empty. No doubt many of our contemporaries will recall what the financial situation was like in those days.

However, thanks to painstaking efforts and close supervision of finances signs of improvement became visible, and, as 1933 neared its end, debts had been liquidated and the sums due to the merchants paid off. At the end of 1933 the Financial Adviser resigned whereupon we assumed complete personal control of the Sultanate's finances and the preparation of its annual Budgets. The improvement in Customs revenues continued (the Sultanate having no other income to speak of) enabling us to raise officials' salaries and to give attention to the welfare of the Sultanate. The financial position has continued to improve until the present day.

The third period runs from 1939, with the outbreak of the Second World War, until 1945. During this period prices rose and consequently so too did Customs revenues. We further increased officials' salaries and undertook much needed reforms in various parts of the Sultanate. From 1933 to this day there has been no financial deficit in the Government's Budget and the Government has been able to build up reasonable financial reserves against emergencies, as well as meeting necessary expenditure in various fields, especially that of defence, which swallowed up about half the Budget. We were anxious to introduce various urgently needed reforms for the welfare of the country, but found that there was not enough leeway either in the Budget or in the reserves to support any sort of planning, for we did not want to overburden the Sultanate's finances and weigh them down with new debts, after having paid off all the old ones. Doubtless it would have been easy to obtain money in various ways, but this could only have been by a loan with interest at a set percentage rate. This amounts to usury, with which I completely disagree, and the religious prohibition of which is not unknown.

By now the financial position of the Sultanate will have been made plain to you by the facts which we have set out for you, and which account for the inability of Government of the time to bring the country up to date. We were fully aware of the many reforms which the country needed, but whilst the eyesight was long, the arm at that time was short. Despite all this, however, we were never at a loss to undertake any work which brought general benefit to the country whenever we found a way to do so. For example, when the opportunity occurred in 1940, during the war, we built the Saidiya School in Muscat, the first Government building constructed after getting over the difficult period. Similarly we made a number of improvements to Government centres and forts in various Wilayets.

In 1958 our friends, the British Government, offered us financial assistance to strengthen the Sultanate's Army; to introduce improvements in education; to set up Health Centres in some of the Wilayets along the coast and in the interior; to build Experimental Farms to raise the standard of farming in the country; to construct roads and other improvements. We accepted this with deep gratitude. There was a time limit to it in that it was to continue only until the finances of the Sultanate improved. It continued until the end of March last year, ie, four months before oil exports began at the end of July 1967. During this interim period we depended upon such financial reserves as we had. Had it not been for our economy and for our reserves, we would not have been able to bear the burden of expenditure during these months. In particular the allocation to the Sultanate Army took up a large part of our resources until the Government obtained its share of oil revenues.

Now the oil flows from the fields at Fahud and Natih through the pipes to the tanks at Mina al Fahl in Saih al Maleh (which ought now to be called Saih al Huluw). Soon the product of another field at Jibal near Fahud will flow to join the output of the first two fields supplying the tanks at Saih al Huluw whence the oil is pumped out to the tankers anchored at Mina al Fahl to be carried away. Thus our dear country becomes among the exporters of oil, and we can insert a new subhead in our Budget 'Oil Revenues'. Yes only now that we know that revenue from oil will be coming in steadily can we consider and plan and estimate how to put into effect the various projects which the country needs. We hope these revenues will continue to increase each year.

We ought at this stage to mention the relationship between the Sultanate and the oil company. The first agreement was concluded in the middle of 1937. The Company paid a rent for the right to search for oil in Sultanate territory and this helped to strengthen the Budget somewhat. In 1964, when oil was discovered in commercial quantities in the Sultanate, the present Company suggested a revision of the agreement signed between the Sultanate and the previous oil company, the new agreement to correspond with similar agreements signed recently between various oil companies and the Governments of the oil exporting countries of the Middle East. The Sultanate agreed and asked the Company to put forward a suggested revision for the Government to study.

In March 1967, after talks between the Sultanate and the Company, Agreements were concluded giving the Government 50% of the oil profits, and the right to 12½% of all oil exported. This accorded with the decision of OPEC, an organisation formed of some of the Middle East oil exporting countries. The Agreement included many other matters bringing advantage and general benefit to the country.

All of this took place during the period in which Mr. F. Hughes was the Company's General Manager and Representative. He was appointed by the Company to negotiate the detailed revision of the Agreement and we found a complete understanding of the situation on his part. Agreement on terms was reached with great ease, thanks to the efforts displayed by him so that the Agreement should benefit both sides.

God willing, 1968 will be the start of a new era for our country which will see the beginning of various plans which will be executed under the supervision of qualified technicians and experts. Firstly we shall begin building offices for various Government Departments; then houses for officials who will come from abroad; then step by step will come various projects such as hospitals, schools, roads, communications, and other necessary works including the development of fisheries, animals and agricultural resources etc. until modern projects spread over the whole of the Sultanate, to each area according to its needs. So long as oil flows the Government will match its flow with continuing development for the welfare of the country. Naturally projects involve much effort and hard work. The progress we see in other countries was not the work of a day, but the result of efforts over long years. It takes time for the results of projects for improvement to be seen and there will be an unavoidable gap between the receipt of oil revenues and the appearance of benefits for the populace. We are straining every nerve to improve the lot of the country both in general and in particular.

An initial task is to increase the salaries of Government officials which we consider need to be increased and to establish a cadre to regularise promotion. We shall reinforce the Government machine by adding to it a number of experts and technicians. This will ensure that the Government has a modern administrative machine. The present situation requires changes in the existing Government set-up.

There are urgent schemes to which we consider we must give priority.

1. Water – work on this project is being pressed ahead, and we hope that a water pipeline to Muscat and Matrah will be laid within 21 months of the date of contract, making pure water available to all.
2. Electricity – all the preliminary stages have been completed and work is going ahead briskly. It is hoped that the Company to which the project has been entrusted will supply electricity to consumers in Muscat and Matrah next summer.
3. Matrah Port – because of Matrah's outstanding natural location, secure commercial position and reliable communications with the various parts of the Sultanate, which make it the commercial capital of the country, we consider that we should make a start on the construction of port facilities in the near future, to which the general Customs Department will be transferred, and where steamers, sailing craft and motor boats may moor to load and discharge. Sufficient warehouses will be provided for the storage and protection of incoming and outgoing goods.
4. Saidi currency – another project which will be given priority and special study is that of currency. The Saidi currency will be based on the Saidi Riyal, sub-divided into ½ Riyal and ¼ Riyal. Baizas will be minted to meet the requirements of the people, denominations being of 100, 25, 20, 10, 5 and 1 Baiza. The necessary announcement about this will be made at the appropriate time.

When we talk about planning we must not forget the oil-bearing area and the Duru tribe who live there. They must be given special attention and must get the projects they need and which suit them.

Other plans will follow later, in order of importance. We must not forget that the area of the Sultanate is more than 100,000 square miles, that its coastline is no less than 1,000 miles long and that its population is estimated at more than half a million.

We shall appoint a body, known as the Development Board, to execute such plans as we decide upon. This body will be responsible for drawing up a Budget for each project and for keeping in touch with experts, technicians and others whom it is necessary to consult in connection with any desired project.

We shall also appoint a special Board for the water and electricity schemes. It will oversee the progress of work and will ensure that the schemes conform with the regulations fixed by the Government to safeguard the needs of the people.

We are now passing through a preliminary planning stage for the projects which enjoy priority because they are for the benefit of all. We are looking forward to a bright future by which we guarantee raising the standard of living of the inhabitants of the Sultanate and increasing the income of the individual. We shall develop the country so as to keep pace with the cavalcade of present day civilisation. We shall ensure every benefit and advantage for the populace and we shall pursue those developments which bring us that which is best and preferable and is consonant with our people's heritage and ancient history. However much we progress and move forward we must keep before our eyes our true religion on which we place our reliance and traditions which are our heritage. There are prohibitions of our religion which are inviolable for ever and there are customs which can be altered without infringing the basic traditions of the country which are among the glories of our worthy ancestors, which are a source of pride and which protect our very existence. The Almighty said in his Book 'Say "work" and God will see your work'.

We ask the Almighty whose works are great to inspire us to do that which is right, to crown our efforts with success, bring us success in our enterprises and grant us victory in our desires. We are humble towards him whose power is sublime and brings us success in what is for the good of our Omani people and our country.

Published: January 1968. Copy in author's archives.

APPENDIX 2: PFLO Policy Intentions for Oman – National Act Programme

The Voice of the Oman Revolution (ADEN) broadcast the PFLO National Act Programme for OMAN between 21 October and 1 December 1974. The following is a summary of the aims of the National Act:

Preamble The Omani people are struggling for self-determination and real democracy, not the false democracy of Qaboos and the British. This is a dictatorship which oppresses and terrorises the majority of the Omani people. Our Omani people will continue to struggle in all ways to achieve the following aims:

First The liberation of OMAN from occupation and imperialism. The following should be our aim:

(a) Cancel all agreements with British and other Imperialist countries;
(b) Eliminate all foreign bases from Oman and the occupied islands;
(c) Deport all foreign troops, advisors and officers.

Second Establish a national democratic rule by the following methods:

(a) Abolish tribal and hereditary rule;
(b) Establish a popular democratic republic;
(c) Establish a people's electoral legislature and a progressive constitution.

Third To provide political and democratic freedom by:

(a) Release of all political prisoners, abolition of the British, American, Jordanian and Iranian intelligence machines, and to provide security and stability for the people;
(b) Abolition of the imposed martial laws and the wall system in towns. Inhabitants should be allowed to travel freely in Oman;
(c) Allowing those people deported for political reasons to return;
(d) Freedom of the press and free expression of opinion.

Fourth The economic policy should be reformed as follows:

(a) All oil companies should be nationalised so that they are controlled by the people;
(b) A strong national industry should be established to exploit the physical wealth for the people of the country;
(c) The establishment of a government bank, nationalisation of the foreign banks which at present control the national economy, and

the domination of the foreign insurance companies;

(d) The expansion of relations between Oman and those countries which respect its independence and the people's control;

(e) The development of fishing and agricultural industries.

Fifth An agricultural policy should be established which would free the farmers from the present feudal system, raise their standard of living and serve the national economy:

(a) Establish an agricultural reform law to encourage the farmers to cultivate the land without differentiating between them on tribal or hereditary basis (i.e. no private ownership of land);

(b) All cultivated land in the possession of monopolist companies and foreign imperialists to be confiscated and redistributed to the farmers;

(c) Redistribute uncultivated land to the farmers and improve water supplies and irrigation;

(d) To encourage the establishment of farmers' co-operatives, and to supply them with seeds and other equipment;

(e) To assist farmers to adopt modern methods;

(f) To liberate farmers from the usurers and brokers and to establish a bank to give low-interest or interest-free loans to farmers;

(g) To encourage trade between the cities and the rural areas and to improve social services in the latter.

Sixth Laws would be passed to guarantee workers' rights and to raise their standard:

(a) The existing labour law should be repealed and replaced by a progressive law. Workers' representatives should help draft the new law;

(b) Unions should be established and workers should have the right to strike;

(c) Workers' representatives should be included in the management of companies;

(d) Technical institutes should be established. Contractors and companies should be compelled to employ Omanis only, who should be given training for high positions;

(e) Health and social security benefits should be provided for all workers and their families;

(f) Unemployment should be fought, good standards of living should be made possible for all. Omanis now living abroad should be able to return and share in the progress.

Seventh The social position of the people should be improved:

(a) Advantages obtained through tribal, social or hereditary position should be abolished;

(b) Women should have social and economic equality with men, and women's movements should be assisted;

(c) Youth clubs and unions should be encouraged;

(d) Free medical service should be available throughout the country;

(e) Building restrictions should be abolished, the construction of good houses should be assisted and all areas should have water and power;

(f) The repressive social laws should be abolished and all citizens should be able to exercise their rights;

(g) Communications and transport should be improved, particularly in the remote areas;

(h) Shepherds should be offered all available help.

Eighth Ignorance and the imperialist educational system should be fought and a national culture established:

(a) The present crazy [sic] and reactionary curriculum should be abolished. A new educated generation should be created, aware of our national culture and Arab history, forward-looking and sympathetic to the people's struggle;

(b) Education should be compulsory and free;

(c) Schools, technical institutes and a national university should be established within a comprehensive educational plan;

(d) Illiteracy should be abolished;

(e) Students should be allowed to establish unions, both to defend their rights and to help in the country's progress;

(f) Attention should be paid to the arts, culture and the Omani civilisation.

Ninth To build a strong, disciplined and well-equipped army, imbued with national spirit.

Tenth Popular armed forces should be established capable of co-operating with the army to protect the nation from conspiracies and foreign expansion.

Eleventh Respect of all principles and religious beliefs.

Twelfth Protection of minority rights and of those foreign communities respecting the leadership.

Thirteenth To work for the reunification of greater Oman (Dhofar to Abu Dhabi) by peaceful means and without foreign intervention.

Fourteenth To unite with the Arab Gulf to resist Irani expansion and to restore Arab Gulf unity.

Fifteenth To align with the Palestinian revolution and offer all potential aid to enable them to return to their country and abolish the Zionist state.

Sixteenth To improve the solidarity between the Arab Omani people and the rest of the Arab nation and to participate in the Arab revolution movement to achieve freedom and progress.

Seventeenth To follow an independent and neutral foreign policy based on the following principles:

(a) To sign no military pacts and not to allow foreign bases on Omani soil;

(b) To establish diplomatic relations with those countries that respect Omani independence and who do not interfere in its internal affairs;

(c) To establish friendship and solidarity with all people who love freedom, justice and international peace;

(d) To accept all unconditional aid from such countries, which would be of mutual benefit;

(e) To support all national liberation movements in Asia, Africa and Latin America and all powers fighting for justice and social progress.

APPENDIX 3: Oman Law on Economic Development
(Unofficial translation)

Sultanate of Oman, the *Official Gazette*, No.75, 15 March 1975

1. *Sultan's Decree 9/75*
We, Qabus bin Sa'id, Sultan of Oman, in the public interest and in accordance with the proposals of the vice chairman of the Development Council, have decreed as follows:
Article 1: Law No. 1/75 on Economic Development, the text of which is attached comes into force with effect from first of February 1975.
Article 2: All ministers within their authority are to implement this law, which shall be published in the Official Gazette.
1 February 1975

Economic Development Law/1975

Designation and Implementation of the Law
Article 1: This law shall be called the 'Economic Development Law/1975' and shall come into force from the first of February 1975.
Interpretation
Article 2: In this law, unless the context requires otherwise the following words shall have the meanings expressed below:

'Council' means the Development Council formed in accordance with Sultan's Decree 41/74.
'Council Secretariat' means the Development Council Secretariat.
'Projects' means any capital projects financed entirely or partly by the State and whether connected with the service sector, public amenities or production.
'Consultant Studies' means any commitments, financed by the State, which are made with companies or firms with the intention of carrying out advisory studies related to capital projects or preparing for the creation of such projects.
'Participation' means state shareholding in the capital of Omani companies whatever their legal form.
'Loans' means loans advanced by the State on easy terms to Omani companies and firms as incentives for increased productive and trading activities and economic growth.
'Protection Privileges' means privileges stipulated in the Protection

of Developing Industry Law 4/74.

'Development Budget' means annual financial credits determined by the State in connection with the costs of 'Projects', 'consultant studies', 'participation', or 'loans' within the meanings expressed in this law.

Terms of Reference of the Development Council

Article 3: The Development Council shall be responsible for the following:

First – To set objectives and a strategy for economic development, to propose policies and measures to carry out these objectives and to lay down development plans in harmony with it. Those development plans will be subject to approval by His Majesty, the Sultan.

Second – To discuss and establish an annual development budget and to refer this budget to the Council For Financial Affairs.

Third – To set and approve priorities for development projects submitted by ministries and government departments before they are implemented, with a view to ensuring conformity with the approved priorities, and to achieving complementarity and consistency of projects in terms of time and subject.

Fourth – To set priorities to requests for consultant studies submitted by government ministries and departments and to authorise them before any commitment is made.

Fifth – To lay down general principles and terms to govern 'loans' and 'participation' to be approved by the council for inclusion in the annual development budget.

Sixth – Approval of protection privileges proposed by the minister concerned, in accordance with the law for the Protection of Developing Industry 4/74, if the proposed concessions include any monopolistic rights or privileges.

Seventh – To co-ordinate the activities of ministries and government departments, in so far as the implementation of the development plans is concerned.

Eight – To receive from ministries and government departments follow-up progress reports on the implementation of projects and consultant studies.

Ninth – To issue an annual follow-up report on the implementation of the development plan.

Tenth – Any other business assigned to the Council by His Majesty the Sultan.

Article 4: Ministries and government departments shall remain responsible, within their respective jurisdictions, for follow-up action and effective implementation of projects and consultancy studies after they have been approved by the Development Council and included in the annual development budget.

Article 5: Final financial commitment will be made on projects and consultancy studies proposed by ministries and government departments in accordance with the terms and conditions and by authorised parties as defined in the laws, decisions and current decrees of the Sultan; provided that prior approval of the Development Council has been given authorising such projects and consultancy studies to be included in the annual development budget and in the development plans.

Annual Development Budget and Development Planning

Article 7: Ministries and government departments shall be responsible, within their respective jurisdictions, for carrying out pre-feasibility economic and technical studies for requested projects and consultant study commitments. Also for estimating the costs before their submission to the Development Council.

Article 8: Ministries and government departments shall submit to the council secretariat a statement of the projects, consultancy studies, participations and loans proposed for inclusion in the annual development budget six months before the beginning of the financial year, together with the economic and technical pre-feasibility studies on which basis they are submitting these proposals.

Article 9: The Council shall discuss and decide on the proposals for the annual development budget, and refer these decisions to the Council for Financial Affairs for inclusion in the overall budget of the State.

Article 10: The first development plans shall cover the period 1976-80. Ministries and government departments shall submit to the Council Secretariat, within their respective jurisdictions, the projects, consultant studies, loans and participations proposed for implementation over this period together with their distribution geographically, estimate of costs, definition of priorities, and pre-feasibility technical and economic studies backing each proposal.

Article 11: Ministries and government departments shall submit to the Council Secretariat monthly follow-up reports on the actual progress in implementing each approved project or consultant study, together with a statement explaining the reasons for differences between the dates and decree of actual implementation and what was aimed at in the original plan.

Article 12: Ministries and government departments shall submit to the Council Secretariat, within their respective jurisdictions, a detailed statement of the projects, consultant studies, loans and participations to which they have been committed before this law took effect and which are being presently carried out.

They shall provide the development council with monthly follow-up reports on their implementation.

Article 13: Each ministry and government department shall designate an authorised officer to be charged with following up the implementation of decisions of the council and with assisting the council in carrying out its tasks.

Article 14: Implementation and follow-up loans and participations approved by the Council shall be the responsibility of a development bank, to be established and regulated by a decree from the Sultan in accordance with the proposals to be put forward by the Council.

Exception

Article 15: Exception from the provisions of this law may only be granted by a decree from the Sultan.

Issue of Regulations

Article 16: The Vice-Chairman of the Development Council may issue statutes and by-laws necessary to implement this law and achieve its objectives.

INDEX

For Product Safety Concerns and Information please contact our EU
representative GPSR@taylorandfrancis.com
Taylor & Francis Verlag GmbH, Kaufingerstraße 24, 80331 München, Germany

www.ingramcontent.com/pod-product-compliance
Lightning Source LLC
LaVergne TN
LVHW010619300926
849162LV00001B/4
9781041331490